The View of Life

Translated by John A. Y. Andrews and Donald N. Levine
With an Introduction by Donald N. Levine and Daniel Silver
and an Appendix, "Journal Aphorisms, with an Introduction"
Edited, Translated, and with an Introduction by John A. Y. Andrews

The View of Life

Four Metaphysical Essays with Journal Aphorisms

GEORG SIMMEL

The University of Chicago Press
Chicago and London

John A. Y. Andrews is a consultant for the Rhode Island Department of Human Services'
Medical Assistance Program (Medicaid). He has a BA in religious studies from Yale University
(1976) and an MA in sociology from the University of Chicago (1982). Donald N. Levine is
professor emeritus of sociology at the University of Chicago and author of *Powers of the Mind*
(2006). Daniel Silver is assistant professor of sociology at the University of Toronto.

The University of Chicago Press, Chicago 60637
The University of Chicago Press, Ltd., London
© 2010 by The University of Chicago
All rights reserved. Published 2010
Printed in the United States of America

19 18 17 16 15 14 13 12 11 10   1 2 3 4 5

ISBN-13: 978-0-226-75783-4 (cloth)
ISBN-10: 0-226-75783-8 (cloth)

Originally published in German as *Lebensanschauung: Vier metaphysische Kapitel*
Duncker & Humblot, 1918

Library of Congress Cataloging-in-Publication Data

Simmel, Georg, 1858–1918.
   [Lebensanschauung. English]
   The view of life : four metaphysical essays, with journal aphorisms / Georg Simmel ;
translated by John A. Y. Andrews and Donald N. Levine ; with an introduction by Donald N.
Levine and Daniel Silver and an Appendix, "Journal Aphorisms, with an Introduction" edited,
translated, and with an introduction by John A. Y. Andrews.
   p. cm.
   "Originally published in German as Lebensanschauung: Vier Metaphysische Kapitel.
Duncker & Humblot, 1918"—t.p. verso.
   Includes bibliographical references.
   ISBN-13: 978-0-226-75783-4 (cloth : alk. paper)
   ISBN-10: 0-226-75783-8 (cloth : alk. paper) 1. Metaphysics. 2. Life. 3. Death.
4. Individuality. I. Levine, Donald Nathan, 1931– II. Andrews, John A. Y. III. Simmel, Georg,
1858–1918. Fragmente und Aufsätze. English. IV. Title.
B3329.S63L413 2010
193—dc22   2010004863

♾ The paper used in this publication meets the minimum requirements of the American
National Standard for Information Sciences—Permanence of Paper for Printed Library
Materials, ANSI Z39.48–1992.

Messo t'ho innanzi: omai per te ti ciba;
Ché a sé torce tutta la mia cura
Quella materia ond'io son fatto scriba.

Dante to the Reader

I have served you: for you now the meal;
Since all my concern is turned
To that matter for which I was made scribe.

CONTENTS

Lebensanschauung, rendered here as *The View of Life*, stands as the last of Georg Simmel's publications issued during his lifetime. Printed in December 1918 by Duncker und Humblot, the book's four metaphysical essays seek to articulate, at the most basic level, what the world consists in when we approach it from "the view of life."

Simmel began this work in 1914 with his move to Strassburg from Berlin, where he had lived, studied, and worked since his birth in 1858. Deeply enmeshed in Berlin's vibrant cultural scene, Simmel lectured at the University of Berlin without a regular faculty appointment. Jewish, intellectually nonconformist, irreverent toward standard academic etiquette, he was truly a "stranger" in the academy—at once inside and outside, near and distant. Coupled with a personal disposition toward individuality and philosophical conviction in its value, his marginal professional position led to periods of unmatched intellectual creativity and fecundity: pathbreaking work in the philosophy of history and ethics; strikingly original investigations into the nature and consequences of a money economy; foundational statements for the discipline of sociology; bracing interpretations of Kant, Goethe, Schopenhauer, and Nietzsche.

Simmel's writings are essayistic, his topics varied. Nevertheless, his work was animated, often implicitly, by a set of core issues that beat like a pulse throughout his corpus. Most centrally, these concern the genesis, structure, and transcendence of social and cultural forms, together with the nature and history of authentic individuality. As his career progressed, Simmel came to believe that the notion of "life" could unify and deepen these questions. With the move to Strassburg and his appointment to a full professorship, he took up this philosophical challenge to formulate his "view of life."

Alerting his friend Hermann Graf Keyserling that he was readying himself to make "the great leap," Simmel made a decision to develop his philosophical project in the form of a metaphysical treatise. Versions of chapters 2, 3, and 4 appeared between 1910 and 1916 in the acclaimed humanistic journal *Logos*. Simmel revised those chapters in light of the definitive conception of life set forth in the first chapter, "Life as Transcendence," composed expressly for this work. The text was completed in the final days of his life, which ended on September 26, 1918. Not long before he died, Simmel told Keyserling, "Now I am in the midst of very difficult ethical and metaphysical investigations. . . . If I can still finish them, they will amount to my testament. I am at an age [60] where the harvest must be brought in, and no further delay is allowed" (Simmel 1999, GSG 16, 441).

If we take Simmel at his word, we must conclude that Anglophone students of Simmel have not yet come to grips with the full scope of his life's work. It has taken ninety years to produce a complete English translation of the testamentary work of a man whom George Santayana called "the brightest man in Europe," whose ideas shaped the argument of Heidegger's *Being and Time*, and whose extraordinary impact on European interwar intellectual life Jürgen Habermas extolled. Until now, Simmel has been received in Anglophone circles chiefly as a sociologist, or as a protocritical theorist, or, more recently, as a postmodernist avant la lettre. Scholars anxious to turn sociology into an academically respectable scientific discipline have naturally been averse to associating the field with metaphysical investigations (Sorokin 1928) or else dismiss them as of purely antiquarian interest (Kelly 2005). In line with the common tripartite periodization of Simmel's work, the latter prefer to keep Simmel's middle, sociological period inoculated from his later writings.[1]

Postmodernists and critical theorists intent on preserving Simmel's image as an impressionistic, unsystematic essayist wandering through the boulevards of science have naturally been averse to the notion that one coherent vision of

---

1. As, for example, von Wiese (1910); Spykman (1925); Coser (1956); Gassen and Landmann (1958); Landmann (1968); and Freund (1981). Although Gerson (1932) suggests that such periodization can be useful when cautiously deployed, Mueller (1960), Vandenberghe (1997), and Levine (1997) thoroughly debunk this view. Interpretations of Simmel's entire oeuvre in ways consistent with the ideas of *The View of Life* are adumbrated in Weingartner (1960) and Oakes (1980), while Levine (2007) and Silver, Lee, and Moore (2007) review systematically certain hermeneutic implications of this text.

the world unifies Simmel's work as a whole (Frisby 1981; Collins 1994; Weinstein and Weinstein 1991; Capetillo-Ponce 2005; Kron 2000; Scaff 2005; Kemple 2007). For his part, however, Simmel writes in *Hauptprobleme der Philosophie* that the philosophical attitude is defined by a quest to understand "the totality of being," an attitude that resists any presuppositions external to its own movement of thought: "One might well characterize the philosopher as one who possesses an organ that receives and reacts to the totality of being."[2] Given that Simmel counted himself a philosopher, it would appear that by calling *The View of Life* his metaphysical testament he intended this work to represent *his* way of receiving and reacting to the "the totality of being." The Simmel of this work cannot be kept separate from the Simmel of aesthetics, ethics, epistemology, and sociology. Rather, this statement beckons us to the synthetic task of discerning the manifest unity amidst the dazzling diversity of Simmel's oeuvre. As his widow Gertrud Simmel further observed: "He called it the final conclusion of his wisdom—I think it offers a cornucopia for all who understand how to receive that wisdom" (Simmel 1999, GSG 16, 442).

The present translation no longer permits Anglophone readers to disregard Simmel's view of life and a raft of related questions. The time is ripe to ask the following questions: how might the ideas of *The View of Life* inform his work more generally and therewith offer resources to receive his wisdom? How did those ideas silently shape *Being and Time*, one of the most influential philosophical works of our time? How does the freshly composed opening chapter recast the earlier chapters? What does it suggest for future explorations in sociology?

The Meaning of *The View of Life*

As Simmel demonstrates in his studies of figures like Kant and Goethe, Schopenhauer and Nietzsche, Rembrandt and Stefan George, the great challenge for readers is to hear how a truly original thinker's voice expresses his "deepest and ultimate personal attitude to the world" (1910, GSG 14, 30). With *The View of Life* Simmel has done us the favor of revealing his own deepest and ultimate personal attitude, yet it requires patient and careful reading in order to fathom it.

The very title of this work contains a subtle double meaning. It purports to set forth how the author views life, yet the title also carries a sense grasped

---

2. "Man kann den Philosophen vielleicht als denjenigen bezeichnen, der das aufnehmende und reagierende Organ für die Ganzheit des Seins hat" (Simmel 1910, GSG 14, 16).

only as readers work their way through the text. Resonating with the great turn in twentieth-century philosophy away from system building and toward "experience" as a principle of inquiry and a model for successful existence, this is the bold claim that everything that humans manifest, including the most sublime moments of high culture, warrants being interpreted from the point of view of life itself.

To see how this claim unfolds and how much meaning is packed into it, it may be useful—given the layered complexity of this work—to introduce it by way of a genealogical sketch; that is, by considering its last three chapters in their earlier versions first, then reviewing the first chapter and asking how it recasts the others and brings them into a coherent whole.

What became the second chapter, "The Turn toward Ideas" ("Die Wendung zur Idee"), first appeared in the 1916 edition of *Logos* under the more tentative title "Proto-forms of Ideas: Studies toward a Metaphysics" ("Vorformen der Idee: Aus den Studien zu einer Metaphysik"). The *Logos* essay lays out Simmel's conception of life as generating "axial turnings" (*Achsendrehung*) that reverse the order of things, a conception left largely unaltered in the *View of Life* version. Objectified forms can bring back to the life process ideas and values that channel the stream of life in new directions. This takes place through the creation of diverse worlds—in present-day language, cultural systems—such as the worlds of value, art, science, religion, law, and the like. The world of music, for example, arises from using rhythms and melodies to express emotions directly, such as at times of grief, when on the warpath, or for public celebrations. The musical elements thus created can, however, evolve into forms that are cultivated for their own sake, above and beyond any practical situation.

Once this happens, the worlds become embodied in systems of symbols that Simmel was wont to designate as objective culture. The sonata form evolves from Haydn and Mozart to Beethoven and Brahms in accord with internal musical logic, not according to changing practical needs for funereal, battle, or festive music. As this evolution proceeds, the worlds of objective culture become increasingly incommensurable. None can be reduced to or described solely in terms of another. Each has the power to subsume all of the contents of human experience in its own distinctive way. In Simmel's words, "the forms or functions that life, for its own sake, has produced from its own vitality now become so autonomous and definite that conversely life serves them and arranges its contents into them; and the success of this arrangement serves just as much as an ultimate realization of value and meaning as did previously the introduction of these forms into the economy of life" (1916b, GSG 13, 253). The world of art, for example, can represent both social interactions and religious symbolism in paintings or poetry. Similarly, in the world of religion,

Chapter	Title	Theme	Earliest Adumbrations	*Logos* Title, Date
II	"The Turn toward Ideas" ("Die Wendung zur Idee")	two-stage emergence of cultural forms	1881; 1900	"Proto-forms of Ideas" ("Vorformen der Idee"), 1916
III	"Death and Immortality" ("Tod und Unsterblichkeit")	death as immanent in life; mortality as individuating; fate; transmigration of souls	1884; 1898; 1908 (chap. 2)	"Toward a Metaphysics of Death" ("Zur Metaphysik des Todes"), 1910; "The Problem of Fate" ("Das Problem des Schicksals"), 1913
IV	"The Law of the Individual" ("Das individuelle Gesetz")	reframing the categorical imperative	1892	"The Law of the Individual: An Essay toward the Principle of Ethics" ("Das Individuelle Gesetz: Ein Versuch Über das Prinzip der Ethik"), 1913

art can be seen as a vehicle toward spiritual transcendence and certain experiences of social interactions like the giving of gifts—as Simmel himself argued (1912, GSG 10)—can appear as phenomenological sources of religiosity. In sociology, furthermore, the production and consumption of artworks can be viewed as elements in social interaction and religious activities can be seen as embodied in social forms such as exchange, domination, and conflict.

Because the same contents of our lives can be taken up into diverse worlds, these worlds can appear to break existence up into discontinuous fragments if approached only in their own terms: "Life as a whole appears as a fragment in that each of its particular pieces—regarded from the viewpoint of the autonomously created, fully shaped form of that piece—is naturally only a fragment" (1916b, GSG 13, 282–83). Here, Simmel's discourse resonates with his analyses of objective culture, to be discussed below. This revolves around the conception of an ever-expanding diversification of life-spheres, to the point that individuals deeply immersed in one can scarcely communicate with others, and individuals enmeshed in several suffer from acute internal conflicts. Simmel's thoughts on all this parallel Weber's discussion of the autonomy (*Eigengesetzlichkeit*) of different life-spheres and the unceasing war among competing gods in modern life, and Niklas Luhmann's more recent radicalization of the theory of functional differentiation.

From the theme of life as a culture-generating force, one that produces multiple cultural systems that constrain one another and the life process itself, Simmel turns in the third chapter to another dimension of life: the way in which death serves to delimit and organize the human self. He stitched together this chapter, "Death and Immortality," out of three components: a *Logos* article of 1910, "Toward a Metaphysics of Death" ("Zur Metaphysik des Todes"); a *Logos* article of 1913, "The Problem of Fate" ("Das Problem des Schicksals"); and material added for the 1918 version, mainly on the physiological process of ageing and on the meaning of immortality.

The earliest of these texts turns on the point that death is not an abrupt happening that occurs simply at the end of life, but rather that *death figures as an ever-present moment that colors all of life.* "Just as we are not already present in the instant of our birth, but rather something of us is continually being born, so too we do not die only in our last instant" (1918c, GSG 16, 299; *View*, 65). Awareness of this condition differs from the "primitive" notion that when someone dies he must have been killed. Rather, our view of life deepens when we include death as a constitutive feature of life. This conception, Simmel argues, contrasts with the view of Christianity, which removes death as an inherent quality of life—and thus, he adds in 1918, confines the view of life exclusively to its positive elements, making what the ever-present possibility of death can do to lives not part of our real life.[3]

Furthermore, Simmel observes, the possibility of death serves to bound life and give it form—just as, he notes elsewhere, the picture frame is needed to provide a boundary to a painting (1918b, GSG 13). In contrast to inorganic things, living beings define their limits (and thus themselves) internally, from within and out of their own vital center. This process of defining a self proceeds spatially when an organism reaches maturity and actively maintains equilibrium with its environment; it proceeds temporally when an organism defines itself internally by the fact that it is mortal and exists in reference to its own end.

Material incorporated from the 1913 essay constitutes an excursus on the concept of Fate nestled within a discourse on immortality. The category of Fate differs from Immortality in that it connotes a desire to reach beyond the mere contingency of events by linking them with the intentions of a subject. By removing this contingency, the course of life and of the world become a single fact. Only when some external event impinges on a person's life in ways that prompt it to take a new turn is some external occurrence deemed fateful. Fate, thus, signifies a synthesis of subjective tendencies and objective events through the act of the living individual.

3. For more on this theme, see Theunissen (1984).

The fourth chapter, "The Law of the Individual" ("Das Individuelle Gesetz"), relates the notion that human lives are delimited and individualized by an immanent sense of death to a notion of life's distinctive ideality and lawfulness. Simmel worked through a preliminary version of this idea in the 1913 *Logos* article by the same name, to which he appended the subtitle: "An Essay toward the Principle of Ethics" ("Ein Versuch über das Prinzip der Ethik"). Here, Simmel holds that law is not necessarily an enemy of life. Following Kant, he argued that "Is" and "Ought" are two equally fundamental aspects under which life is always lived. When I am observed as thinking, I function at the same time according to the norms of logic governing how I should think (1918c, GSG 16, 350–51; *View*, 102–3); when I simply converse, I nonetheless act according to norms governing how I should treat my conversation partner. If "Ought" really is an aspect of life, then the relevant ethical question is not how supra-individual, universally valid "ideal" norms do or do not govern our "actual" private, personal, individual lives, but how a norm is living and emotionally charged rather than rigid and asensual. A genuine law, in other words, makes demands on my whole self, including my being and my feelings. Like happiness, health is not a unitary norm—involving set standards of muscle mass, motility, strength, and the like—to which we all aspire, but a holistic, personalized, individuated way of approaching each and every moment of my life as a whole. This is what Goethe called the deeper lawfulness expressed in his notions of responding to "the demands of the day" and seeking to "become who you are." Life is not wild and lawless, but neither does it proceed under universal and supra-individual norms. The Law of Life is what persons legislate for themselves as their own Law of the Individual.[4]

The View of Life, then, reshapes these core statements in ways that align them with Simmel's culminating stance on the essence of the life process and thereby brings them into a coherent view. This animating view appears in chapter 1, "Life as Transcendence": *just as all human activities have boundaries that can be stepped over, the life process itself contains an essential feature of "transcendence," in that it continually produces forms which it then moves beyond.* As Simmel described his intention, the decisive point about the reworking of the *Logos* essays is that in *View* "they are all held together by the same metaphysical concept of life set forth in the first essay and, as parts of the unfolding of its potential, reveal its ultimate meaning" (1918c, GSG 16, 236n1; *View*, 19n).

For one thing, every element in the life process reaches out to the future. Since humans inexorably create limits and the conditions for transcending them, every sense of the present moment harbors some projection into the future (a notion adumbrated in the introduction and opening chapters of

---

4. For a discussion of "The Law of the Individual" in Simmel's early writings, see Koehnke (1996).

Hegel's *Phenomenology of Spirit*). We experience both the present moment and the reality of some transcendence of that moment by fusing it with some particle of the future. This restless movement defines something as "vital." Conversely, to say that something capable of transcending its limits has become or is becoming stuck within those limits is another way of saying that it has died, or is dying.

In illustrating this point, Simmel refers to ways in which daily experience has been altered by the inventions of the microscope and telescope. These instruments afford a new purchase on everyday reality by relocating it in a wider context, which allows us to live in that reality as though outside it—seeing, for example, sunrise as a movement of the sun and then grasping it as a result of the earth's rotation (1918c, GSG 16, 215–16; *View*, 4).[5]

The discussion of boundaries and border crossing as a constitutive feature of vitality—life as "reaching out beyond itself" (1918c, GSG 16, 221–22; *View*, 8)—sets the stage for what Simmel believes is a deeper insight: the inherent dialectical structure of the life process. He articulates this by saying that life is not only "more-life" but also "more-than-life." As "more-life," all living creatures manifest a creative, flowing, continuous aspect. This involves not just preserving one's life, but also enhancing and reproducing it.

As "more-than-life," however, living human beings do more than other species can; they generate "objectified" forms. These forms channel and direct life's energies as though from above. Once created out of the life process, these forms exist on their own. The most energized lives pour themselves into something more than life—a moral code, political power, truth, beauty, wealth, and so on. "Life is compelled to exist solely in the form of its own opposite, produced immediately by it, in the form of *forms*" (1918c, GSG 16, 352; *View*, 104). Unformed life processes contain a constant demand for forms; conversely, forms separated from life processes are dead. This duality appears wherever there is life, albeit the effort to grasp it conceptually poses a dilemma in revolutionary moments where our lives and their guiding forms seem to come unglued.

As the master concept of *The View of Life*, Simmel's distinction between more-life and more-than-life frames its three remaining chapters. Whereas the earlier publications had subtitles that connote work in progress—"*toward* a metaphysics of death" or "an *essay toward* a principle of ethics"—these working glosses disappear from *View*. Thus, the static "Proto-forms of Ideas" gets

---

5. Simmel expresses this duality with a number of other examples, most notably perhaps in a description of "lived time" vs. "mechanical time." In the latter, the present moment is atemporal, a point disconnected from a lost past and a remote future. In lived time, the present, through objectified structures as well as memory, contains a relation both to the past and to the future, as we continuously press ourselves forward into a projection of what we might possibly be.

swept up into an active, more-than-life process in the chapter newly titled "The *Turn* toward Ideas." The final version of the discourse on differentiation of cultural forms in "Proto-forms" gets supplemented with a contrasting perspective grounded in late Simmel's newly crystallized view of life. This occurs prior to the passage on fragmentation cited above. Developing his theme of fragmentation there, Simmel writes, "We continually circulate through multiple levels, each of which in principle represents the world-totality according to a special formula, but each of which takes our life along only as a fragment" (1918c, GSG 16, 244; *View*, 25). To that, he then adds:

> The aspect is different, though, if we view life from its own standpoint, rather than from these levels that extend beyond it to their own totality. Here the attachment of life's contents to discrete—as it were self-existing—worlds loses its essential meaning. Such an attachment now appears as a belated abstraction and hypothetical transplanting of pieces that, as experienced, do not exhibit mutual delimitation and discontinuity at all. They are united in the dynamic of the life process like waves of a stream; it is in each case *one* life that produces them as its pulse-beats, and because they are inseparable from it they are not ultimately distinguishable from one another. (1918c, GSG 16, 244; *View*, 32)

This new perspective, which Simmel did not have time to develop further, views life as a continuous flow, coursing through and uniting all its separate manifestations. But by anchoring the diverse worlds of cultural forms in a common vital substratum, Simmel adumbrates a worldview that contrasts with Weber's war of gods and Luhmann's cacophony of functional systems by pointing toward a realm of being that all share or have in common. This is akin, for example, to Durkheim's view that what appeared to be morally incompatible spheres of modern life represent a "moral division of labor" on behalf of a more complex organic societal system. Above all, it resembles, ironically, the overarching conception of a universe of action with which Talcott Parsons clothed his general theory, which links mutually irreducible bounded systems distinguished by functional differentiation through tracing them all to a universal field of meaningful human conduct.[6]

---

6. In his late work on the human condition, Parsons (1978) links the whole universe of action more pointedly than ever to a fundamental energy substratum outside that field, yet also—drawing on the core ideas of his "cybernetic hierarchy"—links them to a supernatural "ultimate reality" above. Simmel would presumably respond that the very notion of the latter is something that itself emerges out of the life process.

The 1918 version of this chapter adds one other significant point that was not included in the 1916 text. When describing the various worlds of art, religion, eudaimonism, eroticism, and science, Simmel adds to the last of these a fresh consideration of the nature of truth. Whereas previously he had subscribed to a pragmatic theory of truth, according to which propositions are not useful because they are true but rather they are true because they are useful, in *The View of Life* he expands on a few passages from the 1916 version that caution against a complete reduction to pragmatism and acknowledge the importance of inner processes and not just practical conduct for determining what is true. In *The View of Life*, Simmel adds a claim that truth may be established not only by pragmatic adequacy, but in the "living out of a capability," the "clarification of inner tendencies," or the "self-expression" of a being. In this perspective, thought figures as only one among a number of essential organic processes that constitute our living actuality. *Truth, therefore, becomes a manifestation of the entirety of life.* Accordingly, different life forms necessarily encompass different truths that are inseparable from both their practical context and their inner processes.

> Of course, the *content* of such a truth depends upon what the life in question wants from the world. Truths to an Indian yogi and to a Berlin stock jobber, to Plato and to an Australian aborigine, lie so incomprehensibly distant from each other that conducting these existences on the basis of their notions of the world would be utterly unthinkable if for each of them "life" did not mean something different than for the others, and thus provide for each a special knowledge basis correlative to him. (1918c, GSG 16, 257; *View*, 34)

For Simmel, this is a strikingly novel formulation about the nature of truth. It represents a bolder claim than what he wrote at the beginning of *Sociology*, where he noted that the idea of scientific completeness was a self-deception, and that "the individual can reach completeness only in the subjective sense of communicating everything that he has been able to see" (1908a, GSG 11, 31). This new formulation resonates with Simmel's definitive attempt—one that draws on deep engagement with the Romantic tradition—to transpose Kant's categorical imperative from a doctrine of universalizability to an imperative of authentic individuality, the task of the fourth chapter, "The Law of the Individual."

The discussion of death in *The View of Life* adds two new topics that could be taken to reflect Simmel's own approaching death as a painful cancer of the liver wore on. For one thing, it includes passages that deal with physiological processes of ageing. "Every death from illness in advanced age can also be seen as a death of senescence, because the organs themselves have been altered pathologically by age" (1918c, GSG 16, 299; *View*, 65). More concretely, Simmel adds that ageing entails an increased division of labor among cells, which ultimately produces so radical a specialization of functions that those cells atrophy and waste away. In other words, Simmel here draws with a new intensity on his own life experience as an ageing person.

In addition, the revised chapters on death adds a novel discourse concerning the topic of immortality, presenting its experiential dimensions through the view of life as simultaneously more-life and more-than-life. Here Simmel imports the core of his 1913 article on fate to confront the topic of immortality—the Christian doctrine of the eternal soul in particular. Christianity, he argues, proceeds from an untenable assumption: that souls exist in their life-forged individuality beyond the bounds of that very life. In contrast, he presents Goethe's view: that only the genuinely individual, the "irreplaceable," actually dies; where individual persons live like other members of their species, the "immortality of the species devours the mortality of the individual" (1918c, GSG 16, 325; *View*, 82), and their lives beget more-life. Those (like Goethe) who stamp the life process with their own distinctive form of existence generate something more-than-life, more than the perpetuation of the species. This means, he adds in 1918, that in their mortality they are constituted as incomparable, individuated *selves*: "only individuality . . . can actually die" (1918c, GSG 16, 330; *View*, 86). Thus, instead of a doctrine of eternal souls, Simmel's analysis locates the experiential roots of the sense of individual immortality in ongoing life process. From this insight, he moves boldly to conceptualize immortality in a way that could avoid the logical difficulties of both the Christian and the Hindu conceptions.

The 1918 version of "The Law of the Individual" in the fourth chapter reframes Simmel's recurring critique of Kant so that it rests more firmly on the new "view of life." What Simmel does here is recast Kant's dualism—life's actuality vs. the Ought—in the terms of a dualism of life process vs. emergent form where, as Simmel stated earlier, life creates forms that later hem it in. Reconstructing Kant's theory of an objective morality that is universal to all people and applies to their individual, discrete acts, Simmel looks for an objective morality that is unique to each individual but is universal to all acts in that individual's life process.

Much of this theoretical development appears in a new excursus, which addresses the question of how, after the Ought is brought in as internal to life process, one is to retain any objective moral judgment.[7] For Simmel, Kantian ethics judges morality based on the correspondence between self-enclosed acts and moral principles. But life is a single process that encompasses the constituent acts, acts that cannot be judged as moral in isolation. The whole of life enters into each discrete action of the individual, such that there is a universality of the individual, not of the act or moral principle. We cannot, however, deny the objectivity of this individualized morality. Such denial causes humans to slip into pure amoral individualism. Rather we must recognize that the "individual law," the universality of the individual, has a certain objectivity or "materiality" to it. This conception, Simmel argues in a final added passage, means that the whole life is responsible for every act, and every act for the whole life.[8]

The View of Life as Capstone to Simmel's Corpus

The key ideas developed in *The View of Life* represent notions present throughout Simmel's corpus. But only in *View* are they fully crystallized and interconnected. The proto-forms of Simmel's view of life appear chiefly in his earlier work on cultural forms, social forms, forms of individuality, and the topic of death.

Cultural Forms

Simmel's 1881 dissertation on music stands as the first place to look for continuities with his later ideas about the relation between cultural forms and the life process. This short text draws on two ideational banks that fund Simmel's exegeses on the relation between forms and the life process: the ideas of his teacher, anthropologist Moritz Lazarus, on the adaptive foundations of cultural forms, and Darwin's ideas of the evolutionary significance of singing. Together, these sources led Simmel to treat music as forms that arise within the needs of the practical life process, then become autonomous forms, cultivated for their own sake—prefiguring his late notion of "more-than-life."

7. "So long as the Ought is seen as removed from life and opposed to it in principle; then admittedly no impediment exists to rational calculation with self-contained constructs, exhaustible by their concept, that submit to a universal principle on the strength of this concept. But as soon as the form of life itself is recognized in the Ought, such discontinuity is excluded; the stream of the Ought accompanies (though flowing on an entirely different level) that of the actual life, whose steadiness does not take refuge in precisely cut concepts and rejects the logical hierarchy of such concepts" (1918c, GSG 16, 374; *View*, 118).

8. This is fundamentally incompatible with Kant's formalistic ethics. Kant denies individuals the "creative aspect of the ethical realm," the continuous integration of the total life and the ongoing act.

Subsequent publications exhibit a continuous, if intermittent, development of these notions, evolving five lines of argument: (1) cultural forms arise within the life process; (2) cultural forms become autonomous and objectified, independent of adaptive needs; (3) objective cultural forms serve to advance cultivation, or "subjective culture," through processes by which they get incorporated in the individual's personal development; (4) objectified forms come into conflict with ongoing life processes; and (5) in the condition of late modernity the pressures of life process come to exert dominance over cultural forms.[9]

Publications of the 1890s broach the first two of these arguments, anchoring at least two sets of cultural forms in the life process: ethical values and ways of knowing. The early work on moral science (1892–93) locates the genesis of moral values, not in any rational a priori, but in the life of communities with their need for moral control over members. (His ideas on this matter parallel those of his American contemporary, William Graham Sumner [1907]). Soon after, Simmel wrote on the relation between Darwin's theory of natural selection and cognitive forms (1895). Here Simmel stakes out a core notion, parallel to the views of pragmatist philosophies, that ideas arise from efforts to solve experienced practical problems. Simmel touches on this further in 1908 in his introduction to *Sociology*. This view prefigures (and was cited by) work a century later under the rubric of evolutionary epistemology (Campbell 1974; Coleman 2002).

Simmel broaches the notion of the autonomization of cultural forms when he discusses problems of the philosophy of history. In his 1892 discussions, writing in a neo-Kantian mode, Simmel identified forms of historical understanding as distinct and essential components of the act of writing history. Only later, in 1916, would he explicitly articulate the relationship of historical reconstructions to the dynamics of the life process (Simmel 1916a, GSG 13). Explicit theorization of the autonomization of forms appears in Simmel's discourse about philosophy itself. There he talks about the generation of totalizing forms, which he designates as "worlds." Within this perspective, the work of the philosopher is to articulate a coherent view of the "whole of knowledge and, indeed, the whole of life."

The fourth issue in Simmel's evolving thought about cultural forms comes to the fore in 1900 with the first edition of *The Philosophy of Money*. There Simmel formulates his notion of a conflict between autonomous cultural forms and the ongoing life process carried by individuals, whose appropriation

---

9. For overviews of the relevant primary and secondary literature pertaining to this complex of issues, see Levine (2001), Gessner (2003), and Levine (2008).

of those forms he calls "subjective culture." Over the next dozen years, Simmel found this tension between objective and subjective culture increasingly problematic, designating it in 1911 as a tragedy and in 1916 as a serious crisis.

In his very last statement on this topic, published the same year as *The View of Life*, Simmel reversed his position dramatically. Instead of viewing the ongoing life process as threatened by the hypertrophy of objectified cultural forms, he found the ascendance of the idea of Life and the explosion of vital energies so relentless that cultural forms could no longer exert the kind of constraint that they had throughout history. Confronting this denouement, Simmel exclaimed, "we gaze into an abyss of unformed life beneath our feet. But perhaps this formlessness is the appropriate form for contemporary life" (1918a, GSG 16, 207; this poetic English translation appears in Etzkorn [1968], 25).

Social Forms

The notion of forms as generated by the life process and their subsequent obsolescence due to changes in the ongoing life process, thematized in the essays from 1911 that culminate in *The View of Life*, was foreshadowed in several earlier publications. Articles of the mid-1890s on factors that enable social groups to persist (Simmel 1895; Simmel 1897–99) consider this dynamic in the case of logical forms, legal codes, and functionally specialized social structures. Logical forms, for example, are but organs for comprehending the totality of things. As soon as logic strives for self-sufficiency, attempting to be the conclusion rather than a medium of understanding, it becomes obstructive to the preservation, extension, and unification of knowledge. Similarly, law comprises a coherent set of formal norms to which relationships among group members ought to conform, but changes in the latter often find themselves in conflict with the former. More generally, the self-preservation of a society sometimes requires it to discard "service organs"—or institutional forms—that have been created to serve it. When an organ proves inadequate to its task, recourse must be had to the unmediated living interaction of group members in order to perform more effectively the function that the organ was originally developed to serve.

The forms vs. life process problematic was also adumbrated in a 1908 article, "Die Treue" (Faithfulness) (Simmel 1908b).[10] In this piece, incorporated in the final version of his essay on the persistence of social groups, Simmel treats faithfulness as a concrete example of how a "fluctuating, constantly developing life process" gives rise to a relatively fixed, stable form, which then

---

10. With a companion piece "Dankbarkeit" (Gratitude), this article turned into the very last excursus inserted in his *Sociology* of 1908.

becomes a constraint against that life process (1908b, GSG 8, 401). In the case of faithfulness, he notes that form arises from elements within the relationship, as contrasted with forms like legal norms, which are imposed from the outside. He illustrates this dynamic with the linguistic form of polite address ("Sie," "vous"), which often becomes unsuited to represent the actual intimacy that has evolved within a personal relationship. However much the actual relationships they circumscribe pulsate and change, faithfulness offers society an indispensable inertia that keeps relationships ongoing independent of their initial motives.

Forms of Individuality

In addition to the many places where Simmel prefigures the first two chapters of *The View of Life*, it is easy to point to a long line of writings that anticipate the ideas of the fourth chapter, "The Law of the Individual." Indeed, if there is any leitmotiv in Simmel's corpus it is manifestly the theme of individualization and freedom. The dynamics of modern individualization form the central problematic of *Über soziale Differenzierung* (1890). Modern society is portrayed as a highly differentiated social world wherein individuals are liberated from a variety of customary constraints in ways that enormously expand their freedom of action. There is a transition in form, for example, from the relatively small-scale organization of groups containing homogeneous members to an expanded scale of association in which group members differ from one another (chap. 3), and from a condition in which shared beliefs embody the lowest common denominator of mental activity to one that permits individualized intellectual achievement (chap. 4).

As Simmel's work went on, he came increasingly to distinguish between two forms of individualism, a distinction that he articulated most fully in a late essay on eighteenth- and nineteenth-century views of the individual (1917a, GSG 16, 122–49). In addition to treating individualism as an outcome of the secular dissolution of restraints due to urbanization, commercialization, and industrialization, he went on to celebrate the ideal of individuality. He did so in a variety of ways. Already as early as the chapter on the Categorical Imperative in volume two of the *Einleitung in die Moralwissenschaft* (1893), he questioned the adequacy of universalizability as a touchstone for an ethic of individuality. His depiction of monetarized society included an analysis of how money enhances the freedom to be one's true self (Levine 1981). In addition, he portrayed with enthusiasm several exemplars of individuality, such as Rembrandt, Goethe, Schopenhauer, Nietzsche, and Stefan George. Finally, in his posthumously published lectures on pedagogy, he advocated a complex of educational principles and practices whose core intention was to help students develop as complete, individual personalities (Levine 1991).

Death

Death and immortality became increasingly salient for Simmel in the days leading up to World War I. His 1914 "Germany's Inner Transformation" comes close to valorizing death on the battlefield. The "absolute situation" of confronting death generates "authentic history." The tedium of day-to-day bourgeois life vanishes. Germany, Simmel writes, cannot know what it will be like on the other side of the war, yet this very uncertainty generates the life-affirming qualities that war offers (1917b, GSG 15, 276 and passim).

Nevertheless, the meaning of death for life, as well as the psychological dimensions of immortality and the relationship between immortality and individuality, are questions Simmel explored in a number of contexts throughout his career. Understanding dying and the afterlife figure large in his early enquiry into Dante's psychology (1884, GSG 1). A decade later, his analyses of how social groups maintain themselves presume that "the unity [of a social group] is of longer or shorter duration, until, like everything earthly, it at last yields to decomposing forces" (1897–99, GSG 18, 85).[11]

A decade later, a kindred assumption enters his analysis of the two-person group. At first, his treatment of dyads—in a two-part piece on the influence of numbers on the form of groups in the *American Journal of Sociology* of 1902–3 (1902a, 1902b)—omits any reference to the matter of mortality. As revised in *Sociology* (1908), however, the topic surfaces in a surprising gloss.

> Both the lives of the individual and that of the association are colored in specific ways by the representation of their respective deaths. . . . Death stands before us, not like a fate that will strike at a certain moment but, prior to that moment, exists only as an idea or prophecy, as fear or hope, without interfering with the reality of this life. The fact that we shall die is a quality inherent in life from the beginning. In all our living reality, there is something which merely finds its last phase or revelation in our death: we are, from birth on, beings that will die . . . [T]he dyad . . . [is] a group that feels itself both endangered and irreplaceable, and thus [is] the real locus not only of authentic sociological tragedy. (1908a, GSG 11, 102)

11. Prior to its publication in German, this paper appeared in French in 1896, and in English, in the *American Journal of Sociology*, in 1898.

Because dyadic relations require greater levels of individual commitment, they are more clearly marked by a sense of mortality than are larger social groups. In this sociological context, Simmel anticipates—in language nearly identical to that of his ensuing metaphysic of death—the more general relationship between individuality, mortality, and the tragic that he would later root in the very constitution of life as such.

Finally, we can find a hint of receptivity to thinking about death in Simmel's pronounced lifelong interest in pessimism. This appears already in his first year of academic teaching, in a lecture course titled About Pessimism, and in a philosophical paper on that subject the same year (1887, GSG 2). It would figure significantly as an interpretive gloss in his repeated engagements with Schopenhauer and Nietzsche, as when he writes of Schopenhauer that his descriptions and evaluations of human life are dominated by "the deepest substance of his pessimism," or how Nietzsche deals with the pessimistic notion of the purposelessness of life (1907, GSG 8, 63, 67).

The View of Life in Philosophies of Life and Existence

Schopenhauer and Nietzsche were of great interest to Simmel in another respect. It was through sustained dialogue with them, as well as Goethe, and then Bergson, that he developed the core ideas of his philosophy of life. What is more, Simmel's metaphysical chapters on life deeply influenced later philosophy, most significantly Heidegger's *Being and Time*. These lines of influence, development, and critique present numerous connections for future scholarship to pursue.

Simmel treated Schopenhauer and Nietzsche as exemplary figures for thinking through what it would mean for life to function as the metaphysical basis of a post-Christian form of existence (1907, GSG 10, 167–408). Schopenhauer's Life, as Simmel interpreted it, epitomizes a world without the final telos provided hitherto by the Christian God. What remains is life as a vast, purposeless flow, unguided from without or within. Individuality and fixed forms are illusions. Life is directionless striving, constant suffering without redemption, punctuated by monotonous cycles of boredom. By contrast, Nietzsche's view of Life is for Simmel indelibly marked by Darwin. It aims toward no final purpose but nevertheless manifests evolutionary movement. Life is expansive, self-overcoming; more-life is a goal internal to life—we need not seek an external purpose to life, for life itself is its purpose.

According to Simmel, Schopenhauer and Nietzsche were still wedded to a metaphysics of the Will. Simmel believed that Bergson's understanding of life went wider and deeper, counting life itself as the more basic metaphysical category.[12] Life for Bergson offers a modern analog to the Greeks' Substance and the medievals' Creation. Simmel saw in this conception an opening to his own project of articulating the world from the standpoint of life.

Yet for Simmel, Bergson's understanding of life remained insufficiently dialectical. Bergson's Life does contain its own purpose—more life, reproduction, expansion, increased capacities. Nevertheless, Bergson remains a partisan of "flow" against "fixity," unable to "extinguish their absolute opposition" and provide "a way of manifesting a unity of metaphysical life" (1914, GSG 13, 69). Bergson views form as inherently extravital, the enemy and contrary of life. Not incidentally, Bergson does not thematize death or tragedy as internal to life. Simmel writes, "It is as if [Bergson] never noticed the tragedy that life, in order to exist, must transform itself into something that is not life" (1914, GSG 13, 63). Simmel, as we have seen, rejects this separation between life process and life-form, and with it the denial of death and tragedy as constitutive features of life. One might consider the hypothesis that Simmel's own conception of Life infuses Bergson's metaphysics with Nietzsche's keen sense of life's tragic structure.[13]

The View of Life played an important but largely subterranean role in twentieth-century philosophical discourse, mainly in Germany. Simmel's conception of life contributed to the midcentury development of philosophical anthropology, especially in the work of Arnold Gehlen and Helmuth Plessner. *View* might also have had some unacknowledged influence on Karl Jaspers both on the latter's psychology of worldviews (Grossheim 1991, 40) and on his notion of the Axial Age (Levine 2004). Later in the century, Hans Joas found Simmel's notion of the "immanence of transcendence" a key to understanding "the genesis of values" (Joas 1994).

The "Four Metaphysical Chapters" of *The View of Life* exerted their greatest impact, however, on Martin Heidegger's *Being and Time*. Hans-Georg Gadamer once remarked, "Already around 1923, Heidegger had spoken to me with admiration about Georg Simmel's late writings. That this was not merely a general recognition of the philosophical personality of Simmel, but rather indicated Heidegger's reception of specific stimulus in matters of content, is clear to anybody who today reads . . . the four 'Metaphysical Chapters' gathered under the title *The View of Life*" (Gadamer 1972, 229). Gadamer recalls another statement by Heidegger in which Heidegger reportedly said,

---

12. For more on the relation between Simmel and Bergson, see Fitzi (2002).

13. Felsch and Gagern gloss the difference thus: "The historicity of the Bergsonian organism is heterogeneous, self-enclosed continuity; the historicity of the Simmelian organism is dialectically teleological" (2000, 87).

"Simmel's 'Four Metaphysical Chapters' were of fundamental significance for my introduction to philosophy" (Gadamer 1986/87, 24).

Michael Grossheim traces this influence in painstaking detail, concluding that, had Heidegger been forced to write *Being and Time* five years earlier, it would likely have been called *Being and Life*. Readers of both *The View of Life* and *Being and Time* are immediately struck by the similarity between their conceptions of death and temporality, even if Heidegger tended to play down his affinity with Simmel in print (Jalbert 2003; Grossheim 1991). Heidegger follows Simmel in approaching temporality not by way of the conditions of the possibility of historical science, but by treating life as *being* "truly past and future" (Jalbert 2003). In addition, each treats death as immanent to life, connecting this fact to the possibility of authentic individuality and fatefulness in human existence (Krell 1992). Grossheim finds powerful affinities between Heidegger's notion of "Dasein" as projecting possibilities into the future and Simmel's conception of life as more-life, as well as between Simmel's notion of the "Law of the Individual" and Heidegger's "Call of Conscience." To be sure, Heidegger eventually rejected both the language of "life" and the language of "viewing" as ways of articulating the distinctive mode of Dasein's being. But Simmel's notions of life, death, temporality, and transcendence provided Heidegger with key insights that have reverberated through and beyond the twentieth century.

The View of Life as a Stimulus to Future Social Thought

With the insights of *The View of Life* before us—the final key, as Frau Gertrud Simmel suggested, to the treasures of Simmelian thought—what might follow from bringing its ideas to bear on future scholarly inquiry? We believe it may open a door to a treasure of new insights in a wide array of fields—from aesthetics, ethics, and psychology to epistemology, metaphysics, philosophy, and theology.

To begin with, consider Gertrud Simmel's report that Georg himself had longed for another twenty years of intellectual strength so as to pursue in new directions the lines of thought it had opened to him (Simmel 2004, GSG 20, 297; *View*, 189). A fragment from his posthumously published file "Metaphysics," translated in this book at the conclusion of the journal aphorisms (190–92), offers tantalizing hints as to where these investigations might have led. In that fragment, Simmel proposes a new discipline, "philosophy of life." This discipline would treat life as a synthesis of process and content, aiming to articulate the basic forms through which that synthesis proceeds. For instance, when we study a painting, Simmel would ask, "what are the effects of treating

it as an element in a system of relations that form the course of a life, in contrast to those that form a cognition or a world of values?" (Simmel 2004, GSG
20, 298; *View*, 191). This question resonates with his earlier remarks about
subjective culture as the cultivation of persons, and with his late suggestion
of another perspective on the meaning of truth, within which Truth becomes
a manifestation of the entirety of life. Although no one can say how Simmel
would have answered the question, these thoughts stand to stimulate an effort
to explore what might follow from leveraging the ideas of *The View of Life* into
a new kind of life-infused set of philosophical inquiries.

Writing as sociological theorists, let us now proceed to ask, what would it
mean to fold the insights of *The View of Life* back into the discipline of which
Simmel himself was a preeminent founder? How can we extend Simmel's insights in directions he did not live to pursue?

The distinction between more-life and more-than-life stakes out terrain
that has almost never quite been explored in sociology. Sumner's important
distinctions between folkways and mores, and between crescive and enactive
institutions, lie adjacent to that terrain. This topos would imply investigat-
ing mechanisms, dynamics, and cases of how processes of generation differ
from processes of reproduction. It would examine the relation between ongoing processes of social interaction and processes of the institutionalization of
social and cultural patterns. This could offer one way of bridging the contributions of Simmel and Parsons, since Simmel's sociology was devoted almost
exclusively to the former and Parsons's primarily to the latter. Above all, taking
it seriously might entail a shift in sociological perspective, beyond that which
informs much of Simmel's own sociological writings as well; away from static
representations and analyses in general toward one that from the outset looks
at the seeds of changes—becoming, evolving, transforming, and dying—which
may germinate in all social and cultural formations.

The key idea of the second chapter governs questions about how symbolic
systems work to channel and redirect human life. This connects with Weber's
notion of the role of ideas in history, and Parsons's concept of constitutive
symbolism. More recently, it has become central to a large research program
represented by Shmuel Eisenstadt and others regarding Axial Civilizations.
A systematic research program might investigate mechanisms, dynamics, and
cases of how those complexes become objectified and how they function to
redirect social and cultural activities.

The importance of the awareness of death in life has been barely treated
by mainstream sociologists, apart from some seminal statements and analyses by Parsons and an emerging subfield of "mortality studies." The ideas that
Heidegger drew from Simmel and developed by connecting awareness of

death with authentic individuality might well be drawn on to inform such sociological work. In addition, Simmel's ideas in the third chapter on fate and contingency might form a useful bridge between sociology and similar work in philosophy, such as Odo Marquard's "defense of the accidental" and Alexander Nehamas's writings about Nietzsche, Proust, and life as a narrative constructed out of fortuitous events to form permanent and harmonious motifs.

Perhaps most fruitful for sociological examination are the notions of the fourth chapter. This would involve returning sociology to the themes and interests of earlier American thinkers such as John Dewey, William Isaac Thomas, and David Riesman, with their concern for identifying and promoting the growth of persons who manifest high levels of creativity and autonomy. One might also find this set of Simmelian ideas resonating with contemporary writings such as Bernard Williams on virtue ethics, Charles Taylor on the "ethic of authenticity," and Zygmunt Baumann on the postmodern ethics of "life in fragments." It would entail analyses of the conditions that promote or inhibit the development of authentic individuality, particularly in families, schools, and voluntary associations. The converse of that relationship might open up entirely new areas for inquiry, directing attention to the implications for social organization and culture of the ascendance of increasing numbers of persons so oriented. That might amount to a Simmelian utopia.

To read this short, daunting masterpiece—no less than to translate it!—puts uncommon demands on the patience, care, and imagination of the reader. The reward is indeed a cornucopia of wisdom, one that offers a searching account of how the pinnacles of human thought—all the great systems of cultural symbolism; human reflections on death, destiny, and immortality; and the form and content of the moral law—come into being in virtue of a single grand source: the force that through the green fuse drives the flower.

REFERENCES

Coleman, Martin. 2002. Taking Simmel seriously in evolutionary epistemology. *Studies in History and Philosophy of Science* 33 (1): 55–74.

Collins, Randall. 1994. *Four sociological traditions.* New York: Oxford University Press.

Campbell, Donald T. 1974. Evolutionary epistemology. In *The Philosophy of Karl Popper*, ed. P. Schilpp, 413–63. LaSalle: Open Court.

Capetillo-Ponce, Jorge. 2005. Deciphering the labyrinth: The influence of Georg Simmel on the sociology of Octavio Paz. *Theory, Culture & Society* 22 (6): 95–121.

Coser, Lewis. A. 1956. *The functions of social conflict.* Glencoe, IL: The Free Press.

Etzkorn, Peter K., trans. 1968. *Georg Simmel: The conflict in modern culture and other essays.* New York: Teachers College Press.

Felsch, Phillip, and Moritz von Gagern. 2000. Die Seiten und die Zeiten des Lebens: Individuum und Gesellschaft bei Bergson, Durkheim, Simmel. *Simmel Studies* 10:66–92.

Fitzi, Gregor. 2002. *Soziale Erfahrung und Lebensphilosophie: Georg Simmels Beziehung zu Henri Bergson.* Constance: UVK.

Freund, Julien. 1981. Introduction à Georg Simmel. In *Sociologie et épistémologie*, trans. I. Gasparini, 7–78. Paris: PUF.

Frisby, David. 1981. *Sociological impressionism: A reassessment of Georg Simmel's social theory.* London, UK: Heinemann.

Gadamer, Hans-Georg. 1972. *Wahrheit und Methode: Grundzüge einer philosophischen Hermeneutik.* 3rd edition. Tübingen: Mohr.

———. 1986/1987. Erinnerungen an Heideggers Anfänge. *Dilthey-Jahrbuch* 4:13–26.

Gassen, Kurt, and Michael Landmann. 1958. *Buch Des Dankes an Georg Simmel.* Berlin: Duncker & Humblot.

Gerson, Hermann. 1932. Die Entwicklung der ethischen Anschauung bei Georg Simmel. PhD diss., University of Berlin.

Gessner, Willfried. 2003. *Der Schatz im Acker: Georg Simmels Philosophie der Kultur.* Weilerswist: Velbrück Wissenschaft.

Grossheim, Michael. 1991. *Von Georg Simmel zu Martin Heidegger: Philosophie zwischen Leben und Existenz.* Bonn: Bouvier.

Jalbert, John E. 2003. Time, death, and history in Simmel and Heidegger. *Human Studies* 26 (2): 259–83.

Joas, Hans. 1994. *The genesis of values.* Chicago: University of Chicago Press.

Kelly, Russell. 2005. Georg Simmel. In *Blackwell's encyclopedia of sociology*, ed. G. Ritzer. Mass.: Blackwell.

Kemple, Thomas M. 2007. Allosociality: Bridges and doors to Simmel's social theory of the limit. *Theory, Culture & Society* 24 (7–8): 1–19.

Koehnke, Christian. 1996. *Der junge Simmel: In Theoriebeziehungen und sozialen Bewegungen.* Frankfurt: Suhrkamp.

Krell, David Farrell. 1992. *Daimon life: Heidegger and life-philosophy.* Bloomington, IN: Indiana University Press.

Kron, Thomas. 2000. *Individualisierung und soziologische Theorie.* Opladen, Germany: Leske & Budrich.

Landmann, Michael. 1968. Introduction to *Das individuelle Gesetz: Philosophische Exkurse*, ed. Michael Landmann, 7–29. Frankfurt: Suhrkamp.

Levine, Donald N. 1981. Sociology's quest for the classics: The case of Simmel. In *The future of the sociological classics*, ed. Buford Rhea, 60–80. London: Allen and Unwin.

———. 1991. Simmel as educator: On individuality and modern culture. *Theory, Culture and Society* 8 (3): 99–117.

———. 1997. Simmel reappraised. In *Reclaiming the sociological classics*, ed. Charles Camic. London: Blackwell.

———. 2001. Le posizioni contraddittorie di Simmel sulla cultura moderna. *Rassegna Italiana di Sociologia* 42 (4): 541–48.

———. 2004. Note on the concept of an axial turning in human history. In *Rethinking civilizational analysis*, ed. S Arjomand and E Tiryakian, 67–70. London: Sage.

———. 2007. Soziologie und Lebensanschauung: Zwei Wege der, Kant-Goethe-Synthese bei Georg Simmel. *Simmel Studies* 17 (2): 239–63.

———. 2008. Simmel's shifting formulations regarding the antinomies of modern culture. *Simmel Studies* 18 (2): 239–63.

Müller, Horst. 1960. *Lebensphilosophie und Religion bei Georg Simmel.* Berlin: Duncker & Humblot.

Oakes, Guy. 1980. Introduction to *Essays on interpretation in social science*, by Georg Simmel, 3–94. Totowa, NJ: Rowman and Littlefield.

Parsons, Talcott. 1978. *Action theory and the human condition*. New York, NY: The Free Press.

Scaff, Lawrence A. 2005. The mind of the modernist: Simmel on time. *Time & Society* 14 (1): 5–23.

Silver, Daniel, Monica Lee, and Robert Moore. 2007. View of life: A Simmelian reading of Simmel's testament. *Simmel Studies* 17 (2): 262–90.

Simmel, Georg. 1884. Dantes Psychologie. In vol. 1 of *Georg Simmel Gesamtausgabe*, ed. Klaus Christian Köhnke, 91–177. Frankfurt: Suhrkamp.

———. 1887. Über die Grundfrage des Pessimismus in methodischer Hinsicht. In vol. 2 of *Georg Simmel Gesamtausgabe*, ed. Otthein Rammstedt, 9–19. Frankfurt: Suhrkamp.

———. 1890. Über soziale Differenzierung. In vol. 2 of *Georg Simmel Gesamtausgabe*, ed. Otthein Rammstedt, 109–295. Frankfurt: Suhrkamp.

———. 1892. Die Probleme der Geschichtsphilosophie. In vol. 2 of *Georg Simmel Gesamtausgabe*, ed. Otthein Rammstedt, 297–424. Frankfurt: Suhrkamp.

———. 1893. Einleitung in die Moralwissenschaft, 2nd volume. In vol. 4 of *Georg Simmel Gesamtausgabe*, ed. Klaus Christian Köhnke. Frankfurt: Suhrkamp.

———. 1895. Über eine Beziehung der Selektionslehre zur Erkenntnishtheorie. In vol. 5 of *Georg Simmel Gesamtausgabe*, ed. Hans-Jürgen Dahme and David P. Frisby, 62–74. Frankfurt: Suhrkamp.

———. 1897–99. The persistence of social groups. *American Journal of Sociology* 3:662–98, 829–36; 4:35–50.

———. 1900. Philosophie des Geldes. In vol. 6 of *Georg Simmel Gesamtausgabe*, ed. David P. Frisby and Klaus Christian Köhnke. Frankfurt: Suhrkamp.

———. 1902a. The number of members as determining the sociological form of the group I. *American Journal of Sociology* 8 (1): 1–46.

———. 1902b. The number of members as determining the sociological form of the group II. *American Journal of Sociology* 8 (2): 158–96.

———. 1907. Schopenhauer und Nietzsche. In vol. 10 of *Georg Simmel Gesamtausgabe*, ed. Michael Behr, Volkhard Krech, and Otthein Rammstedt, 167–408. Frankfurt: Suhrkamp.

———. 1908a. Soziologie: Untersuchungen über die Formen der Vergesellschaftung. In vol. 11 of *Georg Simmel Gesamtausgabe*, ed. Otthein Rammstedt. Frankfurt: Suhrkamp.

———. 1908b. Treue: Ein Sozialpsychologischer Versuch. In vol. 8 of *Georg Simmel Gesamtausgabe*, ed. Alessandro Cavalli, Volkhard Krech, and Otthein Rammstedt, 398–403. Frankfurt: Suhrkamp.

———. 1910. Hauptprobleme der Philosophie. In vol. 14 of *Georg Simmel Gesamtausgabe*, ed. Rüdiger Kramme and Otthein Rammstedt, 11–157. Frankfurt: Suhrkamp.

———. 1911. Der Begriff und die Tragödie der Kultur. In vol. 14 of *Georg Simmel Gesamtausgabe*, ed. Rüdiger Kramme and Otthein Rammstedt, 385–416. Frankfurt: Suhrkamp.

———. 1912. Die Religion. In vol. 10 of *Georg Simmel Gesamtausgabe*, ed. Michael Behr, Volkhard Krech, Gert Schmidt, and Otthein Rammstedt, 39–118. Frankfurt: Suhrkamp.

———. 1914. Henri Bergson. In vol. 13 of *Georg Simmel Gesamtausgabe*, ed. Klaus Latzel, 53–69. Frankfurt: Suhrkamp.

———. 1916a. Die Krisis der Kultur. In vol. 13 of *Georg Simmel Gesamtausgabe*, ed. Klaus Latzel, 190–201. Frankfurt: Suhrkamp.

———. 1916b. Vorformen der Idee: Aus den Studien zu einer Metaphysik. In vol. 13 of *Georg Simmel Gesamtausgabe*, ed. Klaus Latzel, 252–98. Frankfurt: Suhrkamp.

———. 1917a. Grundfragen der Soziologie. In vol. 16 of *Georg Simmel Gesamtausgabe*, ed. Georg Fitzi and Otthein Rammstedt, 9–150. Frankfurt: Suhrkamp.

———. 1917b. Der Krieg und die gestigen Entscheidungen. In vol. 16 of *Georg Simmel Gesamtausgabe*, ed. Georg Fitzi and Otthein Rammstedt, 7–58. Frankfurt: Suhrkamp.

———. 1918a. Conflict of modern culture. In vol. 16 of *Georg Simmel Gesamtausgabe*, ed. Georg Fitzi and Otthein Rammstedt, 181–208. Frankfurt: Suhrkamp.

———. 1918b. Das Problem des Portraits. In vol. 13 of *Georg Simmel Gesamtausgabe*, ed. Klaus Latzel, 370–81. Frankfurt: Suhrkamp.

———. 1918c. Lebensanschauung. In vol. 16 of *Georg Simmel Gesamtausgabe*, ed. Georg Fitzi and Otthein Rammstedt, 209–425. Frankfurt: Suhrkamp.

———. 1999. Editorischer Bericht. In vol. 16 of *Georg Simmel Gesamtausgabe*, ed. Georg Fitzi and Otthein Rammstedt, 426–42. Frankfurt: Suhrkamp.

Simmel, Gertrud. 2004. "Aus der nachgelaßnen Mappe 'Metaphysik.'" In *Georg Simmel Gesamtausgabe*, vol. 20, ed. Torge Karlsruhen and Otthein Rammstedt, 297–301. Frankfurt: Suhrkamp.

Sorokin, Pitirim. 1928. *Contemporary sociological theories*. New York: Harper.

Spykman, Nicolas. 1925. *The social theory of Georg Simmel*. Chicago: University of Chicago Press.

Sumner, William Graham. 1907. *Folkways: A study of the sociological importance of usages, manners, customs, mores, and morals*. Boston: Ginn.

Theunissen, Michael. 1984. Die Gegenwart des Todes im Leben. In *Tod und Sterben*, ed. Rolf Winau and Hans Peter Rosemeier, 102–24. Berlin: de Gruyter.

Vandenberghe, Frédéric. 1997. *La sociologie de Georg Simmel*. Paris: La Découverte.

Von Wiese, Leopold. 1910. Neuere soziologische Literatur: Kritische Literaturübersichten. *Kölner Zeitschrift zur Soziologie* 11:11–20.

Weingartner, Rudolf. 1960. *Experience and culture: The philosophy of Georg Simmel*. New Haven: Yale University Press.

Weinstein, Deena, and M. A. Weinstein. 1991. "Georg Simmel: Sociological flaneur bricoleur." *Theory, Culture & Society* 8:151–68.

Wolff, Kurt H. 1950. *The sociology of Georg Simmel*. Glencoe, Ill.: Free Press.

NOTE ON THE TRANSLATION

The first English translation of the first essay was published as "The Transcendent Character of Life" in the volume *Georg Simmel on Individuality and Social Forms: Selected Writings*, edited and with an introduction by Donald N. Levine (University of Chicago Press, 1971). Building on the Levine translation, John A. Y. Andrews executed a complete translation of *Lebensanschauung* in 1998. Andrews's manuscript lay dormant until 2007, when Levine enlisted a team of knowledgeable colleagues at the University of Chicago to review that translation: Monica Lee, Robert Moore, and Daniel Silver. Each team member took primary responsibility for carefully reviewing an essay, comparing it to the original text, and, through collaboration and consensus with Levine and Andrews, revising and honing the translation. In 2008 Andrews produced the first English translation of the posthumous *Fragmente aus dem nachgelassenen Tagebuche*.

Although the translators tended to follow Simmel's constructions in the German original—eschewing, for example, the injection of section headings, which Simmel never favored—at times they modulated his extravagantly long paragraphs and split his enormous sentences into manageable portions. They kept some sentences intact in order to represent the flavor of Simmel's prose; his long German sentences are carefully balanced and weighted in emphasis.

Certain word renderings have a significance or pervasiveness that also begs remark, among them the following:

+ *Wirklichkeit*—which is conventionally translated as "reality"—is often rendered here as "actuality." Occasionally, "reality" is used, although Simmel himself fairly consistently uses *Realität* for that term.
+ *Sollen/das Gesollt*, etc.: English has simply no comparably supple rendering for the various forms of *sollen* that Simmel employs in the fourth essay, "The Law of the Individual." The equivalent verb in English is "should," but this doesn't help very much—it would seem absurd in English to speak of "the Should," "the Shoulded," etc. The translators have opted for "the Ought," "the obliged," and the like as somewhat more natural and reflective of Simmel's takeoff point in ethics—though as Simmel makes clear, his conception of the realm of the Ought is far broader than that of traditional ethical concerns.
+ *Geist*, a notoriously difficult word to translate, is rendered either as "Mind" or as "Spirit," according to the context.
+ *Seele* has often been rendered as "soul"; *seelisch* as "psychic" or "psychical."

1

Life as Transcendence

Man's position in the world is defined by the fact that in every dimension of his being and behavior he finds himself at every moment between two boundaries. This condition appears as the formal structure of our existence, filled always with different contents in life's diverse provinces, activities, and destinies. We feel that the content and value of every hour stands between a higher and a lower; every thought between a wiser and a more foolish; every possession between a more extended and a more limited; every deed between a greater and a lesser measure of meaning, adequacy, and morality. We are continually orienting ourselves, even when we do not employ abstract concepts, to an "over us" and an "under us," to a right and a left, to a more or less, a tighter or looser, a better or worse. The boundary, above and below, is our means for finding direction in the infinite space of our worlds. Along with the fact that we *have* boundaries always and everywhere, so also we *are* boundaries. For insofar as every content of life—every feeling, experience, deed, or thought—possesses a specific intensity, a specific hue, a specific quantity, and a specific position in some order of things, there proceeds from each content a continuum in two directions, toward its two poles; content itself thus participates in each of these two continua, which collide in it and which it delimits. This participation in realities, tendencies, and ideas that are a plus and a minus, a this-side and a that-side of our here and now, may well be obscure and fragmentary; but it gives life two complementary, if also often colliding, values: richness and determinacy. For these continua by which we are bounded and whose segments we ourselves bound form a sort of coordinate system through which, as it were, the locus of every part and content of our life is identified.

For the most decisive meaning of the constitution of our existence through boundaries, however, this property of determinacy forms only the point of departure. For although the boundary as such is necessary, yet every single specific boundary can be stepped over, every fixity can be displaced, every enclosure can be burst, and every such act, of course, finds or creates a new boundary. The pair of statements—that the boundary is unconditional in that its existence is constitutive of our given position in the world, but that no boundary is unconditional since every one can in principle be altered, reached over, gotten around—this pair of statements appears as the explication of the inner unity of vital action. Out of countless cases I shall name merely one that is very characteristic of the turbulence of this process and of the persistence of our life through it: knowing and not knowing about the consequences of our actions. We are all like the chess player in this regard: if he did not know with a reasonable degree of probability what consequences would result from a certain move, the game would be impossible; but it would also be impossible if this foresight extended indefinitely. Plato's definition of the philosopher as he who stands between knowing and not-knowing holds for man in general; the slightest consideration shows how every step of our life without exception is determined and made possible by the fact that we perceive its consequences, and likewise because we perceive them only up to a certain point, beyond which they become confused and finally escape our vision altogether. Moreover, it is not only the fact that we stand on this border between knowledge and ignorance that makes our life what we know it to be; life would be completely different if the boundary were definitive in each instance, if with advancing life (both in general and in regard to every individual undertaking) the uncertain did not become more certain, and that which is most surely believed more questionable. The inherent displaceability and displacement of our boundaries means that we are able to express our essence with a paradox: we are bounded in every direction, and we are bounded in no direction.

Yet the essential fluidity of our boundaries immediately implies or signifies something further: that we also *know* our boundaries as such—first the particular boundaries and then the general ones. For only someone who stands outside his boundary in some sense knows that he stands within it; that is, knows it as a boundary at all. Kaspar Hauser did not know that he was in prison until he came into the open and could see the walls from without.[1] In the theoretical realm, for example, our direct experience and our introspective imaginative representations can only identify graduated phenomena within certain magnitudes. Beyond a certain degree, speed and slowness are not actually conceivable for us; we have no real picture of the speed of light or of the slowness with which a stalactite grows because we cannot project ourselves into such tempi; nor can we effectively imagine temperatures of 1,000 degrees or absolute zero; what lies beyond red and violet in the solar spectrum is not optically accessible to us at all; and so forth. Our imagination and *primary* apprehension stake out areas from the infinite fullness of reality and the infinite modes of apprehending it, probably so that the magnitude of stimuli that are thereby delimited suffices as a basis for our practical conduct. But this very reference to such boundaries shows that we can somehow step over them, that we *have* stepped over them. Concept and speculation, construction and calculation induce us to move beyond the world that we have, so to speak, in sensible reality, thereby revealing this world to us as bounded, by enabling us to look at its boundaries from the outside. Our concrete, immediate life posits an area that lies between an upper and a lower boundary; but consciousness of this account depends on the fact that life has become more abstract and advanced, thus transcending its boundary, and thereby confirming the reality of a boundary. Life holds the boundary fast, stands on this side of it—and in the same act stands on the other side of it and views it simultaneously from within and from without. The two aspects belong equally to its establishment, and just as the boundary itself partakes of both its "this side" and its "that side," so the unified act of life includes both boundedness and the transcendence of boundary, despite the fact that this, considered as a whole, seems to present a logical contradiction.

This self-transcendence of the spirit occurs not only in individual episodes, around whose quantitative limit we occasionally impose a broader boundary so as to recognize it as a true limit for the first time by bursting it. This process also governs the most dominant principles of consciousness. To illustrate, one of the most enormous steps mankind has made to go beyond a boundary, which at once results in an otherwise unattainable knowledge of our boundedness, lies in the broadening of our sensible world by the invention of the

---

1. Kaspar Hauser (ca. 1812–33), mysterious foundling and reputed lost prince of the House of Baden. Hauser's account of his childhood alleged that he had been kept incommunicado in a darkened cell for as long as he could remember, until released in his teenage years by a mysterious masked man. Though generating much speculation at the time, many key aspects of his self-account have since been debunked.—Trans.

telescope and the microscope. Formerly, man had a world defined and limited by the natural use of the senses, a world thus harmonious with his total organization. But since we have built eyes which see at billions of kilometers what we normally observe only at very short distances, and others which disclose the finest structures of objects at an enlargement that would have no place in our natural perception of space, this harmony has been disrupted. A most thoughtful biologist put it this way:

> A being whose eyes had the structure of a giant telescope would be formed quite differently from us in other regards, too. It would possess completely different faculties for making practical use of what it would see. It would fashion new objects, and above all would have a vastly longer life span than ours. Perhaps even its conception of time would be fundamentally different. As soon as we become aware of the disproportion between the space and time relations in such worlds and those of our own existence, we need only to remind ourselves that we could not walk on stilts a half kilometer long. But whether we enlarge our sense organs or our locomotive organs beyond their due is in principle the same: in both cases we break through the natural fitness of our organism.

We have thus transcended the compass of our natural being in certain directions; that is, the adaptation between our total organization and our world of perception. We now have around us a world that, if we consider man a unified being whose several parts are in appropriate relation to one another, is no longer "ours." Looking back from this world, however, which was won by transcending our being through its own powers, we regard ourselves in a hitherto unheard of cosmic diminution. As we push our boundaries out into the realm of the measureless, our relations to such vast spaces and times press us back in our consciousness to the magnitude boundary of an infinitesimal point. A similar situation applies with respect to the overall structure of our cognition. If we assume that the determination of truth depends on the fact that a priori categories form the given material of the world into objects of knowledge, what is "given" must nevertheless be able to be formed by these categories. Now either we conclude that our mind is so arranged that nothing at all can be "given" to it which does not fit these categories, or we determine the way in which a "givenness" can take place from the outset. Whether this determination of fact takes place one way or another, there exists no guarantee that the given (be it given in the sensible or the metaphysical manner) will even actually enter completely into the forms of our genuine or definitive cognition. Just as little as everything that is given us from the world enters into the forms of art, just as little as religion can possess itself of *every* content of life, so little perhaps is the totality of the given accommodated by these forms or categories of cognition. However, the fact that, as knowing beings and within the possibilities of cognition itself, we can even conceive that all the world might not enter the forms of our cognition; the fact that, even in a purely problematical way, we can imagine that there might be a given something in the world that we simply *cannot think of*—this represents a movement of the mental life beyond itself; a breakthrough and attainment of something beyond not only a single boundary, but beyond the mind's limits altogether; an act of self-transcendence, which alone sets the immanent limits of cognition, no matter whether these limits are actual or only possible. This formula holds no less true for each particular version of the general principle. The one-sidedness of the great philosophies expresses most unambiguously the relation between the infinite ambiguity of the world and our limited interpretive capacities. The fact that we know this one-sidedness as such, however—and not only individual instances of it, but one-sidedness as a necessity in principle—this places us above it. We deny the boundary the moment we know its one-sidedness, without ceasing thereby to stand within it. This is the only thing that allows us to be released from our despair about it, about our finiteness and mortality: that we do not simply stand *within* these boundaries, but by virtue of our awareness of them have passed beyond them. That we ourselves know our knowing and not-knowing, and that we again know this more embracing knowledge, and its infinite potential—this is the real infinity of the mind's vital movement. Every limit is herewith transcended, but of course only through the fact that it is set; that is, that there exists something to transcend. It is only with this self-transcending movement that the mind shows itself to be something absolutely vital. This carries over into the realm of ethics expressed in the idea, which has arisen ever again in numerous forms, that the moral task of man is to overcome himself. This notion appears all the way from a completely individualistic form:

> Von der Gewalt, die alle Wesen bindet,
> Befreit der Mensch sich, der sich überwindet.
> [From the force all creatures heed
> He who transcends himself is freed.]

to that of the philosophy of history:

> *Der Mensch ist etwas, das überwinden werden soll.*
> [Man is something that is to be overcome.]

Logically considered, this, too, presents a contradiction: he who overcomes himself is admittedly the victor, but he is also the defeated. The ego succumbs to itself, when it wins; it achieves victory, when it suffers defeat. Yet the contradiction only arises when the two aspects of this unity are hardened into opposed, mutually exclusive conceptions. It is precisely the fully unified process of the moral life which overcomes and surpasses every lower state by achieving a higher one, and again transcends this latter state through one still higher. That man overcomes himself means that he reaches out beyond the bounds that the moment sets for him. There must be something at hand to be overcome, but it is only there in order to be overcome. Thus even as an ethical agent, man is the limited being that has no limit. This hasty sketch of a very general and not especially profound aspect of life may serve to prepare the way for the conception of life to be developed here. As a point of departure, I will take up a consideration of time.

Taking the term in its full logical strictness, the present does not encompass more than the absolute unextendedness of a moment; it is as little time as the point is space. It denotes exclusively the collision of past and future, which alone make up *amounts* of time; that is, time as such. But since the one is no longer, and the other not yet, reality adheres to the present alone; this means that reality is not at all something temporal; the concept of time can be applied to reality's contents only if the atemporality they possess as *present* has become a "no more" or a "not yet," at any rate a nothing. Time is not in reality, and reality is not time. We acknowledge the force of this paradox, however, only for the logically observed object. The subjectively *lived* life will not adjust to it; the latter is felt, no matter whether or not it is logically justified, to be something real in a temporal dimension. Common usage indicates this, if in an inexact and superficial way, by understanding of the term "present" not only the mere punctuality of its conceptual sense, but also always a bit of the past and a somewhat smaller bit of the future. (These "bits" vary greatly in size according to whether the present in question is of a personal or political, cultural or geological nature.)

Considered now more deeply, the reality of life at any moment carries its past within it in a very different way from that of a mechanical phenomenon. The latter is so indifferent toward its past, out of which it has emerged as an effect, that the same condition can in principle be produced by a number of different causal complexes. On the other hand, the hereditary material out of which an organism develops contains countless *individual* elements, such that the past sequence which leads to *its* individuality can by no means be replaced by another: the results have not vanished without a trace into the true net result, as is true of mechanical effects, which can result from the most diverse combinations of causes. The protrusion [*Hineinleben*] of the past into the present first appears in full purity, however, when life has reached the stage of consciousness [*Geist*]. At this level it can take two forms: objectification in concepts and structures, which from the moment of their appearance become *tale quale*[2] the reproducible possession of countless succeeding generations; and *memory*, with which the past of the subjective life not only becomes the cause of the life of the present, but also continues over into the present with its contents relatively unchanged. Insofar as previous experience lives in us as memory, not as an atemporal content but linked in our consciousness with its position in time, it is not entirely transformed into its effect (as in the mechanistic and causal mode of observation). Instead, the sphere of actual, present life stretches all the way back to the moment of its formation. Of course, the past as such does not thereby rise from the grave; but because we comprehend an experience not as a present thing, but rather as one that is attached to some moment in the past, our present is not focused on one point, as is that of a mechanical existence, but is, so to speak, extended backward. At such instances we live beyond the moment back into the past.

It is similar with our relation to the future, which is in no way adequately characterized by defining man as the "goal-setting" being. The somehow remote "goal" appears as a fixed point, discontinuous with the present, whereas what is decisive is the immediate carryover [*Hineinleben*] of present will—and feeling and thought—into the future: the living present consists in the fact that it transcends the present. With every exertion of the will in the here and now, we demonstrate that a threshold between "now" and the "future" is just not real, and that as soon as we assume such a threshold, we stand at once on this side and on the other side of it. The concept of "goal" permits the continuous movement of life to coalesce about one point (whereby it manages to satisfy most of the demands of rationalism and of practice); it swallows up the stretch of uninterrupted temporal life between "now" and "later," and thereby it creates a gap on whose respective sides the present point and the goal-point stand firmly fixed. Insofar as the future, just like the past, is localized at some point, however indefinite, and the life process is disrupted and crystallized into the logical differentiation of three grammatically separate tenses, the immediate continuous stretching of itself into the future, which every living present signifies, gets concealed. The future does not lie ahead of us like some untrodden land that is separated from the present by a sharp boundary line, but rather we live continually in a border region that belongs as much to the

2. "As is."—Trans.

future as to the present. All theories that locate our psychic essence in the will merely express the fact that psychic existence projects out beyond its narrow present, so to speak; that the future is already encompassed within it. A mere wish may well be aimed toward the distant, not yet living future, but the actual will stands directly outside the contrast between present and future. At the very moment of willing we are already beyond it, because the logically apparent but necessary unextendedness of the will's activity could not accommodate the establishment of the *direction* in which life must move further—to describe it as virtually established in this punctuality would be a mere word to conceal the incomprehensible. Life *is* truly both past and future; these are not just appended to it by thought, as they are to inorganic, merely punctual reality. In procreation and growth, before life reaches the level of consciousness, the same form must be acknowledged: that life at any given moment transcends itself, and its present forms a unity with the "not-yet" of the future. As long as past, present, and future are separated with conceptual precision, time is unreal, because only the temporally unextended (i.e., the atemporal present) moment is real. But life is the unique mode of existence for whose actuality this separation does not hold; the three tenses in their logical separateness are applicable to it only through subsequent analysis, following the mechanistic model. Time is real only for life alone. (The whole ideality of time in Kant is perhaps deeply linked to the mechanistic element in his worldview.) Time is the—perhaps abstract—form in our consciousness of that which is life itself, as experienced in inexpressible, immediate concreteness. Time is life seen apart from its contents, because life alone transcends in both directions the atemporal present-point of every other reality and only thereby realizes, all by itself, the temporal dimension (i.e., time). If we retain the concept and fact of the present at all, as we are both justified and indeed compelled to do, then this essential structure of life signifies a continual reaching out beyond itself as something in the present. This reaching out by life into that which is not its actuality, but such that this reaching out nevertheless *shapes* its actuality—is, therefore, not something that has merely been tagged onto life but rather, as it takes place in growth, procreation, and the spiritual processes, is the very essence of life itself. This mode of existence does not restrict its reality to the present moment, thereby pushing past and future into the realm of the unreal. Instead, its unique continuity is sustained outside of this separation—its past actually exists into its present, and its present actually exists out into its future. This mode of existence is what we call life.

The statement that life takes place in the form I have characterized as a "reaching out beyond itself" is grounded in a truly antinomial relation. We conceive of life as a continuous stream proceeding through successive generations. Yet the bearers of this process (i.e., not those who have it, but those who are it) are *individuals* (i.e., closed, self-centered, unambiguously distinct beings). Although the stream of life flows through—or more accurately, *as*—these individuals, it nevertheless dams up in each of them and becomes a sharply outlined form. Each individual then asserts itself as a complete entity, both against other individuals of its kind and against the total environment with all its contents, and it does not tolerate any blurring of its periphery. Here lies an ultimate, metaphysically problematic condition of life: that it is boundless continuity and, at the same time, boundary-determined ego. Furthermore, vital movement is somehow held still not only in the "I" as a total existence, but also in all experienced contents and objectivities, as at a single point. Wherever something with a definite form is experienced, life is caught up as it were in a blind alley, or feels its streaming crystallized in and given form by that something; it is bounded. But since life's further flowing is incessant all the same—since the persisting centrality of the total organism, of the "I," or its more relative contents, cannot nullify the essential continuity of the flowing—the idea arises that life pushes out beyond the given organic, or spiritual, or objective form; that it overflows the dam. A purely continuous, Heraclitic flux which lacks a definite and persistent "something" would not contain the boundary over which a reaching out is to occur, nor the subject *which* reaches out. But as soon as "something" exists as a unity unto itself, gravitating toward its own center, then all the flow from within its bounds to beyond its bounds is no longer agitation without a subject; rather, it somehow remains bound up with the center, so that even the movement beyond its boundary belongs to the center; it represents a reaching out in which this form always remains the subject, and yet which proceeds nonetheless beyond this subject. Life is at once flux without pause and yet something enclosed in its bearers and contents, formed about individualized midpoints, and contrarily it is therefore always a bounded form that continually oversteps its bounds; that is, its essence. Certainly the category I call here "the reaching out of life beyond itself" is thus meant only symbolically, only with an indication that it can probably be improved. Taken in its essence, however, I hold it at all events to be a primary one. So far it has been described only in a schematic and abstract way, thus producing only the bare sketch or form for the concretely filled life. Insofar as life's essence goes, transcendence is immanent to it (it is not something that might be added to its being, but instead is constitutive of its being).

The simplest and most fundamental instance of what is meant here is self-awareness, which is also the original phenomenon of the living human spirit.

The "I" not only confronts itself and makes itself—as knower—the object of its own knowing, but it even judges itself as a third party, esteems or deprecates itself, and so puts itself *above* itself—for all that, it moves beyond itself constantly and yet remains in itself, since its subject and object are here identical. In the intellectual process of knowing itself the self spreads apart this identity, without thereby mutilating it (because the latter is not rigidly substantialist). The surmounting of the knowing consciousness over itself as known rises to the infinite: I know not only that I know, but I also know that I know this; writing down this sentence I lift myself yet again above the previous stages of this process. A difficulty in thinking appears here. It is as if the "I" were so to speak always chasing after itself, without ever being able to overtake itself. The difficulty disappears, however, as soon as "reaching beyond itself" is recognized as the primary phenomenon of life, occurring here in its most sublimated form, completely detached from all accidental content. By virtue of our highest, self-transcending consciousness at any given moment, we are the absolute above our relativity. But as the further advance of this process again relativizes that absolute, the transcendence of life is revealed as the true absoluteness in which the contrast between the absolute and the relative is collapsed. Through such an elevation above the contrasts inherent in the basic fact that transcendence is immanent in life, the eternally felt conflicts in life come to rest: life is at once fixed and variable; of finished shape, and developing further; formed, and ever breaking through its forms; persisting, yet rushing onward; bounded and free; circling around in subjectivity, yet standing objectively over things and over itself—all these contrasts are but unfoldings or refractions of that metaphysical fact: the innermost essence of life is its capacity to go out beyond itself, to set its limits by reaching out beyond them; that is, beyond itself. The ethical problem of *will* discloses the same form as that which the mental self-transcendence of life manifests in its consciousness of self-awareness. We can conceive of the course of human will only through the image that a plurality of intentional strivings is typically alive within us, from which a higher will selects one that shall develop further and culminate in action. It is not in those desires for whose emergence we generally do not feel responsible, but in this ultimate will that we experience what we call freedom and what establishes our responsibility. It is naturally one and the same will that is spread open in this process of self-transcendence, just as it is one and the same "I" which separates in self-awareness into object and subject. For the former, however, the multiplicity of contents gives rise to a dichotomy and a choice, something that does not come into question for the theoretical self-awareness. The infinite regress of this latter also has a certain analogy here. We often sense that even a decision made by exerting the will against itself does not correspond with our real will; there remains a still higher authority within us that could quash that very decision. On the other hand, the feeling that life has been fully attained can be described symbolically by saying that the course of practical self-appraisal, no matter how high it climbs, never finds a check, or paradoxically, the will also really wills our will. Everyone is familiar with the peculiar malaise of situations where we have chosen to do something in practice that we do not regard as our ultimate will. Perhaps many difficulties in the problem of freedom, like the problem of the self, result from hardening stages of the processes just mentioned into substantiality, a process which language can scarcely avoid. When this happens, such stages appear as closed, autonomous parties among which only mechanical interplay is possible. This would be otherwise if one saw in it all the primary phenomenon in which life reveals itself as a continuous process of self-transcendence, and in which this self-accentuation and constant abandonment of itself is precisely the mode of its unity, of its remaining in itself.

A deep contradiction exists between continuity and form as ultimate world-shaping principles. Form means limits, contrast against what is neighboring, cohesion of a periphery by means of a real or an ideal center to which, as it were, the ever on-flowing sequences of contents or processes are bent back, and which provides that periphery with a firm hold against dissolution in the flux. If one takes seriously the concept of continuity—the extensive depiction of the absolute unity of being—such peculiar stability of an enclave of being is not admissible; it precludes discussion about the continual destruction of forms, because something that could be destroyed would not be able to arise in the first place. For this reason Spinoza was unable to derive any positive *determination* from the conception of absolute, unified being. Form, on the other hand, cannot be altered; it is eternally invariable. The form of an obtuse-angled triangle remains forever just that; and if shifting the side makes it an acute-angled triangle, its form, in whatever moment of the process I catch it, is absolutely fixed and absolutely different from that of any other moment, no matter how slight the deviation. The expression—the triangle has changed "it-self"—imparts to it, in anthropomorphic fashion, a lifelike subjectivity which alone (as shall be discussed further) is capable of self-change. Form, however, is individuality. It can be identically reproduced in countless bits of matter, but that it should exist twice as pure form makes no sense. That would be as if the sentence—two times two equals four—could, as ideal truth, exist twice, although it can of course be realized by countless centers of consciousness. Equipped with this metaphysical uniqueness, form impresses on its bit of matter an individual shape, makes it peculiar to itself as distinguished from differently formed items. Form tears the bit of matter out of the continuity of

the next-to-one-another and the after-one-another and gives it a meaning of
its own, a meaning whose determinate boundedness cannot be reconciled with
the streaming of total being, if the latter is truly not to be dammed up. Now
if life—as a cosmic, generic, singular phenomenon—is a continuous stream,
then this not only provides the basis for its profound opposition against form:
an opposition that appears as the unceasing, usually unnoticed and incidental
(but also often revolutionary) battle of ongoing life against the historical pattern and formal inflexibility of any given cultural content, but thereby it also
becomes the innermost impulse toward culture change. Moreover, individuality as distinctive form seems to have to withdraw from the continuity of life's
flux, which admits no closed structures. This is indicated empirically in that
the highest peaks of individuality, the greatest geniuses, almost consistently
produce few or no viable offspring because women, during periods of emancipation when they strive to advance from their status as "women in general"
to a stronger expression and justification of their individuality, seem to show a
declining fertility. Among strongly individualized men of higher cultures one
feels, through numerous indications and disguises, a hostility against their
function, against being a wave in the ongoing stream of life that surges through
them. That is by no means only a presumptuous exaggeration of their personal significance—a desire to distinguish themselves qualitatively from the
masses—but it is instead an instinct for the irreconcilable opposition between
life and form, or, in other words, between continuity and individuality. The decisive element here is not at all the nature of the latter, its characteristic pecu-
liarity or uniqueness; but rather the for-itself, in-itself character of individual
form in contrast to the all-embracing continuous stream of life, which not only
dissolves all form-giving boundaries but even prevents them from coming into
being. Nevertheless, individuality is everywhere something alive, and life is everywhere individual. So one might suppose that the whole problem of incom-
patibility of the two principles is one of those purely conceptual antinomies
which appear whenever immediately lived reality is projected onto the plane
of intellectuality: there reality inevitably breaks up into a plurality of elements
that did not exist in its primary objective unity, and that now, rigidified and
logically independent, show mutual discrepancies whose reconciliation the intellect may try, subsequently and seldom successfully, to accomplish, because
the latter's intrinsically analytic character prevents it from creating pure syntheses. But this is not altogether the case. That duality lies embedded in the
very depths of the feeling of life, but there it is of course surrounded by a living
unity and is recognized as a duality only where it steps over the edge of that
unity, so to speak (as happens only in certain culture-historical situations);
only at this border does it deliver itself up as a problem to the intellect, which

(because by its character it cannot do otherwise) as an antinomy projects it back even onto that ultimate stratum of life. This stratum is dominated by something which intellect can only call the overcoming of the duality by unity, but which is in itself a third principle beyond duality and unity: the essence of life as the transcendence of itself. In *one* act, it creates something more than the vital stream itself—individual structure—and then breaks through this form that has been etched by a blockage in that stream, which lets the stream reach out beyond its bounds and plunge back again into the ongoing flux. We are not divided into life free from limits and form made secure by them; we do not live partly in continuity, partly in individuality, the two asserting themselves against each other. Rather, the fundamental essence of life is precisely that internally unified function which, albeit symbolically and inadequately, I have termed the transcendence of itself, and which immediately actualizes as *one* life what is then split—by feelings, destinies, and conceptualization—into the dualism of continuous life flux and individually closed form. But should one prefer to characterize the one side of this dualism as life pure and simple, and the other as individual structure which makes a simple contrast to the former, then one should seek further to achieve an absolute concept of life which subsumes that view, still aloof to contradiction, within itself and is therefore merely relative. Just as there is a broadest concept of the good that includes both good and bad in their relative sense, and a broadest concept of beauty that embraces the contrast of the beautiful and the ugly, so life in the absolute sense is something that includes life in its relative sense and in its respective opposite, or unfolds itself to them as its empirical phenomena. Self-transcendence thus appears as the unified act of the building up and breaking through of life's bounds, of its *alter*, as the character of life's absoluteness—which makes its analysis into autonomized opposites quite intelligible.

Schopenhauer's "will to life" and Nietzsche's "will to power" doubtless lie in the direction of concrete fulfillment of this idea of life; although Schopenhauer feels boundless continuity to be more decisive, Nietzsche places more stress on individuality as circumscribed by form. Perhaps because they understand life's transcendence one-sidedly as volitional, it has escaped them that what is decisive, what constitutes life, is the absolute *unity* of both aspects. In fact, though, this unity holds for all dimensions of vital movement. Thus, life has two mutually complementary definitions: it is *more-life*, and it is *more-than-life*. The "more" does not arrive by accident to augment a life already stable in its quantity; instead, life is the movement that, for each of its parts, even when these are comparatively pitiful, at every moment draws something into itself in order to transform it into its life. No matter what its absolute measure, life can only exist in that it is more-life; so long as life is present at all, it begets vitality, because sheer physiological self-maintenance involves continual regeneration. This is not one function that it exercises among others; rather, insofar as it does this it *is* life. If, as I am furthermore convinced, death is immanent in life from the outset, this, too, is a stepping out of life beyond itself. While remaining in its center, life stretches out toward the absolute of life, as it were, and becomes in this direction more-life; but it also stretches out toward nothingness, and just as it persists and yet increases itself in *one* action, so also it persists and declines in *one* action, *as* one action. Here again is that *absolute* concept of life, of more-life, that includes the more and the less as relativities and is *genus proximum* to both. The deep relationship man has always perceived between birth and death, as if some formal relation existed between them as life catastrophes, finds here one of its metaphysical pivots: both events are attached to the subjective life and transcend it, both rising above and falling below it, so to speak. Life, beyond which they extend, is nevertheless not conceivable without them. To climb beyond oneself in growth and reproduction, to sink below oneself in old age and death—these are not additions to life; rather, such rising up and spilling over the boundedness of the individual condition is life itself. Perhaps the whole idea of the immortality of man simply signifies the accumulated feeling, heightened into a uniquely immense symbol, for this transcendence of life beyond itself.

The logical difficulty raised by the statement that life is at once itself and more than itself is only a problem of expression. If we wish to express the unified character of life in abstract terms, our intellect has no alternative but to divide it into two such parts, which appear as though they were mutually exclusive and only subsequently merge to form that unity. Once these parts are fixed in mutual opposition, the duality admittedly yields a contradiction. It is naturally an *ex post facto* reconstruction of immediately lived life to characterize it as a unity of boundary-setting and boundary-transcending, of individual centeredness and of reaching out, because describing it this way divides it precisely at this point of unity. For conceptual expression, the constitution of life in its quantity and quality and the transcendence of this quantity and quality can only touch each other at this point, so to speak, whereas actual life that goes on there encompasses both sides, constitution and transcendence, as a real unity. As I indicated above, spiritual life *cannot* do otherwise than present itself in forms: in words or deeds, in patterns or any sort of contents in which psychic energy currently realizes itself. But from the very moment of their emergence these formulations of its patterns possess an objective significance of their own, a fixity and inner logic, with which they confront the life that created them; the latter is a restless onward streaming that not only overflows any particular definite form, but overflows every form because it is *form.* Because of this basic contrast in essence, life cannot enter into form at all—beyond every attained structure it must at once seek out another one, in which the play—necessary structure, and necessary dissatisfaction with the structure as such—is repeated. As life it needs form; as life, it needs more than a given form. Life is thus caught up in the contradiction that it can only be lodged in forms and yet cannot be lodged in forms, that it passes beyond and destroys every one it has created. This, of course, appears as a contradiction only in logical reflection, because the individual form exists as an intrinsically valid, real or ideally fixed structure, discontinuous with other forms, and in logical antithesis to movement, streaming, reaching further. Life as immediately experienced is precisely the unity of "being formed" and "reaching out or flowing beyond form," which manifests itself at any single moment as destruction of the given current form. Life is indeed always more life than that accommodated in the form currently allotted to and grown from it. Insofar as psychic life is perceived in terms of its contents, it is in each case finite and self-bounded: therefore it consists of these ideal contents, which now have the form of life. But the process reaches beyond any given form and indeed beyond itself. We conceive, feel, desire this and that—they are tightly circumscribed contents, and this thing is something logical that is merely realized now, something that is completely definite and definable in principle. Yet, as we experience it, something else is also there, something inexpressible, indefinable, that we feel of every life as such: that it is more than every assignable content; that it swings out beyond every content, regarding it not only from the inside out (as is the nature of the logical content statement) but likewise from without, from what is beyond it. We are in life's content and at the same time outside of it; in receiving this content—and no other given element—into the form of *life,* we discover, by that very fact, more than its content.

Thus the dimension is suggested into which life transcends itself when it is not only more-life, but more-than-life. This is always the case when we call ourselves creative, not just in the specific sense of a rare, individual power, but in the sense—obvious for all imagination—that imagination produces a content that has a sense of its own, a logical coherency, a certain validity or permanency independent of its being produced and borne by life. This independent character of the created product speaks as little against its origin in the pure, exclusive creativity of the individual life as does the origin of physical offspring from no other potency than that of the parent, which is called into question by the fact that the offspring is a fully independent being. And just as the creation of this autonomous being, thenceforward independent of the creator, is immanent to physiological life and, in fact, characterizes life as such, so too the creation of an independently meaningful content is immanent to life at the level of the spirit. The fact that our ideas and cognitions, our values and judgments stand completely beyond the creative life in their meaning, their objective intelligibility and their historical effectiveness—this is the exact characteristic of human life. Just as life's transcendence, within the plane of life itself, of its current, delimited form constitutes more-life (although it is nevertheless the immediate, inescapable essence of life itself), so also its transcendence into the level of objective content, of logically autonomous and no longer vital meaning, constitutes more-than-life, which is inseparable from it and is the essence of spiritual life itself. In general this signifies nothing other than that life is not merely life (although it is certainly also nothing else), but is rather absolute life, because it embraces the relative contrast between life in the narrower sense and content independent of life. As the definition of spiritual life one can even declare that it produces something with a meaning and law unto itself. This self-alienation of life, this confronting of itself in an autonomous form, can only appear as a contradiction when a rigid boundary is established between its within and its without, as though they were two self-centered substances, rather than conceiving of it as a continuous movement whose unity at every point is divided into those opposing directions only by the spatial symbolism of our expression. Having made this assumption, however, we are able to look at life only as the subject's continual reaching out into what is foreign to him, or as the production of something foreign to him. But the latter is by no means thereby subjectivized; rather, it persists in its independence, in its being more-than-life. The absoluteness of its otherness is much too watered down, mediated, or made problematic by the idealistic view that "the world is my idea"; and this also implies that actual full transcendence would appear impracticable, illusory. No, the absoluteness of this other, of this *more*, that life creates or into which it penetrates, is precisely the formula and condition of life as it is lived: it *is* from the outset nothing other than a reaching-out-beyond-itself. This dualism, sustained in full sharpness, not only fails to contradict the unity of life, but is indeed the very way in which its unity exists. In life as volition this finds an extreme expression in the prayer: "Lord, Thy will be done, and not mine." Logically it appears utterly perplexing that I both do and do *not* want something to occur. This paradox disappears with the insight that, just as in the theoretical and productive spheres, life here has raised itself (in the form of an autonomous structure) above itself, and in this development has so remained within itself that it genuinely knows the will attributed to *that* structure as its own; it is thus a matter of indifference whether or not its lower level (which is still so firmly held that it is still described as "my" will) corresponds or differs in its content with the higher level (which is nevertheless one's own will also, since the "I" *wishes* its fulfillment). It is here, where the process knows itself from the start to be transcendent and feels the will of the transcendent object to be ultimately its own, that transcendence reveals itself as the immanent condition of life perhaps most strikingly of all.

One of the ultimate concerns of the modern worldview can be thus characterized. Man has always been aware of certain realities and values, certain objects of belief and validities, for which there is no room in his seemingly strictly circumscribed space, because he feels the latter to be filled up by his immediately distinctive, self-centered substance. At first he expresses the certainty of this awareness in that he consolidates all such things in separate existences outside of life. He beholds them in the sharply separated beyond and lets them react back from there onto life (although, to be sure, in what manner is unknown). Against this naivete arises critical enlightenment, which recognizes nothing "beyond" the subject; it throws back everything located in the beyond within the bounds of subjective immediacy, and thus declares as illusion whatever tends to persist nevertheless in independent confrontation. This is the first step of the great tendency in intellectual history: to place back into life itself, by means of a mighty revolution, everything that had been established outside of life in its own existence and which came to life from beyond. But since at this point life is conceived as absolute immanence, everything remains in a subjectivization (albeit with manifold nuances), a denial of the form of the beyond, and one fails to notice that with this delimitation of the subject he has in fact made himself dependent on the idea of the beyond, and that it is only in and from this beyond that the boundary could take shape in which life was caught and busied itself in the unbreakable circle of the self. Hence, the attempt is made here to conceive of life as something that *constantly* reaches beyond the bounds of its beyond and which finds its essence in this reaching beyond. It is an attempt to find the definition of life in general in this transcendence, to retain firmly the consistency of its individual form, to be sure, but only in order that it may be broken through by the continuous process. Life finds its essence, its process, in being more-life and more-than-life; its positive is as such already its comparative. I am well aware of the logical difficulties that confront the conceptual expression of this way of viewing life. I have tried to formulate these difficulties, in full presence of the logical danger, because *possibly* we have here reached the level in which logical difficulties do not command immediate silence—because this is the level from which the metaphysical root of logic itself is ultimately nourished.

2

The Turn toward Ideas

With the word "world" in its broadest, most complete sense, popular consciousness thinks it apprehends the sum of all things and events that are at all real, whether comprehensible to us or not. In fact, it apprehends something else altogether: even if the entire infinity of world contents were given to us piece by piece, we would only have one and another and yet another—that together these pieces comprise "a world," though, is something added to this mere existence of many particulars, a *form* in which they must be apprehended. Only spirit is capable of fashioning a unity of all, of gathering it into a web that it itself has spun. When we speak of "world," we mean an entire range, of whose contents only a miniscule portion is accessible to us. This can only be clarified by saying that we are somehow in possession of a formula that allows even the unknown to attach to the known and to combine with it into the unity of *one* world. World in the full sense is thus a sum of contents freed by spirit from the isolated existence of

Earlier versions of the second through fourth essays have appeared in *Logos*. The second essay is essentially only enlarged, but not very much altered, while the other two, though retaining their basic themes, are to be seen as new works. The decisive point, however—which could not emerge in the separate publications—is that they are all held together by the same metaphysical concept of life set forth in the first essay and, as parts of the unfolding of its potential, reveal its ultimate meaning.

each piece and brought into a unitary coherence, into a form that is capable of including known and unknown.

But it still does no good to say, "this is all unity and therefore one world," because sheer unity is an utterly feeble abstract concept. It can only be realized where a *definite* unity, a specifiable principle, a somehow differentiated law, a coloration or rhythm, or an understandable sense ties the particular realities together. A whole series of such unity-creating principles probably contributes to the popular "world": space, time, universal interaction, and causation by *one* divine creator. If we did not perceive these as universally valid schemata to which all actual things submit and which, reaching beyond each particular element, put them in connection with every other particular element—then we would have merely particular things, but not *one* world, and thus not a *world*. Philosophical "world"-views arise as this somewhat diffuse unity is concentrated into sharply defined, exclusive master concepts. With such concepts— of being or becoming, of matter or spirit, of harmony or thoroughgoing dualism, of purpose or godliness and many others—philosophers approach reality, known and not yet known (whether or not these concepts themselves arise from particular experiences), and where any such concept represents the defining, appropriative energy of their perceiving, the mere sum of real elements is formed into a world for them. To say that philosophers do violence to the world with the one-sidedness of their principles is a wrongly formulated accusation. Only through such principles does the world come to be in the first place—though naturally a particular principle can be inadequate, too narrow for the facts, or self-contradictory. Indeed, in that case it brings no world into existence. Perhaps there is then one based on a *better* principle, but without such one-sidedness there is no world at all. What everyone else does when speaking of the world, philosophers achieve only in a more decisive, though correspondingly more one-sided, conceptualization. Now for any particular thinker, the choice of which leading concept creates his world as such evidently depends upon his characterological type, upon his way of existing in relation to the world, which grounds the way his thinking relates to the world.

But there is still another type of concept we use to designate varieties of the spirit's activity, a type so embracing that through its formative powers the theoretical infinity of possible contents coalesces in each case into a "world" united by a consciously *special* character. Above all this is true of the great functional types of the spirit, through each of which it develops (presumably) the same totality of contents into a distinctively self-enclosed world subservient to an unmistakable general principle: the world in the form of art, in the form of knowledge, in the form of religion, in the form of gradations of value and significance in general. Seen purely ideally, no content can escape being known, taking on artistic form, or being evaluated religiously. These worlds are mutually incapable of any mixture, any overlap, any intersection, because each already expresses the entire stuff of the world in its special language, though obviously in any particular case boundary uncertainties arise, and a bit of the world formed by one category may be assimilated into the other and there treated anew as raw material. In each of these spheres, we catch a glimpse of an inner, substantive logic, one that certainly provides scope for great diversity and contradiction, but also binds the creative spirit to its objective validity. And we imagine these formations, once created, to be entirely independent in their sense and value from whether and how often they are adopted by individuals and actualized in their minds. As works or acts of sanctity, as systems or imperatives they have a self-sufficient, internally coherent existence in which they are freed, both from the psychic life whence they have emerged and from that which adopts them.

Now we cannot grasp the stuff of the world in its purity; rather, grasping already means putting it into one of those great categories each of which, in its complete elaboration, forms a world. For example, if we imagine the color blue, then it is perhaps as an element of the sensorially operative world, the locus of our practical life. To this sense probably also belongs, generally, that imaginary notion in which we have distilled only the color from the accompanying circumstances in which the world of reality entangles it. In the abstractness of the pure world of knowledge, however, blue is significant in a completely different sense: there it is a specific oscillation of ether waves or a specific place in the spectrum or a specific physiological or mental reaction. Yet another sense identifies it as an element of the world of feeling, in lyrical sentiments regarding the blue heaven or the blue eyes of the beloved. It is the same and yet, with regard to its worldly significance, a completely differently oriented blue when it belongs to the religious domain, perhaps as the color of the Madonna's robe or generally as a symbol of the mystical world. The stuff formed in this way into an element of quite diverse worlds is surely not a "thing-in-itself," because it cannot be grasped without thereby being formed; it is not a transcendent thing that becomes a phenomenon by being known or valued, religiously ordained or artistically fashioned. The stuff of the world is entirely contained in these respective composites: it is not borrowed from a more independent existence. "Contents" have an existence sui generis. They are neither "real" (for they only become that), nor are they merely the abstraction of the diverse ways they are categorized, for they are not something incomplete like the abstract concept vis-à-vis the concrete thing; nor do they have the metaphysical existence of Plato's "ideas." For although with "ideas" he is on the way to "contents," he does not reach the conceptual purity of the latter because he apprehends them logically and intellectually, but thus one-sidedly. He takes logical form-ing and connection for the utterly pure, not an already specifically prejudiced, point of view. Just as a bit of physical matter appears in any number of forms but cannot exist without *some* form or other—and the concept of its pure, formless materiality, though logically justified, is nonetheless an abstraction that no type of intuition can attain—so too, perhaps, the same holds true for the stuff (as I call it) of the worlds that, each with its own basic theme, form this stuff into totalities (even if these can be finalized only at the point of infin-ity). It is exactly this capability in principle of drawing material into its overall compass that permits me to call reality as a whole—and similarly the artisti-cally creatable, the theoretically knowable and the religiously construable—a world. Seen from the viewpoint of the human spirit, there is by no means only *one* world, if world means the connectedness of all possible givens that become a continuum via any absolutely valid principle. Continuity is indispensable for the concept of a world: that which stands in no relationship at all, immedi-ate or nonimmediate, does not belong in *one* world. If someone says there is only *one* world, he means without exception the locus of our practical interest, for the necessity of life allows humanity to glance so seldom beyond this that the artistic, religious, purely theoretical contents appear only as more or less isolated particularities. For most people the so-called real world is the world absolutely, and its practical preponderance hides the fact that those contents formed differently belong to their own worlds, into which the jurisdiction of the actuality-form does not extend.

Inside the historical realizations of these worlds the picture admittedly looks different. Absolute knowledge, absolute art, absolute religion do not exist. No definite notion connects any longer with the absolute generality of these ideas; they lie so to speak in the infinite—where, for example, the lines of all possible artistic production whatsoever intersect; therefore "art in gen-eral" perhaps cannot be defined. Only a historical art ever exists, that is, an art conditioned by circumstance in its technique, its expressive possibilities, its peculiarities of style; but such an art obviously cannot accommodate each of the infinitely many contents of the world. To take quite a singular example: just as not every emotional experience can be expressed in every lyric style, similarly there is a general limit to the latitude with which the artistic forms developed up to any historic moment are applicable to the world's contents. The maxim proclaimed particularly by artistic naturalism—that there is no world content that cannot be formed into a work of art—is artistic mega-lomania: here naturalism is laying claim to the entire sphere in which art in general and as an absolute principle *could* form the stuff of the world, on behalf of an art that is necessarily limited in its formative power and realized by us within a particular historical instant. Certainly the artistic procedures of Giotto or Botticelli cannot encompass the color impressions of the Degas ballerinas. But this expanding process clearly will never end, and it is equally certain that art is able to form an absolutely complete world according to its idea, and that every given art can only fragmentarily realize this possibility-in-principle. It is obvious that the same is true with the religious world. Often enough, attempts are made to assemble the entirety of things and of life into a seamless religious world. Yet even with relatively limited material this has not succeeded, and there always remains something of the world's stuff that is not ruled by religious categories—though it would surely be *possible* even for those contents not grasped by the historical religions to be formed in religious fashion, so that ideally (and therefore really) one religious world exists. This may also be seen in the "real" world. There are certain world-contents that, for example, are fully meaningful within art and by its particular logic are coherent in themselves and with others, without being able to exist under the category of reality:[1] in principle and perhaps for a higher or differently organized spirit these too would belong to the "real" world. Obviously even artworks and religious notions can be regarded as realities and thus as pieces of the real world; yet by their meaning they now belong along with their (in the former respect "real") content to particular total-worlds. These latter must pay for their hypothetically world-scale completeness in that, within historical life, they always appear as individually one-sided and consequently are not capable of comprehending the entirety of possible contents. That this circumstance nonetheless suits the reality principle to a relatively higher degree lies simply in its connectedness with outward life-praxis, which does not give individual differences, one-sidedness, and accidental developments nearly as great a scope, but holds us to a relatively consistent attitude whose formulations develop more into gradual enrichment than into mutual repulsion.

Now one might maintain not only that the representations and elaborations of the principles art, religion, value, etc., are determined by historical accident, but also that the existence of these principles in the first place is attributable to the historical development of mankind; that in a higher sense it is ultimately through accident and the mere facticity of our mental apparatus that these categories and not totally different ones exist and form worlds; it has in fact been asserted recently that the category "art" belongs to a now al-

---

1. Here one must not confuse "world" a priori with the "real world"; rather, "world" is the quite general form of which "reality" is a particular determination.

most ended human epoch. Even if we admit this thesis (without entering into its metaphysical argumentation) it in no way threatens this discussion. We are dealing only with the fact that these worlds exist ideally, whether necessarily or not, and that as worlds they are coordinated with that of actuality. If we assert their contingency, we must also admit the very same for actuality. Even the fact that we grasp possible contents in the form of actuality cannot be shown as necessary—there are in fact dreamy, "actuality-alien" persons before whom the contents of existence glide as mere images, and who never properly grasp the concept of "actuality." As seldom as this occurs in *full* measure among such people, it is nonetheless an indicator that actuality is not something absolute against which all other worlds are relative, accidental, and subjective—rather, they all stand ontologically on the same level, whether we declare this level as a whole to be an objective or a historically subjective one.

Now the individually lived life has a peculiar relationship to these world-entireties which lie in an imaginary pattern around us, and which we seem with every spiritual productivity more to discover and conquer than to create. Every objective process of consciousness belongs, by its content and meaning, in one of these worlds. It is as though they were merely separate levels through which life continually oscillates, adopting or interpolating a piece, sometimes from this level and sometimes from that, sometimes (with certain contents) standing as though in undifferentiated form between them. Actually all of our thought-contents are accompanied by the more or less distinct feeling that each one belongs *somewhere*. Even the fantastical, the paradoxical, the subjective is only relatively isolated: if one looks more closely, it belongs in a limitless continuum on the same level, even if this level is marked for now or for us only by this one element. Thus all our psychic contents, whether actively or passively experienced, are likewise fragments of worlds, each world signifying a specially formed totality of world-contents in general. In the theoretically comprehensible "actual" world this process is familiar to everyone: we all know that our knowing is piecemeal. Similarly in the ethical realm: we all know how small a part of what the value-formed world could and should be is traced not merely by our actions, but even by our consciousness of duty. In these cases the fragmentary character of our life-contents is brought home to us by a *claim* applying to all and transcending all. But this fragmentary character of our life also exists, if less obtrusively, in all other cases—each demonstrable content is drawn from a total context (in whose logic it has a definite and necessary place) into the vital flux, which springs from its own source and transcends those worlds. Thus above all the ever-present "fragmentariness" of life seems to me to present a world-view-like meaning that is beyond mere elegiac contemplation. We continually circulate through multiple levels, each of which in principle represents the world-totality according to a special formula, but each of which takes our life along only as a fragment.

The aspect is different, though, if we view life from its own standpoint, rather than from these levels that extend beyond it to their own totality. Here the attachment of life's contents to discrete—as it were self-existing—worlds loses its essential meaning. Such an attachment now appears as a belated abstraction and hypothetical transplanting of pieces that, as experienced, do not exhibit mutual delimitation and discontinuity at all. They are united in the dynamic of the life process like waves of a stream; it is in each case *one* life that produces them as its pulse-beats, and because they are inseparable from it they are not ultimately distinguishable from one another.

: : :

So far, the discussion has treated ideal worlds as given phenomena without inquiring about their psychological-historical or analogic genesis, or about the larger unity in which, for all their transcendence of life and reality, they are still intimately entwined with life. This, though, is my real task.

After all, it is evident that those realms emerge as wholes from lived human life, even though in life's immediacy they appear in an entirely different, embryonic form, emerging and vanishing under different conceptual names and with accidental and empirical causes. Or, better expressed: the same thing occurs here in the form of life as exists there in the form of ideality in a world of its own. First of all there are products of life, like all of its other manifestations, subordinated to and serving it. Then comes the great transformation through which the realms of the idea arise for us: the forms or functions that life has brought forth, for its own sake and out of its own dynamic, become so autonomous and definitive that life in turn comes to serve them, subordinating its contents to them—and this successful subordination is just as ultimate a realization of value and meaning as was the earlier introduction of these forms into the economy of life. The great spiritual categories indeed build upon life, even when they are still entirely trapped within it and still lie entirely on its level. Yet to that extent they retain something passive with respect to life, something moderately yielding, something submissive to it, because they must orient themselves towards its overall demand and must modify what they perform for life according to it. Only when that axial rotation [*Achsendrehung*] of life occurs around them do they become truly productive; their objectively true forms are now the dominant ones, they absorb the stuff of life and it must

yield to them. We should think of this as a historical process, as the μεταβασισ
εισ αλλο γενοσ,[2] with which science arises out of knowledge acquired only for
the sake of practical ends, and with which, likewise, art, religion, law, etc. arise
from certain vital-teleological elements. To pursue this process in all its lines,
to discover everywhere the turning point of form out of its vital and into its
ideal validity amid the gradual transitions of actual consciousness, lies naturally far beyond our capacity. The present discussion touches only the principle and the inner meaning of this development, only the characterization of
its stages in high contrast, ignoring the mixings and blurrings with which they
occur historically.

Here we cannot very well avoid speaking of vital purposivenesses [*Zweck-
mäßigkeiten*] that the spiritual functions, defined as world-constructs, serve.
Before I trace how this predetermination works out in particular sequences,
I must therefore try to clarify the essential structure of the principle of purposiveness [*Zweckmäßigkeitprinzips*]. When I noted that certain functions,
formed within life and embedded in its webs of purpose, become independent
centers and tendencies that press life into service—this can easily appear to be
the typical occurrence that the means to an end psychologically become ends.
(The example for this, an example whose clarity is as extreme as its historical
effect, is, as everyone knows, money. For on the one hand there is nothing
in the human world so absolutely without real value and so completely mere
means, because it has in fact arisen exclusively as an economic medium; on
the other hand, there is no earthly thing that appears to so many people as
the end of all ends, as the definitively satisfying possession, the terminus of
all striving and effort. The transformation thus seems to have proceeded more
radically here than anywhere else.) Actually, though, the spiritual structures
of the two patterns are completely different. The development of means into
ends remains thoroughly enclosed in the general form of the teleological, and
merely allows the psychic accent of the final element to retreat a level. If someone, like the miser, declares himself satisfied with possessing money instead of
obtaining pleasures for it, this makes a difference in the material but not the
essential form of valuation. The objectively rational division of a sequence is
not binding for the consciousness of value, but instead cedes to it the choice
of a point where it will peak. This is because in and for itself that sequence is
indeed interminable. No aim, however rational or immediately satisfying, is
immune to being discovered to be the way-station for a yet higher one; the

---

2. *Metabasis eis allo genos*, "change into another genus," a phrase found in Aristotle's *Posterior Analyt-
ics* and used often by Kierkegaard, denotes a logical fallacy in which one shifts from one discipline or
logical structure into another. Simmel was fond of this phrase and used it in the third and fourth essays
as well.—Trans.

chain of earthly life-contents does not break off definitively at any one link, and the designation of a final one never remains an immutable decision of will or feeling. On countless occasions we would have neither the courage nor the strength to act if we did not apply our full concentration, our generally available consciousness of value, towards the next level on the teleological ladder. However transient a means it may be when considered objectively, we must treat this level as though, so to speak, our entire wellbeing depended upon it alone, because for the present it is indispensable. If we were to give it only as much interest as its true importance objectively amounted to, and if we directed our full intensity of valuation only toward the most distant ultimate aim, we would be fragmenting our energy for the practical task in the most dysteleological way. That which contradicts the meaning of teleology in the deepest sense, and really denies it—the means usurping the position of the end—thus in fact becomes one of teleology's most sublimated forms.

But the turning which marks the rise of ideal constructs stands outside the means-ends category altogether. Insight into this possibility (to be explored below) requires another thought: that the means-end category overall has a much narrower significance at the deepest layer of human existence than we tend to ascribe to it, misled as we are by its role in superficial praxis. The bodily organism comprises the domain of all-dominating purposiveness. I certainly do not believe that the organism's ultimate, formative essence is described thus, any more than mechanism (under which we can categorize its phenomena with unlimited success) suffices for it. Yet however merely heuristic or symbolic it may be, once the teleological viewpoint is applied to organisms as physical it finds confirmation in the most astonishing degree, increasing with every new psychological discovery. The more precisely an animal creature is directed toward the immediate consequence of its physicality (i.e., the narrower its radius of action) the more unconditionally it is imprisoned in purposiveness. The most complete purposiveness exists *inside* the body; it diminishes to the degree that the vital movements reach beyond the body, because they then have to deal with a resistant world, accidental with respect to life. This purposiveness approaches its maximum peril and possibly its minimum realization where the conscious spirit and will set off into arbitrary distance from inner-bodily, structurally given movements and their immediate effect.

Man, because he has the greatest radius of action, because his goal-setting is located at the widest and most independent remove from the vital automatism of his body, is least aware of his teleology. That is what one can call his freedom. The creature that sticks to automatism has indeed the greatest purposiveness of life, but pays for it with its strict linkage to bodily apriority. Freedom means precisely the capacity to break through purposiveness; it exists to the degree that the organic being's behavior reaches beyond the limits of its nonwill-fully regulated body. Here, naturally, I mean not only locomotion—where the body as a whole merely traverses space for the sake of nourishment, safety, or procreation—but rather the qualitative and differential engagements of man with the environment. The more developed (i.e., the freer) the person is, the farther removed is his behavior from the purposiveness invested in his body-structure as such and in its nonwillfulness. On account of this distance that exists between the physical givenness of the human organism and its practical behavior, man can in principle be described as the nonpurposive creature; he is relatively free of the purposiveness that rules in the essential nonwillfulness, and thus purposiveness, of lower organisms.

Man has reached a level of existence that stands above purpose. It is his distinctive value that he can act without purpose. By this we mean only ac-tions as wholes, though these may or must be teleologically constructed within themselves; that is, the particular action sequence is built of means that lead to one purpose, but the whole is not in turn situated in an overarching general teleology. Such sequences naturally do not fill life up completely; instead life is purposive in its largest parts—that is, it unfolds in sequences whose final ele-ment proceeds as means to a further purpose; in other words, ultimately to life as such. Here and there, though, man lives in the category of the nonpurposive. If we describe the character of such sequences by calling its final elements purposes unto themselves we merely bring their unique meaning back to pur-posiveness again on a deeper level. Yet this purposiveness is a mere transition, a mere level of development. If we were pure spirit (i.e., if our behavior were no longer considered a part or continuation of the nonwillful purposiveness of our bodily organization) then we would be independent in principle from the category of purpose.

Often, too, the purpose is in fact the low and contemptible element in an activity, and obviously not merely when an end draws inherently value-neutral means into its ethical negativity. Rather, means can possess a value which they are not at all capable of shedding, but which, when put to the service of a rep-rehensible end, brings the baseness or noxiousness of the action as a whole to its highest perfection, so to speak. If a businessman—merely to hoard more and more money, or perhaps to buy the most wretched gratifications for it later—puts into play the highest energy, intelligence, tirelessness and daring, a value still remains to these qualities as *character indelibilis*. Even when prac-ticed utterly without purpose, in some sportlike fashion or in the arrogance of a vigor that seeks only to be discharged, attractiveness and significance adhere to them. But in the former case they are enveloped by the evil and demeaning purpose, which in a remarkable conjunction cannot destroy their value and yet can affix the reversed sign to it. As foolish as moral indignation is towards the principle that the end justifies the means (how else, for example, could the collectivity demand the sacrifice of an individual life!), it also cannot be ignored that often the end itself "unjustifies" the means.

Certainly if we understand "goal-setting" as the consciously rational form of purpose and of the arbitrarily extended sequence of means, then only man is a goal-setting creature. Yet this is still only a part of the purposiveness of life, the part that pertains not at all to the comparison with the teleology of animals. With man, the teleologically emergent element not only appears as separate from all purpose, but in doing so it very frequently disturbs and injures our purposive processes. This can only have a meaning, though, for creatures that can place themselves beyond life. All constructs of specifically human existence—and this will be our concern here—certainly appear to have passed through the stage of purposiveness before ascending into the stage of pure being-for-themselves; that is, freedom. Viewed overall, man is the least teleological creature. At the one end of his existence he follows blind instincts that are no longer utterly purposive as with animals, but aberrant, disoriented, and, given the means that our teleology places at their disposal, destructive to the point of madness. At the other end of his existence he is elevated above all teleology. For him, teleology thus stands between those two poles—to be free from it is the lowest degree and the highest—and only through its quantitative expansion and refinement can it evoke the illusion that man is a purposive creature. So far as he is such a creature, he has no freedom, but is bound to what is merely a specially conditioned mechanism. We are free as pure creatures of impulse because there all countereffort has vanished and we live *ex solis nostrae naturae legibus*.[3] And we are free in the ideal realms before which teleology ends. The domain of purposiveness is the middle range of human existence, precisely as it occupies the middle range between intention and result within a particular action-series.

The antithesis of freedom is not coercion, for in the first place the unfolding of events according to the teleology of organic lawfulness cannot be described as coercion, given the cessation of inner countereffort just noted. Only a being that is somehow free can be coerced: to say that natural things, ruled by natural laws, *must* behave this way or that, is a silly anthropomorphic expression. Their behavior throughout is only *actual*, and to say that it is also necessary in the sense of some sort of duress imputes to them an initiative or capacity for human resistance. The antithesis of freedom, rather, is purposiveness. Freedom is not something negative, not the absence of coercion, but an entirely

---

3. "Only from the laws of our own nature."—Trans.

new category to which the development of man ascends once it has left the
level of purposiveness bound to his inner physicality and the continuation of
this purposiveness into action. Freedom is a release, not from the terminus a
quo, but from the terminus ad quem. From this comes the impression of freedom in art, science, morality, and real religiosity; from it also comes its utter
absence of contradiction with causality.

:::

I will trace the achievement of this emancipation in its essentials in the following pages. By way of introduction I will examine it for two areas whose
original entanglement with the teleology of life may seem completely impenetrable—the eudaimonistic and the erotic areas.

Pleasure and pain originally—we may generally agree—are stimuli to vital-
purposive behavior. Feelings of pleasure are the inducements for assimilating
wholesome nourishment, for remaining in a healthy milieu, for propagating
the species; feelings of pain are warning signals against the opposite behavior,
biological penalties that deter against its repetition. While this connection exists even for man, it has also slackened here and there for him. Now for the
first time he can seek pleasure that is destructive to his own wellbeing and
that of the species: yet this is only the sign that the feeling of pleasure has
achieved psychological independence from these benefits and that biological
utility can accompany it in principle as an isolated, marginal phenomenon. If
an animal also undertakes particular actions for the sake of a beckoning pleasure, this is still always merely something secondary behind which stands, as
its real meaning, the vital purposiveness of the elicited action. Man, however,
can make this turning into a definitive one by placing the totality of life at the
service of pleasure. Yet this is only a growth of a means into end once again,
and it forms no truly new sphere vis-à-vis the teleological life-course, even
when developed to the point of perverting this telos. But a truly radical twist
occurs, it seems to me, with the pure meaning of what we call "happiness"
[*Glück*]. The crude psychology of traditional ethics has failed (with rare exceptions) to recognize the *decisive* turn in which this concept is distinguished
from pleasure; the Greeks saw deeper at this point. Schopenhauer may with
justice have made *pleasure* depend upon a preceding necessity, as revealed by
its rootedness in the sequentially unfolding course of life processes. What *happiness* means to us, though (and this is not merely a definitional distinction,
but rather a difference of inner realities that may be called something else as
far as I am concerned)—is admittedly of undoubted value even for corporeal
well-being and thus also for the entire purposiveness of life—yet it signifies

beyond this a final appropriateness, a summit toward which life strives and beyond which, in the direction of this striving, it cannot proceed, just as one cannot go any higher once one reaches the summit of a mountain. Happiness lacks the particularization of pleasurable feeling through which the latter becomes a mere element of the life-context. As soon as we call ourselves "happy," this life-context in its entirety shows instead a coloration that cannot be localized at all; the characteristic emotional tension of pleasure has to a certain extent left its place in the interaction of life-moments and has become, as happiness, a terminus toward which these moments must collaborate. If "reason" appears to stand so distant from our other intellectual faculties that again and again, from Aristotle to Bergson, people have assigned it a different origin than these faculties, produced as they are from empirical-organic energies (and conversely, this itself is a deep symbol of that feeling of distance), similarly I venture the paradox that happiness, in its purity, is something just as new in kind, something just as distinct from our other eudaimonistic experiences, as reason is within *its* range.

Only in the most extreme heights of happiness, never in those of pleasure, do we feel something like grace; it irradiates ongoing life with a brilliance that this life could never otherwise have produced of itself, one that instead bursts forth from a different, inexplicable order. Because of this, pleasure can be sought, and sometimes even with success, but happiness—in the sense that our anarchy of language has not yet garbled—befalls us like rain and sunshine. Nothing shows more starkly the radicalism of this change than the transcendent intensification of happiness to the concept of "bliss." Here now the supervitality of the state of happiness can no longer be doubted; here it has reached the absolute form (and is thus free of all blending with pleasure), for whose achievement one's whole life is risked and often enough even martyrdom results. The emancipation of happiness from all intravital purposiveness is completed and made unmistakable in the concept of bliss.

It is similar, if not exactly parallel, with pain, which must be viewed genetically as deterrence against behavior that is opposed to life's purposiveness. Suffering [Leid] also appears to behave toward pain in a way somewhat corresponding to the way happiness relates to pleasure. With the reservation that linguistic usage here too allows conceptual boundaries to blur, we describe pain as a localized process occurring in a distinctive line. But alongside of it— and sometimes even alongside of pleasure—stands the chronic tonus of our whole being that we tend to call suffering and that does not point beyond itself biologically in any way. The occurrence of pain within life has thereby broken away from its localization and broadened into a coloration of life on whose basis alone life again experiences immanent teleological or dysteleological events. Whereas pain is adapted to life, the streams of life congeal into suffering just as into happiness; the soul *can* find in suffering as in happiness (though with the sign reversed), a consummation, a completion of life, even a redemption from it, a redemption that is the opposite of the role of pain. The fact that we can spiritually feel sorrows that have in principle no teleological significance—this seems to me to be a quite decisive hallmark of the human essence.

This transformation appears even more characteristically in erotic teleology than in the eudaimonistic. Originally given is the biological significance of the attraction of the sexes and the attached feelings of pleasure. As these latter become the psychological aim for whose sake the act is sought, the teleological series is displaced, and procreation becomes a mere, often unwanted, accident of what is really desired. Still, even this aspect can appear—to put it in a somewhat old-fashioned way—as a ruse of nature to achieve its species-goals, even indeed when the erotic intention no longer flows toward the sex as a whole (i.e., no longer goes toward any more or less acceptable person of the other sex, but is fully individualized under the schema *this or none*). For even such a focusing can be interpreted as an instinct for the most suitable partner for the procreation of the most well-favored offspring. Yet the decisive departure of the erotic from the service of life occurs immediately at this point. Regardless of what genetic or homochronous relationship exists between love and sensual desire, they have nothing to do with each other in respect to their meaning and as phenomena. Sensual desire is of species-oriented nature, and where it relates exclusively to an individual this general life-stream is merely canalized, but ultimately flows back into the generality of its source. But love, as love, has the characteristic that it is a pure, self-enclosed internal occurrence in the soul, though it is of course woven around the now utterly irreplaceable image of the other individual. Countless untraceable energies of the personality flow into it, yet it is not merely a way station for these but rather, happily or destructively, it is a definitive thing. The saying: "if I love you, what does that have to do with you?"—expresses the essence of such love negatively, to be sure, but in unsurpassable clarity. As long as love remains in the general case and as long as it remains desire, it is a form that life takes on for the sake of its "purposes." But this form is emancipated, as in Schopenhauer's (here wholly one-sided) view that only the intellect can be emancipated from life; the lover, who has raised himself and the beloved out of the broad and forward-streaming species-life, knows that life exists in order to nourish this value, this new state of being. One certainly cannot describe this as a "purposive relation." But when such a purposive relation, dominant in species-level desire, is transformed—regardless whether this desire still exists *alongside* of the autonomous love and in inseparable connection with it—love has left behind the whole category of the teleological. The latter category defines only its life-bound pre-form, from which it develops into free self-existence [*Selbst-Sein*]. With this the erotic can reach those most sublime levels where the command, "be fruitful and multiply,"—certainly the greatest imaginable antithesis to the viewpoint of Philine[4]—is regarded as high treason against the essence of love. Certainly there is a continuous transition here, and as little, perhaps, as love exists already "pre-formed" in the first prompting towards the other sex, a gradual process of epigenesis nonetheless brings it forth from the latter impulse. Actuality puts the form of continuity between the two categories, which ideally and in their essence are separated by an absolute threshold.

This question does not pertain to the above-mentioned development of "worlds." Rather, and only along particular lines, we are trying to clarify the process that when broadened into other dimensions leads to world-constructs, to the attainment of autonomous forms with unlimited capacity. The cultural domains, properly so-called, are shaped with these forms, so that it can perhaps be said: culture in general arises where categories produced in life, and for life's sake, become autonomous shapers of intrinsically valued formations that are objective with respect to life. As decidedly as religion, art, and science maintain their meaning as such in superpsychological ideality, certain processes of temporally subjective life are nonetheless their embryonic stages; from their viewpoint these processes seem like their pre-forms; or (in the earlier formulation) exactly the same thing appears in the form of life as those which exist in the form of ideality in its own world. In the instant when those formal driving forces or modes of arrangement (i.e., driving forces or modes of arrangement that *form* given contents into a defined world) become the decisive thing for themselves (though previously life and its material constellation of interests was decisive), and produce or form an object from themselves—in each such instant there is produced a piece of those cultural worlds that now stand before life, offering it the stations of its progress or a supply of contents.

Perhaps the pure essence of science, in contrast to otherwise available knowledge, can be comprehended only under this assumption. Practical life is permeated at every step (more than we are in the habit of acknowledging) by cognitive processes: before the emergence of science we acquire on the whole no less and no more knowledge than is required to carry out our practical outward and inward conduct. No less, because in light of our life's dependence upon scientific notions we would not live if a certain amount and a certain adequacy of these did not exist; and no more, because so long as only life as

---

4. Courtesan in Goethe's novel, *Wilhelm Meisters Lehrjahre.*—Trans.

such and as practical is concerned, this "more" would imply an unneeded burden for life, which would really have no place for it at all. Of course, the degree between too little and too much varies extremely according to the individuals and to the historical situations.

The decisiveness of vital determination here is revealed by the fact that contemporary knowledge, however fragmentary and accidental it may appear to other periods, still always presents a somehow closed and satisfactory coherence. Those periods tend not to provide a justification and central foundation—grounded in the logic and substance of these cognitive complexes—for this currently felt unity, and the latter can only lie in the really demanding, sovereignly determining life-situation. By far the preponderant bulk of our scientific ideas presents itself as though called forth and determined by life's purposiveness—though the more exact definition of this purposiveness itself can remain indeterminate in meaning and direction.

This approach even seems to me the only radical means against radical skepticism or theoretical nihilism, for which every so-called truth is from the outset only illusion. We need no evidence to assert that no person would be able to live even for one day if every one of his perceptions of objects were erroneous. Yet we do live. Therefore it is impossible that we always err; we must possess truth enough to balance out the errors that occur, at least to the point where life becomes possible. Of course, the *content* of such a truth depends upon what the life in question wants from the world. Truths to an Indian yogi and to a Berlin stock jobber, to Plato and to an Australian aborigine, lie so incomprehensibly distant from each other that conducting these existences on the basis of their notions of the world would be utterly unthinkable if for each of them "life" did not mean something different than for the others, and thus provide for each a special knowledge basis correlative to him. But in order to avoid a pragmatist reduction, one must be clear that our inner processes, however much they serve our vital behavior in the world, are themselves a piece of this behavior and this world. Accordingly, it is quite one-sided and confused to locate the meaning and aim of our processes of consciousness exclusively in our action (i.e., in our practical relation to the outer world). We are speaking here too of "purposivenesses" that are not even determined by a terminus ad quem. The living out of a capability, the realization or even merely the fully conscious clarification of inner tendencies, being's self-expression in developments and in the forming of receptive or resistant materials—these are values that are coordinate in significance to those measured by the *results* of our conduct. These, too, obviously arise within some sort of dependence upon an epistemological notion that proves its correctness by their fruits. Even the vital value of a thought lies by no means only in what can be seen as a logical or psychological unfolding of its content; rather, its character as an element of our life is a direct quality (more or less valuable) of that very life in which it stands. All too often, we regard our thoughts only with respect to what they *mean*, with respect to their intrinsically powerless, ideal contents (whatever concrete consequences these may perhaps develop); but here the question concerns their other side, the dynamic-real, of which that ideal meaning is the index or symbol. Our thoughts not only *mean* something that one can express with concepts (which are already life-transcendent in themselves), but they *are* something, they are real pulse-beats of real life that within this life (not first mediated by inner or outer operations) more or less effectively "serve" its value-maximum as its ideal telos. This widening and deepening is always implied when I speak in brief of life's purposiveness.

If we regard our life as a biological process, it is interwoven no differently into the reality of the world than plants are, and all of its functions proceed in their purposiveness like the breathing of a sleeper. Now if a perception [*Erkennen*] intrudes into this teleology of our actuality, our status and our efficacy are not yet altered in principle by it: forward-streaming life is only enriched by this waveform. The perception is thus far nothing but one scene of life itself that prepares another and thereby serves the vital overall intention. This has already been expressed for so-called purely sensual propositions. They appear as continuations of the bodily mechanism, which as a whole is teleologically directed. If this latter proposition is retained, then all other propositions adduced to and codetermining life must be of the same nature. The river of life, dominating and dominated, runs through them as through every other of its elements; the categories in which the conscious image of things is produced are mere tools within the vital context. To me it seems inadequate and half-baked to hypothesize that there exists an absolute truth, valid for all beings—the objectively congruent likeness of "actuality"—and that this "actuality" is gradually conquered by the human species such that the more intelligent, acquiring a greater measure of this truth, thereby possesses an advantage over the less intelligent in the struggle for existence, and, accordingly, along the usual paths of selection, that the utility of truth becomes the cause of its adoption and diffusion. As a basic theme, Schopenhauer's treatment of the intellect, insofar as the will employs it, is no different. Even he does not at all doubt the ideal existence of a truth, independent in content from life, that the intellect seizes upon because the life-will, believing its own ends to be attainable with the help of this knowledge of reality, impels it that way. Even apart from any criticism, such a pragmatist theory in any case leaves the essence of *truth itself* unexplained. Interpret it as we may, it is still something inwardly independent of life, that stands only virtually ready to be grasped by it. Here, though, we are dealing with an antithesis to that way of thinking, a contrast that in Schopenhauer's unsatisfactory manner of speaking, may be described thus: in the pragmatist view a truth is drawn into life because it is useful to it; here, by contrast, the spiritual contents that prove supportive to life's development we call true; the destructive, life-limiting we call erroneous. Here with one stroke it is clear that there can and must be different "truths" for different life forms and life-constitutions; that the ever-irritating question about the "agreement" of thought and actuality is resolved, since thought is only one of the organic processes that sustains and makes possible our living actuality within the cosmic actuality such that, when thought faithfully performs this *function*, morphological "agreement" with an object does not even come into question; and, finally, that the difficulty—as the intrinsically concept-free, merely "practical" attitude of man would have it—of "conducting" oneself according to theoretical truths (an attitude with which even today we find ourselves somewhat at odds due to a certain personalizing of the psychic faculties) falls away if these truths are merely the theoretical formulations or the conceptual mirrorings of certain directions which the practical-dynamic contexts of self-developing life produce in itself and in pursuit of its own meaning.

Once we have acquired and processed a complete cognitive world as our possession, things can certainly proceed in reverse. For our empirical everyday usage there first exists a fixed truth that we must adopt and to which we must adjust our actions: here, what is true is that which is useful. Yet the question of how it becomes truth at all and what it originally means is not addressed. This question is only solved in a coherent way if life creates the cognitive as well as all its other functions; here we may say that only what is useful is true. Man is too many-sided a creature to be able to exist in the world in so linearly teleological a manner as a plant. The diversity of his sense-impressions and his surfaces of contact with the world of his concerns require a concentration of their influences, and a preparation for his reaction, that happen via concept-formation and categorical forms. That these can also be described contrariwise as a ground nourishing his diversity of world-connections merely shows that teleology in general offers only a provisional or symbolic expression for the real law of life. As intellectual forms construct the world for our practical life around us, they make possible the factual connection between the contents of the world and ourselves; they exist for the sake of the content processing required for that connection. Outside of this function they have no business in life. To assert, for instance, that causality is only the translation of felt, intentional life-efficacy onto the object-world really means that life has created for itself, within its own essential domain, the form with whose help it attains a pragmatically workable world. The fact which has often perplexed us—that we nowhere "see" the causality we so firmly believe in—derives simply from the fact that causality is a form and condition for our pragmatically real efficacy in the world; establishing causality additionally in a theoretically objective manner, through "seeing," is not in fact required for this purpose (i.e., for our purely factual action whose precondition it forms).

But all such vitally determined "knowing" is still not science: the principle of science simply cannot be attained by any gradual increase (however large) and refinement of this knowing—but rather only in the instant when the relation described so far is reversed, when the contents are of interest exclusively insofar as they comply with the forms of knowing. The character of all science as such seems to me to consist in the fact that certain spiritual forms exist ideally (causality, inductive and deductive reasoning, systematic ordering, criteria for the establishment of facts, etc.) which the given contents of the world, through placement into them, must satisfy. Expressed psychologically: at first men know in order to live, but then there are men who live in order to know. Which *content* is selected to fulfill that demand is truly accidental and depends upon historical-psychological constellations: for science all contents are in principle of equal value because with science, in its most characteristic contrast to vital-teleological knowing, the object as such is a matter of indifference; a value-priority in an object here can only pertain to the technique within science, so that one object is more useful than another in attaining further knowledge. Though in other respects the physiology of man is more valuable to us than that of the bat, and Goethe's biography more valuable than his tailor's, these priorities are based on appraisals from outside of science; they do not proceed from an interest in truth as such. The general expression that in science "truth is sought for the sake of truth" is certainly almost always meant in a moral sense, to ward off external accusations—a sense that does not apply here at all; yet in fact this expression captures the inner, metaphysical essence of science, just as in praxis truth is sought for the sake of life, in religion for the sake of God or holiness, in art for the sake of aesthetic values. If within these last two teleologies other notions are more serviceable than the *theoretically* true ones, then these others are sought instead of the latter.

The complexes in which contents stand within the life-sequence, along with their meaning and their power to compel, are fully dissolved here; the significance (for life) of perceiving them no longer governs their selection and arrangement; these depend instead on the challenge and the possibility of applying the forms of cognition, now seen as values in themselves, to the contents—naturally with the reservation that the thing thus achieved can again be torn away from these surroundings and equipped anew with a vital dynamic, can plunge into the teleological life-stream. Now if this ideocentric attitude were carried out in all possible contents whatsoever—if they all showed the form, the overall interrelatedness, that the autocracy of the laws of knowledge imposes upon them—then science would be complete. If we seek cognitions that arise in the life-stream—guided and impelled as it is by practical necessities, by will and feeling—then however true such cognitions may be, they do not find their place through connection with other truths, because truth is indeed not the concept of an ultimate end dominating them and leading them together; they must first be released from the line of life in order to be science; that is, to belong to the ideally prescribed domain of the merely-true, whose contents are designated and connected only by the fact that they satisfy the norms of cognition. The fact that these norms themselves, not only in their temporal occurrence but also in their qualitative determinacy, derive from the demands of the life laid out before them is here entirely a matter of indifference. It is enough that they are now the bearer of the truth-value that has become genuine (as paradoxical as it sounds); the *basis* from which truth is truth does not appear in their now achieved autocracy.

That the range of the true has now become fully autonomous as science (i.e., that it even has no "basis" any longer) makes it immediately clear why every proof for the authentic existence of the principle of truth leads here to a circle. We can make neither the negative assertion, "there is no truth," nor the positive, "there is truth" (even only as an assertion), without already presupposing the existence of truth. In the self-sufficient form of science truth is a floating complex, *within* which particulars can certainly be proven true by other particulars, but which is obviously incapable of such proof as a *whole*. If science were perfect, then starting with an axiomatically established truth A, by A one would prove proposition B, by B proposition C, etc. And the Z where one would arrive after passing through the entire contents of science would then in turn furnish the basis of proof for the A posited at the beginning as unproven. This is a circle, but not an incorrect one, for only between particular and particular does this form make the course of proof illusory; but the fact that in a totality each member ultimately can only be built on every other, in complete interaction, is the expression of its closed unity and self-sufficiency. Just as the world, conceived as existing absolutely, can only be self-supporting and can maintain itself only through its own motion, so too it can be for the world that arises as a totality (according to its idea) under the category of scientific knowledge. It rests throughout upon the form of the theoretical proof; that this latter is valid, however, can obviously be theoretically proven only through a *petitio principii*. But certainly only, and quite legitimately, within the world of scientific knowledge. In the instant that we allow this world to be enveloped by the life-context and grounded in it, things are different. Now all those contents of knowledge have their "basis," namely one established outside of knowledge. The practical teleology of the whole life (with every allowance for this inadequate expression as I have often emphasized) now provides the proof that a notion is correct or erroneous; as I have already mentioned, the proof that our knowledge cannot be found utterly in error is furnished immediately by the fact that we live at all. Within the relativity of cognition as a particular function in the multiple interweaving of the totality of human life and its unfolding, cognition gains possibilities of being proven; the loss of these possibilities is the price it pays for the sovereignty and own-worldness to which it is elevated as a scientific cosmos, radically overcoming that relativity.

In whatever life-contexts and for whatever goals the forms of logic (in the widest sense) and methodology may have arisen, the decisive thing is that now, in pure autonomy without any further legitimation, they *form themselves* into their object—as a content of *science*. Practical knowledge demanded by and woven into life has in principle nothing to do with science; seen from the scientific standpoint, it is a pre-form of science. The Kantian notion that the understanding creates Nature, and prescribes its laws to it, is valid only for the immanently scientific world. Knowledge, insofar as it is a pulse-beat or a mediation of conscious practical life, does not originate from the distinctive creativity of pure intellectual forms at all; it is borne instead by the dynamic of life that weaves our reality into itself, together with the reality of the world. While the construct [*Bild*] of the particular object may be the same for science as for praxis, the totality of constructs and their relationships that we call science and that comprise the theoretical "world" emerges only through the axial rotation that transfers the definitional basis for cognitive constructs out of the contents and their meaning for life and into the forms of knowledge itself. These now appear as though filled with a quite genuine creative power, and bring forth from themselves a world whose particular lawfulness and sufficiency is not altered by the fact that our effort gives us possession only of particular and often quite disjointed pieces of its ideal condition. For only with that transformation does the logically coherent totality stand ideally before us, of which scientific knowledge appears as the trace. As long as knowledge is only an element of the life-course, coming from it and flowing into it, this is not the issue; the meaning it is called forth to realize is in this case vital purposiveness, the production of a certain being in us and of a certain existential relation between us and things. One could say: life invents, science discovers. There too, knowledge is organized by intention into a unitary whole. It is not the theoretical cosmos of science, though, but the line of practical life, in the sense of inner as well as outer conduct. For science, knowledge produced and used by life is no less a provisional thing on account of the fact that the forms of thought that take over the shaping of world-contents into science are themselves produced in the life process, and comprise only the most essential expression of that practical relationship between us and the rest of existence. The essential character of science is not at all affected by the *provenance* of these forms and demands. For whether they are this or that by qualitative categorization is of no consequence for this essential character in its pure sense and concept; only the fact that it now defines a world, that the contents are now taken up into this world so as to satisfy its forms—that is the fact that distinguishes science in its separation from life.

It becomes somewhat difficult to comprehend clearly the radical degree of this transformation because the isolated content often looks indistinguishable in the vital *pre-form* of science and in *science itself*, and because the distinction is only established through consideration of the whole, through relationships and inner intention. The distinction emerges much more notably where the world of art is constructed from and above the pre-forms produced by life.

It is established that the realm of empirically practical visual perception provides us a view of the world constructed differently in principle than the one that science induces us to recognize as objective. For this latter view of the world, things are distributed in absolute coordination through infinite space but not such that any point is especially emphasized (thereby forcing a gradation of spatial ordering upon them). Moreover, they exist here in absolute continuity, in the same continuity as space itself, and every smallest part is dynamically linked by its restless motion with each of its neighbors. Ultimately this motion signifies a steady flowing; the restless conversion of energies permits no real fixing to a form, no qualitative or spatial persistence of a unique existence. These conditions change completely as soon as a living subject looks at the world. A center or point of departure is now given which transforms the uniform adjacency of spatial things into a graduated or perspectivistic ordering around the head of the observer. Now there exist, accentuated as such, a near and far, a clarity and obscurity, displacements and breaks, intersections and voids, to which no analogy whatever exists in the subject-free existence of things; similarly the continuity of matter (naturally in the sense unaffected by the atomistic problem) is breached by our practical vision, so that one could almost say that this vision consists precisely in the delimiting extraction of specific "things" out of the continuity of existence; we "see" them by forming them as somehow closed units out of that objective continuity or, more correctly, by forming them into it. Thus even the Heraclitic flux of reality, in its objective temporal becoming, is ultimately dammed up by our glance: our way of seeing creates for itself effectively enduring forms, and the Platonic notion that the sensory world shows only eternal unrest and change, while abstract thought alone comprehends truth (i.e., the unaltered thus-ness of forms) is—if not in the absolute then at least in the proximate and empirical sense—roughly the opposite of the actual state of affairs.

Pursuing these fundamental functional modes of our seeing (those supported by life and its practical orientation) out beyond the measure that praxis allots to them, one stumbles upon the creative mode of visual art. For indeed its first achievement is to release its pattern as a self-sufficient unity from the continuous interweavings of real existence, to cut the threads connecting it to anything exterior, and to bring forth a form that, in its meaning, is oblivious to becoming, self-alteration, or passing away. Yet this is not a technique that life necessitates for organizations of our kind within our milieu (a milieu in which separating out an object as "one," as exemplar of a concept, only occurs so as to reintroduce it at once back into the continuously on-flowing life-course)—rather, such forming is an end-in-itself of art. The content, the really objective element, is not something life-determining that must be poured into this form for the sake of just this nexus, but rather is chosen as a relatively accidental thing, so that this artistic form may represent itself in it, so that it may *be*—just as in science all things were equally privileged because, as material for knowledge as an ultimate aim, they are not "privileged" at all, but, rather, are of equivalent value. This is the legitimate element in the assertion that, for the work of art, its objective content is of no consequence. Yet precisely at that point, the assertion is contradicted again for the actual practice of art, because different objects indeed afford quite graduated possibilities of realizing the purely artistic vision in them. Their differentiation in this respect again affords the contents a difference of value for art, from which their differences stemming from other value categories correctly remain excluded. The creative process in visual art can be interpreted as an elaboration of the artistic process of seeing. With nonartists, inner and outer visions are interwoven into the most diverse practical series in such a way that they can indeed render these particular contents and modifications, but the real impulse and pervading telos does not proceed from seeing as such: seeing remains here a mere means of activities already otherwise intended, and where it is not that, it is only of a contemplative variety, a looking that does not translate into activity at all. With the painter in the hours of his productivity, however, the act of seeing appears in a certain sense to translate, for itself alone, into the kinetic energy of the hand. The known fact that many artists, even in the freest reconstruction of nature, only mean to create what they "see" may well also stem from the feeling of this immediate connection; it may only be that these artists interpret as a substantialistic transference of the formal resemblance something that in reality is a functional thing, a thing quite indifferent to the equality or inequality of cause and effect, namely the creative emergence of mere seeing that otherwise mixes its power only supportively and facilitatively into currents from other sources. But this independent, self-accountable self-furthering of the seeing process into the act of the artist clearly corresponds to an independence of artistic seeing itself that is not available to other seeing. Here seeing is isolated from its mingling with practical, nonoptical purposes, it proceeds exclusively according to its most distinctive laws; so that the seeing of the artist has been described with justice as a creative one—but ultimately it can be distinguished from the seeing of men in general only by the modifications just explored.

A rotation has now taken place, in that the seeing function does not come into force for the sake of the contents, but rather the contents are produced for the sake of and through the seeing function—in a pointed expression: in general we see to live, the artist lives to see. Certainly we should not forget that always and really it is the whole person that sees, not merely the eye as an anatomically differentiated organ. Of course, if the eye of the artist actually sees in an especially autonomous and exclusive sense, we do not really mean that his eye functions in a more decided abstraction from real life than with other men. To the contrary, with the creative artist a greater sum of life passes into his seeing, the totality of life more willingly allows itself to be channeled in this direction. Only secondarily and so to speak technically does the artist have more seeing in his life than others—primarily and essentially he has more life in his seeing, just as the following turn of phrase expresses: that form, produced within and for the goals of real life, produces an ideal world where it no longer adapts to the vital order, but instead itself determines or discerns an order to which life (as actuality, as representation, as image) must adapt.

I will mention only a single feature of this relationship between practical-empirical seeing and artistic seeing and creating. Every optical perception signifies immediately a selection from unlimited possibilities; within every immediate visual field we emphasize (for reasons having to do only in exceptional cases with the merely optical) always particular points only; perception leaves a host of things outside of them, as though not there at all, and even in each particular object there are innumerable sides and qualities that our gaze passes over. Our forming of the visual world thus occurs not merely through identifiable physical-psychic apriorities, but continually also in a negative way. The material of our world of visual perception is in fact not what is really there, but rather the residuum left over after the omission of countless possible components—and this certainly determines in very positive fashion the formations, associations, and unitary structures of the whole. Thus, if a noted modern painter said that drawing is omission, then this truth presupposes another: seeing is omission. As far as the artistic process in general can be characterized along this line, it is—with that complete rotation of intention—the further-ance and systematic heightening of the manner in which we perceive the world at all. "Omission" is here an artistically defining function, while in praxis it is a grievous necessity. The artist (this was already discussed) *sees* more than other men; that is, he must have a much larger amount of material than oth-ers, because he "omits" much more and because for artistic creativity what is seen is not, as for life, merely an *element* that is predetermined by an outwardly established vital purpose as well. All of us, as seeing people, are actually frag-mentary or embryonic painters, just as all of us, as thinkers, are scientists in the same way. But the difference appearing only gradually from this viewpoint must not mislead us into viewing the ideal construct as merely a gradual in-crease of the vital process.

The fact that life's reality appears in this perspective as a pre-form of art is also shown in objective instances along with the subjective ones just exempli-fied. The artistic creations of primitive peoples often proceed from the fact that, for example, a stone is roughly reminiscent of a human or an animal form, and this resemblance is then completed by carving, coloring, or other means. The first step is an associative-psychological event, one of those interweavings of optics and conceptualization that practical life wears at every step. Viewed superficially, the more precise elaboration of the resemblance is only a gradual extension of this analogizing. Its significance, however, involves a total rotation in principle. After the given shape has led in the course of the psychic process to the image of a fish, let us say, this image now becomes active for its part and creates from itself—according to the laws that constrain *it* exclusively—a vis-ible form. First the stone shape has led to the idea of the fish, but then the in-tuitive idea of the fish has led to a stone shape. The seeing process, impelled to a perception of form by a linkage with outer and accidental reality, now takes autonomous control of itself: the fact that the shape is seen as a fish is now no longer the thing determined, but the thing determining; seeing now produces the artistic pattern after vital praxis had secured the prize of form in general. The selection, the giving of meaning, the coherence that signifies our "seeing" vis-à-vis objective nature (because only thus is this seeing practically possible), now becomes something decisive for itself. Life no longer carries form; it re-leases the contents of being from the otherwise form-mediated life-nexus in order to arrange itself autonomously in these contents. Thus on the one hand the feeling of freedom that dwells in all art, in its process as in its result, be-comes comprehensible—for here the spirit really creates *ex solis suae naturae legibus*; on the other hand the content of the life process, insofar as it appears purely in its natural actuality and interwoven with the world, is revealed as a pre-form of the work of art.

The feeling of purity and innocence that can serve as art's pervasive domain may be associated with this independence from all the world's "givenness," into whose complexity and value-contingency we otherwise blend seeing and the actions connected with it. Art may depict a highly striking scene: but this striking character only attaches to it insofar as it is experienced; that is, insofar as its content thus stands under an entirely different category than under that of mere looking. We probably misinterpret that purity of art if we regard it as a positive sentiment like the purity that exists under the same noun in the ethical or the religious mode. In these latter cases the concern is purity of life, but with art it is purity from life. Thus artists defend themselves against all moralizing in respect to ethical and religious reproaches: they do not feel at all affected by this moralizing, which deals only with the *life*-form of these reproaches. For regardless how much life has streamed into the artistic creation and how much streams out of it, as artistic it is released from life (where vision is always only one element among others) and is only vision and its "pure" creative consequence (i.e., separated from all life-entanglements). Artistic perception, as the undisturbed domination of the perception process as such, is so little an abstraction that it would be better to describe practical-empirical perception in this way. For precisely because the nonartistic image of things is shot through with aims, associations, centrifugal meanings that are simply not visible—and serves as one of many coordinated means for achieving practical ends—it must abstract from the whole profusion and pure consequence of the *visible* phenomenon as such; praxis does not take in the entire thing perceived, but only the amount of its perception that it requires for completely different purposes.

In practical contexts the thing perceived is perhaps fused with the totality of life and is as little a fragment of it as a living member is a "fragment" of its living body; but here, evaluated purely as a perception, it is a pure fragment, brought into existence by a selection from the possible totality of all ways it may be regarded. Through this interpretation of art it also becomes evident that the work of art is much less deceptive than many an image of reality. For however we may view the latter's ultimate correspondence to the object which constitutes its "accuracy," and with whatever guarantees we may surround it, the chance that it may nonetheless be false is a possibility we may not exclude. Certainly the artwork, too, has captured the object in itself and made it into its faithfully cultivated material. Once this has happened, however, artistic creation then withdraws fully into itself, takes place only for the sake of the demands of its own form and confronts nothing else whose resemblance (or however else the relation may be called) somehow bears upon its artistic significance. Only extra-artistic interests of *life* can give importance to the artwork's relation to the model. But because the artwork only finds its pure value according to immanent artistic qualities, and purports to say nothing at all about the external object as such, as reality, it therefore cannot mislead us about this real thing; it lacks the correlate by which it could become illusion and whose existence causes the possibility of error for the notion of reality, both the vital and the scientific.

I will now further elaborate, in connection with a remote and difficult case, the radical character of the turn from the real, life-entwined image to the artistic image, a turn that allows the reality-view as lived to serve precisely the pure form of viewing (i.e., its inner laws and impulses), and that thus produces the artwork as such in the first place. Ancient Japanese teacups, which are now collectors' objects, are often shot through with fine golden lines with which ruptures or missing chips have been repaired. To the European observer these pieces of stoneware at first have an utterly rustic effect, even raw and accidental, and only with long familiarity do they reveal their beauties and depths. Yet even then they are not "art" in the usual sense, as for instance Chinese porcelains are, but rather operate as a certain middle element between an accidental product of nature and stylized art, a middle element for whose characteristic unity our European aesthetic has no category. They are not even a manner of synthesis of naturalistic art, for no represented content in them, but only the immediate existence of the pattern, is natural. To be sure, an impression of nature is always awakened in color placement or the treatment of surfaces: one is reminded of a stone or a fish-skin, of bark or the tint of clouds. This is not naturalistic imitation, however, but rather—because this alien impression can only be described symbolically—as though nature had now allowed the optical and tactile elements that it puts forth in these objects to grow through in whatever variation by the hand of a Japanese. While in this the ruptures and holes are something purely, naturally accidental and in their unimproved condition obviously operate thus, the golden lines following them produce in extraordinarily many cases, as if by a preestablished harmony, an image truly enchanting in respect to execution as well as the division of surfaces, artistically utterly perfect, one so perfect that it may often be very difficult to believe in the accidental character of the fractures. Perhaps nowhere does our principle appear more strikingly than here, where the artistic process attaches absolutely tightly to the view of nature and where its freedom of choice can only reveal itself in the breadth, the relief, and the tinting of the gold lines. More immediately than anywhere else, what the artist sees has been translated into what he does. But this reversal of the impression from a naturally determined empirical one to an indubitably artistic-formal one reveals that a change in principle must have occurred here. As long as the fracture of the cup remains in its original form, its optical image also is certainly only produced by the synthetic visual process; only so is it determined purely naturally and through the intermingling of our gaze with the givenness of nature. But the optical form, once achieved, now takes over the direction of the artistic activity. If seeing the given reality (as our life-entanglement with it determines) is the pre-form of art, and if art arises where seeing is released from this entanglement—itself leading the life of the creator into its autonomous rhythms—then here it is the empirical image of lines, perceived in the context of reality, that for the ceramic artist becomes the guideline for how he wants to make the cup appear. The artwork arises through emancipation of the visual image from practical life, an emancipation that becomes productive in forming a new creation, but one now subservient to the function of seeing.

If this is indeed the case, then it clarifies the oft-heard paradox that nature appears for each respective epoch as it is depicted in the art of that epoch's artists, and that we regard reality not "objectively" but with the eyes of the artist. Whether or not this is the whole truth, it is a part of the truth at least. Yet the possibility that art defines our way of seeing lies in the fact that seeing has defined art. After our life in the world has developed seeing, the artists remove the seeing function from this context to a specialized development, to the self-sufficient faculty for placing things into a context created only by seeing. And this now operates back upon seeing in the empirical world: the genesis of art out of its vital pre-form has broken the bridge by which art is linked back to life. We are all preexistential painters and are therefore capable, once the real painter has blazed the trail for us, of following him. Artists proceed only roughly like the thinker who, when experience occurs, extracts from it a pure, autonomous causality—but who can only do so because causality itself has already formed that experience. They do not coerce us (as the paradox expresses so far as it applies to the mere phenomenon) to adopt their purely artistic mode of consideration in lieu of a generally nonartistic one that we would have without them; rather, they determine only the particular current development of an apriority, which in its nonartistic functioning is nonetheless a pre-form of art. This is true not merely for painting, but obviously also for poetic art. If we feel and experience as the poets have felt and experienced before us, it is because those categories that bring "art" into being, in pure freedom and answerable only to themselves in their mastery of psychic materials, have collaborated from the outset toward the formation of the inner world.

Indeed, what I have said about the visual arts also defines the poetic art: we are all preexistential poets. Again, though, we should not forget that this expression is a kind of antedating, since the forms in question, operative within the empirical-practical life, are not yet art nor even a "morsel" of art; they are something differing not gradually, but in principle, that is only set to change into art. For poesy, verbal expression must first be considered here. If we regard speech as a mere means of being understood person-to-person, there appears to be no room in this logical process for anything artistic. But this is true only if we are talking about mechanically pouring a specific content of consciousness into another consciousness, so to speak, and where the speaker's discourse is not intended to arouse in the listener a function proper to this listener. Here, certainly, the telegram-style suffices. But beyond content-equivalence between the evoked and the evoking idea, the aims of oral and written discourse tend to require psychic movements of the receiver that are not obtainable in the same logical way and, though stimulated by what is heard, nonetheless proceed from the spontaneity of the hearer in higher measure than the reproduction of purely objective contents. He is supposed to receive what is heard in a certain mood, it should impress itself upon him or contrariwise occupy him only for a moment, he should be brought to the special reactions of assent, of being convinced, of the linkage of practical consequences—and all of this does not follow with logical stringency upon the mere content, but rather, as a new and further element, depends in large part upon the *form* in which that content is supplied. Once the concept "music" is grasped in its broadest sense—as a rhythm of utterance, as a vibration of feeling beyond what can be conceptually established, as that temporal and dynamic ordering of what is presented which is most favorable for our power of comprehension, as an immediate and continuous communication of a psychic state that words and concepts can convey only piecemeal and as though by construction—if all this is understood as the "music" of our utterances, then this "music" is continually required by their practical purposiveness. But only in poesy does this forming first become a self-sufficient value; here in attaining so-called perfection the word-creation has gained its meaning—and not sooner, nor when with this forming it is first placed as means into a life stretching toward future-situated purposes. Thus from the standpoint of life Schopenhauer is right—"Art is everywhere 'at the goal'"—because in terms of life it has no "goal" at all. Teleology is a vital category, not an artistic one. It is obvious without further consideration that as soon as they have experienced the turn to autonomy, those forms shape their sphere of application much more consequentially, more concertedly, and more radically than is possible for them to do in their vital function. For within the latter they retain the contingency of mere means, they are continually interrupted by requirements directed elsewhere, and they attain no logical development directed toward themselves but instead must remain fragments—though not from the standpoint of life in which they have reality, for in life's continuous current each form is (presumably) exactly correct in the measure of its effectiveness in its place and in its quantity, and every "more" of its domination would not complete what is now demanded of it, but rather make it more wanting. Only when seen from the new creation that results through their sole domination, only when seen from the viewpoint of art do those formations of individual life-moments appear as fragments. The frequent description of life as a fragment rounded off to completeness and entirety only in art probably finds its proper sense in this form-principle: the artwork *can* be a whole and in principle a complete thing in itself because it is constituted *entirely* of norms that here have utterly exhausted their meaning in the execution—whereas otherwise these norms are subordinated to something higher, to the norm of life as such that allows them only changing and interrupted application. Life as a whole appears as a fragment insofar as each particular piece of it is naturally only a splinter relative to its form as perfected in autonomous creativity. From this comes the further fact that we can speak of defective art in two entirely different senses. There is *defective* art, insofar as the work is indeed entirely formed for the sake of the artistic intention and remains within the strict bounds of autocratic artistic forms—but does not satisfy the *immanent* demands of art, and is uninteresting, banal, and powerless. And there is defective *art*, when the work, though perhaps not showing the latter impairments, does not yet fully free its artistic forms from their serviceability to life; the transformation of these forms from their existence as means to their existence as values in themselves has not yet taken place in absolute measure. This is the case where a tendential, anecdotal, sensually excitative interest resonates as one somehow decisive in the presentation. Here the work may be of great psychic and cultural significance, since for this it need not be bound to the conceptual purity of a particular category. However as *art* it remains imperfect as long as its formative elements still display something of that significance with which they fit in with the currents of life—however deeply and comprehensively they may have assimilated these currents.

The vital form of poesy is by no means limited to verbal expression. Rather, the inner and content-wise character of looking with which poetic creation is accomplished is pre-formed in innumerable psychic acts by which we render the stuff of life useful to the purposes of life. I will limit myself to a few examples. From time immemorial, it has been said of art in general (though poesy alone will concern us here) that it brings into representation not the isolated individuality of human existences, but always something universal: types of humanity for which the individual named thus-and-so is only an image and a given name. I will leave unexamined whether this is tenable; in any case, if and to the extent that it is correct it appears to place poetic art—and art generally—in opposition to the method of praxis that grasps human phenomena in their actuality; that is, each one as a distinct individual in the uniqueness of its extent, of its position, of its life-meaning. With this, though, it seems to me that our image of people, as formed precisely for the purpose of our practical connections with them, is not characterized sufficiently at all. Seldom are we fully clear how continually we generalize and typify the people with whom we deal. First in a more external, social respect: in dealing with an officer or a cleric, a worker or a professor, even outside of the circumstances of their occupation, we tend to treat them not simply as individuals, but almost self-evidently as exemplars of those general status or vocational concepts—and indeed not only in such a way that this superindividual definition is operative as a real, naturally unavoidable element of personality. Above the flowing unity of life into which it is introduced, this element, coordinated with others and unbroken, stands out much more as a leading one in practice; it establishes the key of the communication. We *see* not the pure individuality at all, but rather, at first and even sometimes at the last, the officer, the worker, often "the wife," etc.; and often enough the personal definition appears only as the specific difference with which that universal is represented. This structure in the concept of the other is the precondition with which our social intercourse is accomplished. But by the same token, it stands out above the more strictly personal characteristics. However decidedly we may sense the incomparability and indissoluble unity in a person's temperament to be—if we imagine it in the fashion that can directly support a practical relationship to it then it seems, beside everything ineffable of the individual, still to be under a psychological general concept or synthesis of such concepts: clever or stupid, torpid or energetic, elated or sad, grandiose or pedantic—or whatever all the generalizations may be that show precisely their universal character in the fact that each pair of opposites apportions the possible directions of a fundamental psychic energy. We may be aware that even an arbitrarily large heap of such universalities still does not comprise a coordinate system in which the genuine personality can be unambiguously located, and we may recognize that with such generalizations we tear it away from its most genuine roots; but within the praxis of life we cannot avoid such conversions of the individual into the universal. And ultimately the representation of the other still contains a transformation of its distinctive reality that so to speak proceeds through this reality toward the opposite side. Unavoidably we regard the reality of the person confronting us (and perhaps even our own as well) in such a way that we flesh out the particular traits (which alone are given) into a whole image; we project the sequentially developing aspect of its being onto the simultaneity of a "character" or a "temperament"; and we ultimately translate the qualitatively incomplete, garbled, undeveloped, and merely suggested aspect of his personality into a certain absoluteness. We see each one—not always, but surely much more often than we become aware of it—as he would be if he were utterly himself, so to speak; that is, if he had actualized the full possibility of his nature, his idea, toward the good or bad side. We are all fragments, not only of a social type, not only of a psychic type describable with general concepts, but even, as it were, of the type that only we ourselves are. And the other's glance fleshes out all this fragmentary material almost automatically into that which we never wholly and purely are. While the praxis of life seems to demand that we assemble the image of the other only out of really given pieces, this very praxis rests, upon closer examination, on those fleshings-out and, so to speak, on idealizations to universality, both of the type we share with others and of that we share with no one else. Thus here, as everywhere, the empirical relativity of our conceptions stands between two absolutes—we place the other person between the absolute of a universal and the absolute of his own subject—to neither of which he coincides.

We need not look further to see that all poetic and artistic representation of persons finds its prototype in this mode of conception continually practiced in the course of life. In a sociological and psychological perspective, generalizations create the conditions on which communication and understanding arise; that perfected image of individuality serves us to a degree as a schema into which we weave the empirical traits and actions of the personality (even regardless of whether it has arisen on their basis to begin with), a schema that brings them into connection and that first makes the person into a firm factor for our calculations and our demands. The artistic image, however, emerges by a complete axial rotation: the main point now is no longer to make the other adaptable to our life-course through the operation of these categorizations; instead, the artistic intention aims to give these forms to a human character, to a possibility of being human. The most complete poetic characters we possess—in Dante and Cervantes, Shakespeare and Goethe, in Balzac and C. F. Meyer—exist in a unity that we can describe only as the simultaneity of the opposing tendencies indicated here: on the one hand they are something wholly general, as though the individual, released from himself, had merged into a typical outline perceptible only as a pulse-beat of the universal life of humanity; and on the other hand they are deepened to the point at which the person is utterly himself only, to the source where his life arises in absolute self-responsibility and distinctiveness, so as only then alone to experience, from his life's empirical processes, his similarities and generalizations with others.

I will also name a second case on an entirely different level. Of the categories of feeling under whose perspectives life's material is arranged, lyric poetry has selected two to pour more often than all others into its art form: longing and resignation. The moments of fulfillment in which life's will and its object interpenetrate without any disparity not only occur on the whole more seldom in lyric poetry, but they attain real artistic perfection proportionately even more rarely there. The reason, it seems to me, is that longing and resignation—or, somewhat preferably, hope and loss—carry in themselves an element of distantiation that artistic detachment and objectification prefigure. If I am not mistaken, common parlance tends to describe longing and resignation as "lyrical sentiments," and I do not know why this affinity should be felt, save on the basis of that characteristic alienation from the achieved totality of life that *possession* brings. For longing as for resignation, the passage of time (if indeed in widely different senses) has to some extent come to a halt; with both, the soul places itself somehow beyond the limitations of time (as Goethe expresses it in one direction: "What I possess I see as though at a distance, and what has vanished becomes reality to me") and therewith creates as much a pre-form of the artistic relation to time as displacement from the genuinely full life, embedded in both affects, places these into the pre-sphere of art. But underneath this apparent external continuity the radical turn occurs: in real experience longing and resignation arise because we are distanced from a certain intense immediacy of life—in lyrical art, by contrast, these affects are especially sought out because they create for us precisely this artistically requisite distance. The affect that life produces as the result of impassivity, of detachment, here becomes the center because it best satisfies the conditions of art.

In still another respect, detachment creates a turning point between empirical life and poetic ideality. It has long been noted that persons and events of the past are especially suitably disposed to poetic treatment in the epic as in drama. In fact, the manner in which the past is presented to us as such is already a pre-form of art: a detachment from all practical interest, a highlighting of the essential and characteristic as against receding insignificances, the power that the spirit exercises here (differently than in regard to immediate reality) in the arrangement and formation of the material into images—all of these characteristics of remembrance of the past are essential shapers of art as soon as they, for their part, adapt themselves to the given material. This even occurs, though less absolutely, in history as a scientific arrangement of images. History, too, forms the lived material of events by means of such categories into an ideal, life-transcendent construction, but in history, *content* imposes still greater claims than in art on the ultimately created result, so that history stands as a kind of conduit between experiential memory (containing those categories in an embryonic state) and (historical) poetry. The relation between history and art tends to be conceived as though artistic forms and qualities were initially given for themselves, and were then employed for sketching the historical image. Though it may operate that way psychologically after the development of both realms, the essential connection proceeds in reverse fashion. We must consider here not only history as researched by scientific method, but also its precursor that certainly prepares forms for it: the process (almost uninterruptedly pervasive in our lives) of making the experienced or transmitted past present in somehow self-contained images. And this continual experience does not presuppose art; instead, it is immediately formed by those categories that are serviceable and fragmentary within life, just as they centrally define and subsume material, and produce the artistic realm as such. Seen at this deepest level, art is not a vehicle of history, but conversely—history by its most distinctive necessity is a second pre-form of art, the first pre-form of which is the manner, self-generating within life, of remembering the past.

Representing the relation of life and art in this fundamental way reconciles an antagonism of motives or orderings that threatens the essence of the idea in general with an inner contradiction. With greater or lesser historical-psychological thoroughness we can trace the development of art, like that of science and religion, out of the course of natural empirical life or even within the latter: in unnoticeable gradations ideal constructs arise from nonideal ones and phenomena as such seem to recognize no absolutely firm distinction, no point of qualitative transition. Nonetheless we maintain that such a point exists precisely in principle, that art (or generically: the idea) draws its meaning and its claim precisely from the fact that it is life's Other, the deliverance from its praxis, its contingency, its temporal flow, its endless concatenation of ends and means. If we recognize that in all of this forms nonetheless operate which, from their position as means or intermediate points, need only be brought into the other position (as values unto themselves and autonomous powers leading to definitive creations) for those ideal constructs to exist—then both requirements are satisfied. The issue now (varying with the outer phenomenon) is that ways of forming, always existing and effective in the most various degrees, become supreme; with this, it hence becomes conceivable that the boundaries between life-construct and artistic construct (as givens) may not always be sharply drawn, that here and there they overlap one another; for example, that everyday speech passes imperceptibly over into poesy and likewise the empirical way of looking passes into the artistic. Yet precisely because the essential difference lies in *intention*—whether those formings offer themselves as means to the stuff of life and its boundless streaming, or whether conversely as values unto themselves they channel this stuff into themselves and thereby gather it into definitive constructs—precisely because of this the difference between naturally real life and art is an altogether more radical one in meaning. Because the whole process in both cases is the stamping of this specific stuff into specific forms and the entire difference turns on the question of what shall be means and what shall be final value—in other words, because at first the process is a purely internal one and is externally expressed only where forms pass out of the contingent, the fragmentary, the intermixed, into the dominant, the whole, the conclusive—the continuity of phenomena is therefore no longer a contradiction of the unmediated turning of its meaning; instead, the structure of the relationship is expressed precisely in the unification of the two.

Certainly it therefore also becomes understandable that in a great work of art we are always aware of more than the mere artwork. If forms of art stem from the dynamic and the productivity of life, in particular cases they will operate all the more powerfully, significantly, and profoundly the stronger and broader the life they bear. The necessary intermediary is of course what we call talent, through which those forms not only can be delivered to the service of life, but also, through the force of an individual, can be turned into an autonomous configuration of the world's stuff. Yet given an equivalent measure of this specific talent, the decisive element now is how intensive and rich is the life that has entered into these forms. Life now no longer flows through these forms to its own practical ends, but has been dammed up in them, it has so to speak transferred its power to them, and with this power (and to the extent of it) the forms now operate according to their own law. If this endowing life is weak and narrow, the symptoms of a mere formalistic artiness and of an empty technical perfection result. Otherwise, however, the impression arises that the whole meaning of the work is not exhausted with its merely artistic value, that beyond the latter something broader and deeper is verbalized in it. If what is proposed here is correct, this impression points not toward a dualism of the operative factors, but toward their integrated arrangement. Life with its biological and religious, psychic and metaphysical meaning does not inspire the work from beyond the artistic forms; instead these forms are forms of life itself, forms which have freed themselves from life as a teleological flow to be sure, but which owe their dynamic and their richness to this very life, insofar as it possesses these virtues. The "more-than-art" that every great art reveals flows from the same source from which it has sprung, now as a purely ideal construction, free of life. Even when they operate in an utterly objective, independently distinctive sense, life then nonetheless transfers its character into forms sprung from itself, and allows itself to be defined by them in turn, so that it stands so to speak before and behind them; it is eternalized in them by the same claims as those by which they are vitalized in it.

Concerning the formation of the religious "world" I will content myself here with suggesting a unique developmental sequence, avoiding all questions concerning the "essence" of religion. For the present we need only establish that religion is an attitude [*Verhalten*] of *man*—regardless to which metaphysical context it belongs and how it is oriented to and defined by the transcendent. Now in fact there are countless life-circumstances, partly intrapsychic and partly interindividual, that have a religious character immediately of themselves, without being conditioned or defined in the least by a preexisting religion; the word "religious" can only be applied to them in that one looks back toward them from a religion known otherwise and senses in them (even though they are not religiously, but purely vitally determined) the characterization now to be called religious. In empirical life, when we "believe" in a person, when we experience in relation to fatherland or to humanity, to the "higher" or the beloved personage the characteristic mixture or tension of meekness and exaltation, of yielding and desire, of distance and fusion; when we know ourselves truly always at once captive and saved, dependent and responsible, when dark longings and a dissatisfaction in all particular things drives us from day to day—then religion arises as these circumstances and affects are released from their earthly causative substances, as they become to a certain extent absolute and create from themselves their absolute object. Certainly this too occurs psychologically in imperceptible gradations, yet ultimately and essentially God is "love itself;" he is the ultimate object of faith and longing, of hope and dependence; he is not a "something" with which we desire to become one and in which we desire to rest; rather, as these passions, objectless from the earthly point of view, radiate into the infinite, we call their object—and the absolute toward which they radiate—"God." Here perhaps more completely than anywhere else has occurred the rotation around forms that life produces in itself in order to give its contents *immediate* context and warmth, depth and value. Now, however, these forms have become strong enough no longer to be defined by these contents, but rather to define purely of themselves; the object shaped by them, corresponding to their no longer finite measure, can now take charge of life.

In by far the greatest part of the history of religion known to us, the whole religious demeanor—sacrifice, ritual, priestly activity, prayer, feasts, asceticism, etc.—has only the one single meaning of gaining the favor of the gods, be it for the duration of the earthly life, or be it for a life awaited beyond the grave. However greatly this religiosity may be distinguished in temperament, constructs, and technique from other teleological measures, in ultimate principle it is coordinated with all such measures, the umbilical cord to the life that bore it has not been cut; and as internalized, sublimated, and even fantastical the "utility" that those religious modes of behavior may afford, they remain in the vital-teleological context. What one notices with wonder and often with awe in the ethnological and frequently in the ancient world—how tightly, almost to continuity, life is filled with religious undertakings, this quantitatively immense permeation of life by the religious—this observation is nevertheless associated precisely with the fact that religion has not yet achieved its entirely pure being-for-itself vis-à-vis life with its daily desires and interests; certainly after this last has happened, after its wholly distinctive and autonomous meaning has been attained, it is woven back into life again. Life has produced it organically as one of its forms, but intrinsic to the determination of this form from the outset is the fact that it reaches outward from the vital context through a radical turning to a centering and discovery of meaning in itself—and thus for the first time makes possible the self-supporting world integrated under the idea of religion. That the gods are only contingent phenomena made absolute is an Enlightenment banality insofar as it purports to present a judgment on the essence of the Divine itself. But if one asks about the way of man toward God—insofar as it proceeds on the human religious plane—then its decisive turning point is indeed the tearing-loose of those forms of the most inward life from their teleologically relative contents, and their becoming-absolute; the object these forms create for themselves in this pure self-existence [*Selbst-Sein*] can itself only be an absolute, the idea of the absolute. The question of the existence of this object and its believed attributes remains indeterminate, as does that of whether such particular attributes are not perhaps residues that those forms carry with them from their empirical contexts, and from which they cannot yet liberate the realm of their proper ideality.

I began these considerations with the observation that "world" is a form through which we assemble the whole of the given—actual or potential—into a unity. Depending upon the ultimate concept directing this unification, multiple worlds arise out of the same material: the world of knowledge, the artistic, the religious. Common usage, however, applies the concept "world" not only in spheres that by their idea permit nothing outside of themselves. Precisely that formal character of the concept very well justifies assigning it also to relative totalities, realms of narrower extent, provided that an ultimate concept performs the function of integration in them. Thus we speak of a world of law, of economy, of practical moral life, etc. For certain contents of existence, an inclusiveness is thus proclaimed on the strength of a unitarily pervasive sense, an autonomy and inner self-accountability, that makes each of these worlds a formal analogy, in miniature, to that all-embracing one. So it is indeed, insofar as it can attain its self-sufficiency and own objective meaning only through the same axial rotation between life and idea. The material of all these worlds grows in the relationships of life, impelled by life's organic powers and its more or less teleological, all-implicating necessities, and it plays this role within the life-whole in quite specific, characteristic forms that are continually suffused by its vital significance. But the worlds free themselves from this significance; they attain a value that is relative only to themselves and whose ultimate authority is their own meaning; and now, as they pulsate in the rest of life, they take on powers and contents. Now for their part they are the shapers of life's material as far as this material possesses an affinity to them, and becoming a world corresponding to their respective leading idea now appears as its ultimate telos; with the reservation that these latter worlds, in principle finished, as in the larger instances discussed above, can plunge back into the currents and developments of life again. I will try to sketch this principle in a few strokes for some of these one-sided totalities, and first for the world of law.

It certainly cannot be doubted that behavior we describe as being lawful and enforceable by law is already found in essence in social situations that have not yet developed either the concept of law or the institutions made possible only through it. The self-preservation of the group must have achieved this, either as instinct and self-evidently practiced custom or by the threat of punishment. We may assume that this behavior by the social totality and the individual towards one another was perceived as "law" in the sense of correct and justified. But the claim did not spring from "law" as a reality-transcendent idea; rather, it and its fulfillment were functions of immediate life whose purposes the group followed, if indeed often by peculiar paths. In this real entanglement with life we must not be misled by the fact that such commandments and prohibitions appear in major, probably overwhelming part under religious sanction. The religious potencies of such primitive situations, the totem and the worshipped ancestor, the fetish and the spirits inhabiting the entire surroundings are indeed themselves elements of that immediate life; even the more highly developed god remains for a long time yet a member of the group itself. Precisely because all later differentiated sanctions of a moral or a legal, a religious or a conventional variety lie as yet unseparated in the norm of "correct" behavior, this norm, and likewise adherence to it, is situated organically and conjointly in the actually unfolding life process as one of its functions. But "law" has its place on an entirely different level. As soon as it exists—though however "purposive" its contents (which in this sense include its forms) may be—it is not this purposiveness that is the meaning of its realization, but rather the fact that these contents are law. It is now no longer a means or a technique whose ultimate purpose has perhaps been forgotten; the continuing consciousness of its purposiveness so little diminishes the new absolute of the legal claim as such that this claim persists even where there is a conscious negation of that purposiveness: *fiat justitia, pereat mundus.*[5] Among the paradoxes rooted in the deepest ground of the spiritual worlds is the fact that the same actuality of the legal category develops in and out of life, but, from the instant in which it now conversely determines life according to itself, its independence proves the value of its objective presence, even to the negation of this life. One can certainly speak of a social "purpose in law." But this pertains only to its content-wise determinants and to the fact that in general the sanctioned form of coercion exists for it. Both of these, born of the teleology of social life, are common to all stages of development. In connection with essential inner meaning, however, they reveal the radical transformation. As soon as we say that a genuine "law" exists (i.e., one that should be fulfilled because it is law) all teleology falls away: law as such is an end-in-itself, and this is only a somewhat more unclear expression for the fact that it has indeed *no* "purpose." The continuity in its contents, the fact that it is sanctioned, and its social utility must not disguise this turnabout in principle. It is very highly significant that probably all primitive laws carry a predominantly criminal character. The idea of an objective order whose every empirical relationship is only a part and an example regulated by it—this idea originally lies far off. Even such a simple norm that the creditor must be made whole does not originally appear as an objective claim of justice, nor as the obligatory realization of a value logic: instead, nonpayment is prosecuted on the debtor as a subjectively forbidden action. This still echoes in later Roman law where, in some purely civil suits, not only did a verdict result on the monetary settlement at issue, but the condemned party also suffered infamy. Instead of the principle that the contract must be maintained—whereby persons are bearers of rights and duties, but remain otherwise entirely outside of consideration so that the process can relate entirely to the concluded contract alone—instead of this, the impulse much more immanent in the entanglements of life is operative: that the wrongdoer should be condemned. Most closely associated with this is the fact that law at the beginning of its development is essentially oriented toward the preservation of "peace" and above all seeks to remove the threat to the collective entity through individual violence and its no less violent individual defense: its peacemaking, as it has been expressed, originally overshadows its doing of justice. The collectivity wills to live, and out of this will and as the latter's means it creates forms that regulate the behavior of the individual. But so far this still remains entirely in the teleology of the collectivity, just as manners of behavior of the individual life are regulated for the sake of its teleology, and here too

---

5. "May justice be done, though the world perish."—Trans.

very frequently by means of coercion that the center of the personality practices upon the particular peripheral impulses. Law exists here in the form of
life; as superindividual as this may be, it is—in an extreme expression of this
intention—an immanent undertaking of life's teleology within the series of its
techniques; from there it first steps into the form of the idea without having
to change something in the phenomenon: merely that previously justice was
good insofar as it serves life, but now life is good insofar as it serves justice.

How decisively law is elevated to its own basis out of the entanglements
of the dynamic totality of life is shown by its distinction from usage and
custom, with which it was originally fused; or rather there appears to have
arisen at the beginning of all higher social-practical development everywhere
a wholly general norm, an undifferentiated consciousness of what in general
should be—this consciousness is naturally religiously colored, only gradually
proceeding apart and upward into the separate structures of custom, law, and
personal morality.

But *custom* remains permanently bound up with the reality of life, in whose
teleological traits the universal imperative arose. Usage and custom are thoroughly bound to subjects that live according to them both. One can naturally
also consider them in abstraction from the latter as an anonymous formalism,
but in this ideal autonomy they have no real meaning; even as *principles* they
only apply as soon as people live according to them in reality, even if with exceptions. They do not support themselves nor rest on an ideal basis independent of life, but instead remain indissolubly attached to the permanence and
purpose of life. They have not shared in the turning to the idea, a turning that
produces the form of a self-supporting, unitary "world" and that has brought
law into being. They remain serviceable to life—in contrast to this, law, by its
idea, has become sovereign. But even here it should not be forgotten that law,
autonomous and life-defining as it is according to its idea, can also still be
encompassed once again by life.

Even in the domain of the economy, though certainly only discernible by
a differentiating eye out of great displacements and concealments, the realm
of an objective life-domain integrated by a concept has escaped, by a turning
in principle, from the original life-context whence its form originated. Surely
there is no practical complex that is so fused to the primary life processes, so
linked to its daily forced demands as the economic. Hunger and the other
needs in question have thrust forth the forms of their satisfaction, and even
the richest and most refined complex of these forms allows no other meaning
than indeed to satisfy those needs as purposively as possible. The fact that the
economy and its mediating values, especially money, can thereby grow psychologically into definitive, particular purposes signifies, as already emphasized,

no change in principle whatever; all thereby remains in the same level and only changes the psychological accents. But the complete rotation through which the economy really becomes a world unto itself surely does arise as soon as it becomes a process occurring according to purely objective, material-technical regularities and forms, a process for which living persons are only bearers, agents of the norms immanent to it and necessary on its account; and the owner and manager are, no different from the laborers and errand-boys, slaves of the production process. The violent logic of its development does not depend on the will of the subjects, nor on the meanings and necessities of their lives. The economy now goes its necessary way, entirely as though men were there for its sake, but not it for the sake of man. Of all those worlds whose forms life's development has produced in and from itself and that have then found their center in themselves and for their part dominate life, surely none at its origin is so unquestionably and inseparably rooted in the most immediate life, so utterly without a hint of its own distinctive meaning as against the teleology of life; and likewise there is none that, after that axial rotation, sets itself, through its pure material logic and dialectic, in opposition to the real meaning and genuine demands of life with such ruthless objectivity, with such demonic violence—as the modern economy. The tension between life and that opposite-of-life that its forms, produced purposively by itself, attain here has reached a maximum—indeed even a tragedy and a caricature.

In the ethical area, finally, I will indicate only a single phenomenon that represents the motive explored here. Specifically, the Kantian distinction between the hypothetical and the categorical imperative really coincides precisely with what I mean. What Kant calls the subjective motive inherently still alien to morality is precisely what I refer to here as a moment of vital teleology: the natural drive, striving toward a maximum of empirical life-fulfillment, building means upon means, many of which fully satisfy the outwardly practical claim of morality. The fact that according to certain moralists "enlightened self-interest" is identical with morality expresses this to perfection. But morality is not yet realized as an idea when the morally requisite occurs merely where the life process spontaneously produces actions that are otherwise also morally requisite; rather, morality is realized only when duty, of itself and as a sole authority, defines the life-course—and with this observation Kant has expressed in its full radicality the turning treated here. We need not agree to this version of the concept of duty and to the value-exclusivity of his moralism. Above all, though, the mediating moment that concerns me here does not enter into Kant's consideration: to him it appears a mere accident and an alien coincidence that actions appear within subjective-vital purposiveness that are in fact morally correct. But I would not admit this meaninglessness of our constitution, which gives its depiction a deeply pessimistic tendency for Kant. Certainly the motivations in both cases are thoroughly distinct from each other. But beyond all contingency in the particulars, they are united in principle by the fact that life out of its own teleological necessities brings into existence forms of action around which, as though around an axle, life tends to be turned, so that those forms exist as an autocratic idea, and of themselves define life and its value. Kant believed he could only save the absolute character of the ideal definition from the relativity of the vital one by making their relationship utterly contingent. But precisely herein lies a certain lack of ultimate trust in that absolute character. If one is entirely sure of it and if one really places it into the autonomous inwardness of conscience, then the absolute in no way suffers from the fact that out of its relative associations life has already produced—beforehand or simultaneously—the kind of behavior it requires, and that, empirically and psychologically, gradual shadings exist between both motivations of these modes of behavior.

:::

Examination of these trains of thought should surely not imply that the deciding principle dominates them all in exactly circumscribed equality. Each series, rather, has as it were an organic unity in which the basic formal process is drawn by its content into its own differentiated characterization. They possess among themselves only the special relationship of "similarity," which does not admit of being combined out of a quantum of equality and a quantum of inequality, but rather is sui generis.

The ultimate meaning of the theme brought forth here, pursued in its most far-reaching case, is the establishment of an organic relationship between psychology and logic. Now it is indeed certain that this may be attained just as little through psychologism as from the peculiar domain of logic; and surely in the same way the mutual contingency of both domains is not supportable over the long haul. I can see here no other way out than a metaphysical one, of which (reaching back into the first essay in this volume) I will suggest only this for the present context. Just as life is a continuous begetting on its physiological level, so that, to use a compromised expression, life is always more-life—so too on the level of the spirit it begets something that is more-than-life: the objective, the construct, that which is significant and valid in itself. This ascent of life beyond itself is not a something added to it, but is its genuine, immediate essence indeed; insofar as it manifests this, we call it precisely spiritual life, and it itself becomes, beyond everything subjective-psychological, an objective something and develops the objective out of itself. Here I will only touch on the basic thought: that creative life (in the pursuit of productive life) continually transcends itself; that it itself sets up its Other before it and thereby establishes this objectivity as its creation, as comprising a developmental relationship with it; that life draws objective meanings, consequences, and norms into itself again and forms itself according to what has been formed by it. That which stands at this turning point we call objectivity, which is transcendent to the subject and is nothing less than a mere camouflage of it. Or better: *both*, as givens, are stages of the development of life as soon as it has become spiritual life which, though it proceeds through the one in order to reach the other, nonetheless shows its unity in the reactive effect of the latter upon the former. In a relativistic process, there arises an objective character and truth, norm and absolute over the subjective psychological event, and independent of it—until even this is again recognized as subjective because a higher objectivity is developed, and so on into the boundlessness of the cultural process. Herein also certainly lies its whole tragic element, the tragic element of the spirit overall: that life often wounds itself upon the structures it has externalized from itself as strictly objective; it finds no access to them; it does not, in its subjective character, satisfy the demands that it develops in their character. That indeed is the painful proof that we are dealing here with a true objectivity in every sense required of it—and in no way with a psychologization of it. What I have put forward here are only several cases of the objectification of life, a demonstration of several points in which it produces what confronts it and in whose autonomous meaning, independent of real life, the metaphysical—not the psychological—character of creative life becomes visible.

3

Death and Immortality

The inorganic body is distinguished from the living one above all by this: the form that defines it is determined from outside—whether in the most extreme sense that it ends because another body begins, by reacting against its expansion, bending or breaking it; or through molecular, chemical, or physical influences, as when rocks form through weathering or lava through solidification. The organic body, however, produces its form from within; it stops growing when its innate formative energies have reached their limits, and these continuously define the particular manner of its extent. The conditions of its overall existence are the same as the conditions of its manifest form, whereas for the inorganic body the conditions of its form reside outside itself. The mystery of organic form lies in the fact that it is limit: it is at once the thing itself and the cessation of the thing, the domain in which the being and the no-more-being of the thing are one. And the organic being, in contrast to the inorganic, requires nothing else for this determination of its boundary. What is more, its boundary is not merely spatial, but also temporal. It is by virtue of the fact that what is living dies—that dying is bound up with its very nature (whether or not from understood or not yet understood necessity)—that its life receives a *form*. Insight into the meaning of death depends altogether on escaping from the notion of "the Fates" in which its aspect is usually expressed: as though at a particular moment the life-thread, spun forth until then as life (and exclusively as life), were suddenly "cut off"; as though death set bounds for life in the same sense that an inorganic body ends spatially where another (with which it has essentially nothing to do) thrusts against it and defines its form as the "cessation" of its being. The proper symbol of this mechanistic view is the skeleton approaching the living being from without. To most people, death seems like a dark prophecy hovering over their life, yet only in the instant of its actualization will it have anything whatever to do with life, like the prophecy about the life of Oedipus that at some point he would kill his father. In reality, though, death is bound up with life from the start and from within. I will leave aside for now the biological dispute on whether single-celled beings are immortal because they only divide into other living beings and never leave a corpse behind (except through the interference of an external force), so that death would be a phenomenon only emergent in life among multicelled organisms. I will also not debate whether for the latter a part or the whole body-substance ultimately perishes. Here we are only concerned with those beings that really die, and whose life is no less intimately connected with death because the life form of other beings does not possess this limitation in the same way from the start. Similarly, our life's attunement towards and pervasive definition by death is not contradicted by the fact that normal life progresses upward for a time and becomes ever more (and so to speak more vital) life; then only after the highest point of its development—which seems farther from death than any earlier point—do the first visible signs of decline begin. Yet even as it becomes fuller and stronger, life nonetheless stands in an overall continuity that is aimed at death. While the metabolism of life substance consists of assimilation and breakdown, and growth presupposes the preponderance of the former over the latter, we already observe a decidedly decreasing assimilation soon after birth. In other words, although still sufficient to produce the appearance of growth, assimilation nevertheless becomes relatively ever more modest even during the growth period, and the cell pigmentation (particularly in the central nervous system) that is identified as a specific change of aging already begins in early youth. From the start, even if hardening of the arteries does not make death identifiable in them pro rata, as it were, the moments of life form a series proceeding unequivocally towards death. From many perspectives, aging is seen as a summation of fermentation processes—starting already at the beginning of life—that wage a lifelong struggle against the constructive forces. In this sense, one mechanistically minded biologist has described death as a physical agent, the material antithesis of life. This antithesis of life, though, originates from nowhere else than from life! Life itself has produced it and includes it.

In every single moment of life we *are* beings that will die, and each moment would be otherwise if this were not our innate condition, somehow operative within it. Just as we are not already fully present in the instant of our birth, but rather something of us is continually being born, so too we do not die only in our last instant.

What we call changes of old age, so says a physiologist, are only the culmination of changes already played out from the first stages of germination. Every death from illness in advanced age can also be seen as a death of senescence, because the organs themselves have been altered pathologically by age. This makes clear, more than ever, the form-giving meaning of death. It does not bound (i.e., form) our life only in the hour of death, but is a formal moment of it that colors all its contents: the boundedness of the whole of life by death influences each of its contents and instants beforehand; the quality and form of each would be different if it could extend beyond this immanent boundary. There is an organization (i.e., a form defined by inner unity) in the temporal succession of life-moments just as there is in spatial juxtaposition, and if this is in absolute contrast to the inorganic (which can disintegrate just as well sooner as later), it is symbolically repeated in the relations of value among men. Some people (so we must say, albeit naturally in the *relative* sense) die because life ends by accident—death does not appear as a boundary, established from the inner essence of the life process. For these people, life has no form at all in the higher sense and they could just as well live arbitrarily short lives as arbitrarily long ones—just like a rock, which reveals the deeper nonnecessity of its form because whether it is larger or smaller is not integral to it at all. This is really a question of the difference between dying and being killed. Naturally, no one can be killed for whom (in contrast to the rock) death is not a possibility. The question is only whether this possibility at some point leads *necessarily* to death. It could even be that the possibility is realized only through being killed, though it makes no difference whether this occurs through dagger and poison or through coronary embolism or tuberculosis bacillus. Perhaps most primitive peoples believe that when someone dies he must needs have been killed—some person or spirit is responsible for it. Here life is not yet grasped deeply enough or, as will be shown later, individually enough to include death in its unity. Artistic character development also recognizes this difference. In the great tragic figures of Shakespeare, we sense almost from their first words the inexorability of their end, not as an inextricable tangle of destiny's threads, nor as a threatening fate, but rather as a deep necessity—I would rather say, as a property of the entire inner breadth of their life—that is merely canalized in the dramatic, ultimately fatal event, and only then achieves a logically intelligible realization in accord with the way of the world. Death belongs among the a priori determinants of their life and of the relation to the world that it establishes. In contrast, supporting characters in these tragedies die simply as the external course of events dictates; they are merely done away with some-how, utterly regardless of the when and the wherefore. Only the tragic figures are compelled to die from within, and the maturing of their destiny as an expression of life is in itself the maturing of their death.

We hold our plans and actions, duties and interpersonal relations (obviously not by conscious consideration, but instinctively and traditionally) from the outset within bounds proportioned to a death-delimited life. But the way this delimiting or forming of life occurs—both as a whole and in its particulars—is determined by the fact that, though we are absolutely certain about the "whether" of the end, we are nevertheless absolutely uncertain about its "when." The life-arrangement of an earthly immortal being would be utterly inconceivable to us; but even that of beings certain of their future death as well as the year and day of its arrival would differ, in a scarcely less inconceivable degree, from the life-disposition familiar to us. One of my friends put it roughly as follows: "How much better life would be, though, if one knew for certain how many more years one had left! Then one could adapt to it, organize life purposefully, one wouldn't have to leave anything behind unfinished or begin anything unfinishable; but one would really be allowed actually to use up the time." Seen from the other side, though, life in this case would probably be subject to an unbearable pressure for most people. Objectively regarded, the proposed advantages would be offset by countless achievements that could not occur because man very often performs at his best only when he undertakes more than he can perform. And subjectively, it is certainly true of the life-will that thanks only to the uncertainty of death's appearance are anxiety over death and depression over its inevitability reduced to a tolerable level, one that to a certain extent secures for man the inner scope of movement for joy of life, development of energy, and productivity of the life known only to us. This is perhaps the most notable case of a form that defines our life and relation to the world in all respects: that a basis in principle for theory or practice is inescapably settled for us while its elaboration and proof, as would be required for concrete life-situations, become quite problematic and even illusory because of an overlying layer of questionable or concealed factors. Thus we may be persuaded that in view of the natural differences among individuals aristocratic systems are the only objectively suitable ones. Because we have no means at all of recognizing the αριστοι[1] with assurance and placing them into the leading positions, however—nor, even if this were done, of guarding the ruling stratum against the corruption of power—this primary belief avails us, so to speak, very little; so little indeed that even some of its adherents declare

---

1. "The best ones."—Trans.

democracy the lesser evil. Similarly, Kant has perhaps persuaded us that in our cognition a priori forms operate that are valid necessarily and without exception for all its objects because they bring cognition as such into being in the first place. But *which* forms these allegedly are we can only declare by empirical investigation, without any similar a priori guarantee and actually only in hypotheses: that in principle we possess absolutely sure cognitions does not assist us even to an approximately sure knowledge of which perceptions these are. This constellation in which the metaphysical-cosmic "middle position" of man expresses itself is repeated countless times and with quite contradictory value implications. We are confined between knowing and not-knowing. We could not lead the life of an empirical person if we had either a much wider or a much narrower knowledge than we actually do. And weighed against the emphasis on the immense and ever wider progress of our knowledge, it should not be overlooked that at the other end, so to speak, a certain amount that we possessed as "certain" knowledge sinks into uncertainty and perceived error. How much of what the medieval person, or even the enlightened thinkers of the eighteenth century or the materialist naturalists of the nineteenth century, "knew" is for us either entirely discarded or at least utterly doubtful! How much of what now is unquestionable "knowledge" for us will, over the short or long term, suffer the same fate! The entire psychic and practical attitude of man implies that—speaking cum grano salis and for the fundamental point—he only apperceives in his environment things that correspond to his convictions and, in ways often fully incomprehensible at a later time, simply ignores counterinstances, however glaring. For astrology and miracle cures, for witchcraft and immediate fulfillment of prayer, no less "factual" and "convincing" proofs were adduced than are now adduced for the validity of universal laws of nature, and I believe it by no means out of the question that later centuries or millennia—recognizing the indissoluble-unitary individuality of every particular phenomenon as its kernel and essence, underivable from "universal laws"—will declare such universals no less superstition than we declare the beliefs just cited. Once one renounces the idea of "absolute truth" (likewise only a historical construction), one could come to the paradoxical idea that in the continuous process of cognition the mass of just-adopted truths is only just balanced by the mass of just-destroyed errors; that, as in a train that never stands still, just as many "true" bits of knowledge climb up the front stairs as "illusions" are thrown down the back stairs.

To this most diversely formed domain of mixtures and comminglings of knowledge and not-knowledge—within which the specifically human life-orientation for the most part stands—knowledge and not-knowledge of death also belongs as perhaps the most striking phenomenon. In the forms in which we live, life is only possible precisely on this basis of knowledge of the fact and non-knowledge of its time-point. This further shows—and the excursus is inserted here for this reason—how unconditionally form-defining death is for life; how it inhabits life, with what is known of it as with what is unknown, both in indissoluble fusion. Because this limit is both fully inflexible for our consciousness and fully fluid, and because every change in the one as in the other would instantly transform the whole of life into something unimaginable, death appears as the seeming "outside" of life that in truth is its "within," forming every element of this "within" as only we know it.

It is among the colossal paradoxes of Christianity that it removes the life-inherent quality from death, yet from the outset places life under the perspective of its own eternity. And indeed eternity is seen not only as a prolongation of life attaching to the last earthly instant—rather, in Christianity the eternal destiny of the soul depends upon the whole series of life-contents, each of which projects its ethical significance as a ground for determining our transcendent future into the infinite, and therewith breaks through its inherent boundedness. Here death can be said to be overcome, not only because life, as a line stretched through time, reaches beyond the form-boundary of its end, but also because life denies the death acting through all the particular moments of life and inwardly limiting them, on the strength of the eternal consequences of these very elements. Here life is composed exclusively of its positive elements; what death can do to it affects only its outer workings, indeed only what is by assumption not our real life. In light of the continuity with which our other-worldly (though certainly not death-containing) existence is determined by that of this world, death has even lost its "sting," its vital significance, in this world. This very pure depiction (as it seems to me) of the basic Christian theme is admittedly quite warped by churchly notions, above all by the peculiar importance—which interrupts the entire metaphysical life-coherence—of the death-*moment*. Because this very moment—through repentance or even by means of ceremonial activity—is supposed to undo the most wicked life of sin, an excessive emphasis seems to me to be placed on a temporal-earthly detail—an emphasis incompatible with the wonderful, overall insight that we are all from the outset the children of God who make only a fleeting sojourn on this earth. Even on earth we live as His children, obedient or rebellious to His will, defiant or repentant, and (as is the essence of life in general) determining our future through every such present instant. But: that the moment of bodily death (which, being physiologically determined, can contribute only a rather superficial dent, as it were, to the eternal fate of the soul) should now alone decide absolutely everything by its defiance or repentance—this seems to me to trivialize and somehow distort the true meaning of Christianity broadly understood.

Still, even this notion can proclaim a religiously significant idea. Life, as it advances, makes us generally hopeless, not always in thoughts, but in being. In old age we no longer believe in the possibility of great changes: it seems somehow illusory to us that we can still accomplish them. In contrast, the advantage of religious natures is that they continually feel themselves in relation to an absolute, in the face of which the quantitative differences of the life process are infinitesimal quantities. For the religious person there is always time yet, because in the eyes or, better, in the being of the Eternal, twenty or seventy years signify no difference at all. That the last instant still suffices for salvation, no matter how long and recalcitrant a life has preceded it—this is the extreme (if also somewhat superficial) expression for the irrelevance of longer or shorter and for the fact that, in respect to eternal (as contrasted with empirical) life, no measure of past time amounts to being "too late."[2]

Death also appears as the shaper [Gestalter] of life from the opposite viewpoint. The given position of organisms within their world is such that they can only remain alive in every instant through some kind of adaptation in the broadest sense of the word. The failure of this adaptation means death. Just as every automatic or random movement can be interpreted as the impulse

---

2. The interweaving of life with death can serve as one symbolic motivation—along with others—for the claim that there is no unquestionable warrant for calling the Divinity "living." Though this may be a beautiful and perhaps unavoidable notion, it is ultimately no less anthropomorphic than that of the old man walking in the garden in the cool of day. He is thought to be living because this appears to offer the only possibility of communicating with Him. Life or sentience is ultimately a specific type of existence, and to think of it as the "highest"—to place all of being into the exclusive alternative of the purely material and the vital-spiritual—merely because human beings on earth do not experience anything else, seems to me to be a narrow-mindedness most radically sublimated in all those metaphysical systems that announce the "spirit" or "life" as the Absolute. Naturally, nothing would be gained if one chose to describe God as the super-vital: even the most careful attempt at precise definition oversteps what we are justified to think. But nothing hinders us, in fact everything entitles us, to remove the constrictedness of the life- and soul-concept from the Absolute, in full disregard of the fact that this constrictedness is the limit of all of our possibilities. Even the attempt to find something freed from this in the concept of "value" would not lead to a more legitimate determination of the divine Absolute, for to me an actualization of values without the basis of life, soul, and spirit seems a mere word. Schelling's absolute "indifference" would seem more satisfying if he did not separate it at once into the poles of nature and spirit and thereby imprison it yet again within the alternative confines of our contingent experience. Spinoza seems farther along when he ascribes to God infinite attributes, of which only two, thinking and extension, are comprehensible. But he still understood these as real determinants of the Divinity—a point that is surely incontrovertible in consequent pantheism, but again signifies anthropomorphism for a transcendent God. From this perspective the negative theology of the mystic is freer and deeper than all earlier or later dogmatics and philosophy of religion.

toward life, toward more-life, it can likewise be interpreted as the flight from death. Perhaps the essence of our activity is a unity, mysterious even for us, that like so many other things we can grasp only through analysis into the categories of conquest of life and flight from death. Every step of life appears not only as a temporal approach toward death, but as positively and a priori formed by death, which is a real element of life. Furthermore, this forming is thus codetermined precisely by the *aversion* to death, by the fact that striving and enjoyment, toil and rest, and all our other ways of behavior considered natural—are an instinctive or conscious flight from death. Life, which we consume in order to bring us closer to death, we consume in order to flee it. We are like people walking on a ship in the direction opposite to its course: while they walk southward, the deck on which they do so is borne northwards with them, and this double direction of their motion determines their current position in space.

:::

This forming of life *in its entire course* by death is so far, as it were, a bit of imagery that of itself does not yet require any conclusions. It is only a matter of replacing the customary notion, which views death merely and so to speak inorganically as the life-ending snip of the Fates, with the more organic notion that death is a formative moment of the continuous life-course from the start. But whether its biotic pervasiveness [*enbiotische Verbreitung*] is seen on the one hand as a prior action or foreshadowing of the singular death-event or on the other as an autochthonous forming or coloring of every life-movement in itself, in any case it really is this pervasiveness, along with the acuteness of death, that establishes certain sets of metaphysical propositions concerning the essence and destiny of the soul. I will not explicitly distinguish the modifications that draw the one or the other sense of death into the following reflections, but it would be an easy matter to separate the proportions of each in these ideas.

The Hegelian formulation—that each thing calls forth its antithesis and proceeds with it to the higher synthesis in which, though transformed, it nonetheless thereby "comes to itself"—reveals its deeper meaning perhaps nowhere more forcefully than in the relationship between life and death. Life calls death forth from itself as its antithesis, as its "other," which the thing becomes and without which this thing would not have its specific meaning and form at all. So far life and death stand on *one* stage of being, as thesis and antithesis. But with this something higher arises over them: values and tensions of our existence that are beyond life and death and are no longer touched by their opposition, but in which life first truly reaches itself, and reaches the highest sense of itself. The basis of this thought is that life as immediately given proceeds completely undifferentiated from its contents. To call the actuality of consciousness a "process" certainly has something hypothetical or constructed about it. For what really exists—what we inwardly see, experience or think—is still always a something, a content (though of course not a stable one, but one content continually following another); yet the fact that this something is borne, pushed forward, and moved on through the consciousness by an energy (at least by something energy-like), and is not simply lifelessly there—this fact does not inhere in consciousness of the object as it immediately presents itself, but instead is the sensation of an obscure unfurling excitation of life [*Lebensbewegtheit*] that does not really occur on the same level. The mere now-thus [*blosse Jetzt-Sosein*] and now-thus, the mere exchange of images, is not yet movement or process, not even if one feels its continuity here much more than its punctuality, as in a line. Yet regardless of whether it behaves this way under the most discriminating examination, in unselfconscious experience the utterly dominant feeling is that something "proceeds," that the image-content is animated as though presented by something powerful and functional. Here content and process comprise a unity that only analysis after the fact divides in two. Yet this separation, particularly for certain of the highest values, seems to me to become possible only because their bearer, their process, is subjected to death. If we lived forever, life would presumably remain indistinguishably fused with its values and contents, and no real impulse at all would exist to imagine these outside of the single form in which we know them and can experience them infinitely often. But in fact we die and thereby experience life as something accidental, something ephemeral, something that, so to speak, can also be otherwise. Only thus could the thought have arisen that the contents of life do not indeed have to share the fate of its process; only thus could we have become aware of the meaning—independent of all transience and ending, and valid beyond life and death—of certain contents. Only the experience of death could have dissolved that fusion, that solidarity of life-contents with life. Yet temporal life attains its own purest intensity precisely with these timelessly meaningful contents: as it takes these (which are more than itself) into itself or pours itself into them, life transcends itself without losing itself, indeed attaining itself really for the first time, for only thus does its unfolding as process achieve sense and value and know, so to speak, why it exists. It must first be able to separate these contents from itself ideally in order to become conscious of them, and it accomplishes this separation with a view towards death, which can certainly end life's process but cannot annul the meaning of its contents.

Here I do not want to overlook an analogy that highlights the foremost of these spiritual structural relationships. The discrepancy that exists between our drives and capacities on the one hand and our real accomplishments (inner and outer) on the other must belong among the motives for the formation of the continuous ego. If our wishes were always completely fulfilled, the act of willing would perish with its fulfillment and a new one, with new content, would begin—the inner process would be fully exhausted with its relationship to reality, and the ego would not emerge from this entanglement with the reality that accompanies it step for step. This emergence occurs, though, when the will outlives its contact with reality because reality does not quiet the will, and when the willing ego still exists where reality is no longer. A harmonious, thoroughly satisfied relation between will and reality would suck the ego-consciousness much more into itself, and would make the ego in its particular course much less recognizable. The "No" and the "too little" of the outer world vis-à-vis our own allows the latter to operate beyond its contact with the world in such a way that the ego *thereby* becomes aware of its independence, and above all of the continuity flowing only from its own impulses. Thus people to whom much remains denied and who are deeply disillusioned by the world's concessions as a rule show a more pronounced and, from a certain point on, a more immutable ego than those for whom everything has always gone smoothly; even their facial lines show (more than is true for these latter) the character of fixity and lasting imprint. Our attitude toward art presents the counter phenomenon. It is relatively easy for an artwork to satisfy us because all the demands that we can make upon it encounter us first from the work itself: it refuses all problems and obligations imposed from without, and what we want from it is determined only by the work itself. It is the unique formation [*eigentümliche Gebilde*] that allows the "idea" which is its perfection, the form with which it satisfies all demands, to shine forth from itself and only from itself—even when its reality does not correspond to these demands ideally inscribed in it. But when this reality does satisfy them, the sense of the artwork as such is achieved—the self-sufficiency that does not permit the will of the beholder to raise value-claims other than those innate in the work itself. Even its deficiency is measured—in a way not to be pursued here—by the work itself, by its individual ideal. By this means the will's relation to the work of art is distinguished in principle from the claims with which the will tends to approach not only all technical-material things, but also other people and even divine forces.

This structure of the artwork seems to me the deeper basis of the fact, which Schopenhauer describes ultimately only in terms of the phenomenon and interprets only speculatively: that in the face of a work of art the will is silent. It can impose no demand in the face of the artwork (of which alone Schopenhauer is thinking)—except in theoretical pedantry or from tendencies alien to art—that is not preformed in the work itself and indeed also satisfied there. At this boundary the will must halt and cannot desire anything at all beyond it. Therefore, as has been said, the volitional ego dies in the artwork and begins afterwards to live anew. Here, then, is the exception to that typical demand for more, and likewise to the typical dissatisfaction with what worldly life has to offer. For this reason even the success of the latter constellation for ego-formation does not enter in here. People who live predominantly in aesthetic enjoyment (obviously utterly distinct from the artistically productive, in whom a profuse superabundance of will tends to exist) tend as a rule to reveal no continuous, persistent ego free of yieldings. They live instead in relatively short episodes, feel themselves without difficulty into all contrarieties, and allow themselves rather to be mastered by things, instead of dominating them from a self-assured ego. This negative circumstance thus attests to the positive one previously shown: as the process of life must be denied by death in order for the contents of life to emerge in their lasting significance, so too the contents of the will must be denied by dissatisfaction so that the process of the will, the willing-personal ego, may be revealed in its transcendence over every specifiable tie to content. Exactly the same formal structure separates the contents from the process as that which separates the process from the contents.

Obviously therefore, this was not *merely* an analogy, but one side of the central life problem playing out between the ego and its contents, a problem that cannot be grasped broadly enough to understand death's significance immanent within it. I must therefore return again to the ego-formation that takes place in the course of life, in a more general construction of the motive than before, because with ego-formation the problem of death develops into a new stage.

The psychic life process highlights ever more clearly and strongly the formation [Gebilde] that can be called the Ego—not only in the discrepancies just emphasized, but also in its growing overall development. I am speaking here of the essence and the value, of the rhythm and, so to speak, the inner sense that pertain to our existence as this special piece of the world, of those things that we truly are from the outset but in the full sense are not yet. This ego stands in a unique third category, requiring closer explication, beyond its currently existing reality and the irreal value-ideal, which is only a demand. At the beginning of its development though, both for subjective consciousness and in its objective sense, the ego is fused most closely with the particular contents of the life process. And just as this life process separates its contents from itself, just as they obtain a significance beyond their dynamic reality, so too it releases from itself, on its other side as it were, the ego—differentiated in a certain sense *uno actu* with the contents, and therewith also distinguished as a special significance and value, existence and claim from the contents that at first exclusively fill the naive consciousness. The more we have experienced, the more decidedly the ego marks itself off as the one and continuing thing in all pendulum swings of fate and conditions of the world. This is true not merely in the psychological sense that perceiving similarity and persistence in otherwise different phenomena becomes easier and more unavoidable the more numerous they become; but also in the objective sense that the ego is gathered more purely in itself, is elaborated out of all the fleeting accidents of experienced contents, and is developed ever more surely and independently from these contents into its own sense and idea.

The thought of immortality enters here. Just as (in the case discussed above) death allows life to founder so as to permit the timelessness of its contents, as it were, to become free, so now, on the other side of the dividing line, death terminates the series of experiences of particular contents without thereby cutting off the ego's demand to perfect itself [*sich vollenden*] forever or to exist further—the counterpart of that timelessness. Immortality, in the longing of many profound people, means that the ego could *escape* from the contingency of individual contents completely. With respect to religion immortality tends to have another sense. Here it mostly is regarded as a possession—the soul wants bliss or the vision of God or perhaps only a further existence; or, in a starker ethical sublimation, it wants a quality with respect to itself: it wants to be saved, or justified, or purified. But all of that does not matter in connection with the present sense of immortality, as that situation in which the soul *experiences* nothing more; in which its sense thus no longer attaches to a content existing, in some sense or other, outside itself. As long as we live we experience objects; with the advance of years and their deepening, the ego certainly emerges more and more as the invariable and persistent element out of all the diversity of contents flooding past, but somehow it still always remains fused with these; the self-removal, the selfness of the soul signifies only an asymptotic approach to the ego, which exists not in any something but only in itself. Where immortality is believed in and every material content served by the soul as an aim is rejected (whether as insufficiently deep ethically, or as utterly unknowable)—where so to speak the pure form of immortality is sought—there death will surely appear as the boundary beyond which all particular contents of life fall away from the ego, and where life's being or process is a mere belonging-to-itself, a pure self-determination. This is the situation that Yajnavalkya depicts.[3] The fully enlightened one, in trance or in transcendent release, "has no consciousness of what is without or within. That is his form of being, in which he is without desire of silenced desire, *even his desire* is without desire. If he then does not see (hear, perceive), he is nonetheless seeing, though he does not see; since for the seeing person there is no interruption of sight because he is nontransitory; but there is no second element outside of him, no other distinct from him, that he could see (hear, perceive). For only where there is an other does one see (hear, perceive) the other. Pure like water, he stands alone as a seer and without a second element." In other words, then: the life beyond has retreated to pure function; it has no object anymore, but has become the mere self, the self-enclosed life of this self (which is only symbolically expressed with those particular functions)—the falling-away of the object occurs for this pure "life" of the ego because this ego *is* the All.

In the thought of immortality, we always bump into something no longer properly thinkable. This surely arises among other things from the fact that we imagine it as a *life* of the soul beyond the moment of bodily death; yet this is probably just an anthropomorphism, which even the most sublime speculations include no less than do the most childish primitive thoughts. It is not at all settled, though, that life is the only form in which the soul can exist. The soul may have yet other, nonconstruable forms at its disposal than just life, and the fact that it can think of timeless, life-transcendent contents is perhaps a kind of proof for this.[4]

The soul cannot *live* without the body, but it can perhaps *exist* beyond the specific form "life." To identify immortality with eternal life belongs among those apparently logical naiveties that confuse the contrary object with the contradictory one. Because the soul in its earthly form only knows itself as living, it imagines (from here on logically enough) its immortality also as a life—but one that is imaginable in no way other than in connection with physiological processes. Therefore—and admittedly *only* therefore—one need not

---

3. Yajnavalkya was a sage of Vedic India and the ascribed author of the *Shatapatha Brahmana* and *Brhadaranyaka Upanishad*. The quotation appears to be from the *Brhadaranyaka Upanishad*, fourth Adhyaya, third Brahmana, verses 21–32.—Trans.

4. Naturally this is a purely speculative thought, like that previously mentioned concerning the "life" of God; but this whole area is shrouded for us in such a deep obscurity—as indeed the question of how the soul in fact emerges from the organization of matter is so hopelessly inconceivable for us—that speculation may here claim a right to be tolerated. Of course, this right is only well founded when it does not have to do with a purely intellectual-combinatorial play of ideas. Rather, speculation may be only the symbol (however stammering and distant) of an inner givenness, directedness, or attitude; the admittedly subjective expression of an existence that as such is somehow an objectivity and no mere caprice.

surrender to the postulate of Bois-Reymond: if he were to believe in a world soul, one would first have to show him that soul's brain.

Proceeding from a fundamental motif already mentioned, to analyze the life process from a different angle impels us yet again to confront the postulate of immortality. Considering every single current conception that holds our attention at all, we feel that all the tensions or deep processes that rise with it or to it do not come completely to expression and fulfillment; some part of these remains left over, which we feel, or at least always can feel, as the unformed, the nonfinite among our finite instants. No single content that has risen to the level of being formulated in consciousness absorbs the psychic process entirely into itself; each one leaves a residue of life behind it that knocks on the door it has shut, as it were. From this reaching out of the life process beyond each one of its identifiable contents arises the general feeling of an eternity of the soul, a feeling that will not be reconciled with its mortality. Furthermore, this feeling extends significantly beyond instances that we experience as particulars. Within every person reside innumerable possibilities to become another person than he has actually become. Even if his "character" were invariant, the same child raised in Periclean Athens, in medieval Nuremberg, or in modern Paris would have produced three phenomena of immeasurable variation. Naturally, not everything can arise from each—the degree and kind of his powers bind him to uncrossable lines—but within these each has downright infinite possibilities. The mere fact that every child, wherever born, could acquire any of the innumerable languages of the earth as his "mother tongue," and would thus experience an irremovable spiritual formation, shows the illimitable elasticity of the human soul. Yet this does not compare with a piece of clay that can be kneaded into countless forms; rather, it signifies activities carried out by the soul itself and contained within it as positive possibilities, as latent orientations of its energy, as organic inclinations requiring only a developmental stimulus. They are neither merely conceptual "possibilities" nor morphologically similar reproductions of an ordained form, but somehow indeed productivities of the soul itself, responses to the world that only it can give, not an echo that mechanically appears only when an outer movement has occurred. Of these innumerable lines of potential life-formation only a single one is ever actualized; we change into ourselves as the only reality in a shadow-realm of unresolved possibilities of ourselves, possibilities that simply have not come to words, but are by no means nothing. Our narrow reality is perhaps shot through with the feeling of these unbounded tensions and potential directions, and equipped with the intimation of an intensive endlessness that is projected in the time-dimension as immortality.

For a singularly defined reality to emerge from our unlimited possibilities, though, obviously requires the developmental stimulus that the surrounding world, likewise singularly defined at any given time, imposes upon us. This relationship to the world furthermore contains a problematic whose requirement for solution appears able to lead only into the hope of immortality: I mean here the *contingent relation* that exists between our individual, innate characteristics and the historical, preexisting environment. In this environment alone can our existence become a definite life, in fact one modified by *it*. Through this process, however, arise not only the above-noted feeling of unreleased powers, of unfulfilled demands, but even that of a limitless contingency of our entire empirical life. Between its two factors—our disposition, individually unmistakable yet containing unconstrained possibilities, and the world in and through which this potential ego is guided to become a real one—there apparently exists no content-connection supported by the unity of a meaning, other than the general adaptation that makes psychic existence in a world possible at all. But the most inward and distinctive tendencies with which the personality comes into the world and the historically given life-conditions are therefore (unless one believes in a mystically preestablished harmony) no less the factors of a pure game of chance, so much so that the dependency of personal development upon the world often enough makes uncertain or invisible to us what we are really and intrinsically intended for. This is the fundamental contingency in all individual life per se, which becomes obvious to us in the flagrant cases of stunted talents, misplaced energies, and inextricable tangles of fate, but which reveals its full dreadfulness as the truly universal aspect that dominates no less (and indeed, precisely) the most favored life also. I believe that many of the sources that nourish the hope of a superterrestrial afterlife— the feelings of homelessness, of being lost, of being driven about aimlessly, of a deep helplessness—derive from this contingency that cannot be rationalized at all: between our being, which is to a certain degree superhistorical because it is already *brought along* in all history and all possible development, and the historically given milieu into which this being is haphazardly placed and to which it can at most achieve a belated and only relative adaptation. This is the more empirical and so to speak more specialized form of the theme treated above: of the attainment of the pure and self-possessed ego that death releases from all its contents. The deep longing to overcome the contingent, the compulsion with which the soul's relationship to its environment leads us in a direction that is not necessary from the soul's point of view, but could also be a different one—this longing cannot be fulfilled more purely than in the mystical notion of the ego that outlives all particular contents and has therewith eliminated the entire duality of existential elements from which life receives its contingency.

Note on the Concept of Fate

Meanwhile, we must not neglect the fact that this contingent character of life together with its compensation in belief is not the only possible way one can look at the problem of the meaning of life. An entirely different way results when life is regarded under the concept of fate. This concept rests upon a double postulate. First, it presumes a subject that contains or represents a meaning, an inner tendency, a demand—of itself and to that degree independent of every "event." Alongside this self-direction of the subject, however, certain phenomena arise and run their course, phenomena which although lacking any genetic connection to it, nonetheless behave toward it in ways that either advance or inhibit it, interrupt its course or connect it with what is distant, accentuate particular points in it or determine its entirety. Admittedly these events remain "contingent" insofar as what causes them and their own unfolding series of events have nothing to do with the subject's own meaning, which they affect and determine. Yet this does not form the basis on which they now become worth attending to, but rather the fact that they collide with that subjective life and thus acquire a meaning *within it*. This meaning does not even have to be a "rational" one, graspable by an idea or even positively teleological; it can be shocking, destructive, or incomprehensible. For just so do the events have a determinate connection—a point of insertion into a life-course animated by inner directives, however antiteleological and opposed to these directives that connection may be.

The specific character of "fate" thus emerges: that a sequence of objective occurrence, proceeding purely causally, is woven into the subjective sequence of a life determined in other respects from within, and by favoring or violating the direction and destiny of this life, it acquires a meaning from it, a relevance to the subject—as though the more or less external occurrence, operating according to its own causality, were nonetheless somehow aimed at connection to our life. Where one of these elements is lacking we do not speak of fate; that is, neither in respect to animals nor in respect to God. The animal lacks the sense of life, the characteristic ideal and individually specific intention, to which an exogenous occurrence could—both decisively for and also determined by that life, whether encouragingly or restrictively—be interpolated. In contrast, for a divine existence there are no events originally foreign to it and necessary in themselves; instead we would have to imagine events as embraced from the outset by the divine being and as proceeding according to his will, without requiring first that a restraint or encouragement such a being experiences from them must transform their contingency into meaning. Human life, though, stands under a double aspect: on the one side we are held hostage to and ordered by cosmic dynamics, but on the other side we feel and lead our individual existence from a personal center, as self-responsibility and somehow in self-enclosed form. By regarding something as fate, we remove the pure contingency between the two. Tangential to the course of the world, the activity and passivity of life in its course have become, in the concept of fate, a *single* fact.

Yet simply from this structure of the concept it becomes clear that in fact not everything whatsoever that befalls us is fate. Innumerable events certainly graze the outer layers of our actual life, but do not affect its individually meaningful directedness, which is thought to be our real ego. One could speak of a *threshold* of fate, of a significance-quantum of these events, beyond which they promote or inhibit the idea of our life, so to speak. Meeting an acquaintance on the street remains in the region of chance; this is true even if one was just intending to write to him and the happenstance thus becomes "noteworthy" (i.e., that it acquires a cachet of the meaningful). By itself, this proceeds back into contingency again, without being joined with a definitive element of life. However, if through further events bound up with it this encounter becomes a point of departure for deeply transformative life changes, then common parlance will depict it as a working of fate, and therewith signify the entirely new category: that a merely peripheral occurrence now belongs integrally, with positive or negative teleology, to the unity and meaning of an individual life.

When we speak of a purely internal destiny, the ego itself has been correspondingly split into a subject and an object. As we are an object of our cognition, so likewise are we an object of our experience. As soon as our own feeling, thought, and willing proceed for us under the category of "event," the on-flowing, subjective, central life is disturbed by this event as by contents of the external world. This disturbance, occurring in the closed compass of our complete personality, we call destiny as soon as we no longer regard it as a mere occurrence purely contingent to the inner meaning of that central ego; as soon, rather, as this causally emergent, *actual* element of our existence adapts to its very *meaning*, and acquires from it a new significance—increasing or deflecting, modifying or destroying. Even towards ourselves we are in a passivity that, assimilated to the central activity of our life and defining it, appears (as it were, by the reflection of activity upon it) as something meaningful, as something teleologically determined for our life.

From all this the consequence becomes evident: the directedness of the inner life-flow decides what is fate for us and what is not; it makes a selection, so to speak, among the events affecting us, and only those able to adapt to its natural oscillations (and even to their distortion and destruction) play for us the role of fate. Just as we can only conceive that which corresponds to our original or acquired mental norms so that it can be formed by them, and our conceptions therefore must match our spirit—so too can we only have as fate that which can be adopted from our most personal life-definition and processed into fate. Mere events, which remain outside this meaning that would envelop them, correspond then to those merely sensory perceptions that admittedly give us some kind of content, but which we do not understand and cannot form into conceptions by ourselves. The Kantian concept of cognition solved the old puzzle of how the world is organized so that it can be conceived by the contingent structure of our mind; the conceived world is a product of the knowing spirit, in that we only know that portion of it which the mind can appropriate for forming. In the same way, the "apparent intentionality in the fates of individuals," according to which a person's destiny and his individual manner of existence on the whole adapt remarkably to each other, becomes comprehensible through this concept of fate. No interpretation based on the "thing-in-itself" or on mysterious correlations and preestablished conditions is required. Just as the world determines what our perceptual content shall be, though only because perception has previously determined what the world can be to us—so too fate determines the life of the individual, but only because this individual has selected, through a certain affinity, those events to which he can partially grant the meaning whereby they become his "destiny." If certain events are seen entirely as fate regardless of the individual, this is because we presuppose certain fate-decisive life-intentions among all men. Accordingly, we must certainly say that if someone's father is murdered and his mother marries the murderer, it would certainly be an overwhelming event for that person; but that it is Hamlet's *destiny* is determined by Hamlet's nature and not through the fact that this event has affected him as any mere someone. Particular "destinies" are essentially determined from without (i.e., the objective factor appears in them as the predominant one); their totality, however, "the destiny" of every man, is determined by *his* nature. If one only goes far enough back, one sees a unity in this that does not come from particular motives, but whose center lies instead in the a priori formative energy of the individual life; just as—in a somewhat scurrilous analogy—unpunctual people always have a sufficient reason for their tardiness in each particular instance, but as a whole they are unpunctual through themselves, not through circumstances. It is a narrowness peculiar to Kant that although for cognition he in large measure proclaimed the formation of the given world material by forms immanent in the mind—the mentally determined "universal legislation" of nature—yet for the practical realm he allowed a priori determinations only as demands, as ideal values. It escaped him that even utterly nontheoretical, practical-real life is human life as we know it only because the world-material affecting us is itself formed, so to speak, by dynamic categories. Just as the world we perceive is not shaken into us like potatoes into a sack (nor is it a mechanical mirror image of an outside-of-us) neither is the world we experience—in both cases it is our *act*; that is, it is determined by the mode of the specific energies with which we "do" at all. Life, understood as a psychic relation to the world, has its a priori just as perception does, even if not formulable with the same conceptual acuity as the theoretical or as what comes to life from the idea, from the Ought. "Destiny" is one of its categories.

Understood in this way, the concept of destiny is of course no longer attached to the claim of immortality, as was our relation to the world under the aspect of pure chance. Yet this in no way eliminates the dark accent that it cast across life, and which appears likewise, analogous to how experience is constructed, by virtue of the categories of cognition. However decisive the personal synthetic energy of the ego may be for forming the perceptual world out of sensory material, the mere fact that the latter is *given*—that its content cannot be constructed from the mind alone—somehow allows something obscure and unresolvable to endure in this world. And just such a thing persists for fate. Certainly we coax a meaning from the outward event (whose origin is contingent with respect to the personal life-teleology) in that it is placed into that teleology and characterized as fate. It nonetheless brings along its givenness, its content arising from another order; there remains a heterogeneous kernel or remnant in which it is not merely our destiny, and which indeed we do not usually consider in practice, save when the subjective undesirability of our fates reminds us that we are at its mercy. In everything we call our fate, the favorable as well as the destructive, there is a *something* not only ungrasped by our understanding, but also indeed adopted by our life-intention, albeit not assimilated to the ultimate degree. This fact corresponds, by the whole structure of fate, to the uncanny feeling that the entire necessity of our life still somehow remains a thing of chance. Only the form of art offers its complete opposite and its transcendence—in tragedy. Tragedy allows us to feel that the contingent, right down to its deepest basis, is a necessity. To be sure, the tragic hero perishes in the clash between some set of givens external to him and his own life intention; but the fact that this occurs is fundamentally prescribed through the latter. Otherwise his defeat would not be a tragic thing, but a sorrowful one instead. In the suppression of that uncanniness of the contingent in the necessary (and indeed not the necessary according to a would-be "moral world order," but according to the life–a priori of the subject) lies the

"reconciling element" of tragedy; to this extent it is always a "tragedy of fate."
For *tragedy* presents the meaning of the concept of fate—that the mere event-
fulness of objectivity is transformed into the meaningfulness of an individual
life-orientation, or is disclosed as such—in a purity that our empirical fate
does not attain, because in the latter case its event-element never *entirely* renounces its independently causal, meaning-alien essence.

∷∷∷

The problematic of death and immortality does not have a uniform relation
to the fact of the "soul" at all; rather, the individuality of the soul differentiates
this relation. Goethe once said that although he was convinced of our immortality, we are not all immortal in the same way—rather, the greatness of our
further existence depends on how great one is. This adjacent thought—that
the soul overcomes death in the measure of its strength, or that its annihilation
becomes more unthinkable the more significant and irreplaceable it is—looms
over a properly opposed association of concepts.[5] If an amoeba or even a frog
dies, the essential, irreplaceable, singular element of the animal would die only
if he were by chance the last of his lineage. Otherwise he leaves a living posterity indistinguishably similar to him; or at the least a high-grade individuality
is not discernible to us here. The animal lives on not only *in* the posterity but,
one can say, *as* this posterity, and is therefore to this degree immortal. Where
individuals are not different, the immortality of the species devours the mortality of the individual. The question of mortality thus only becomes acute at
all in respect to the genuine individual, in the sense of the nonrepeatable, the
irreplaceable.

   If these concepts and those of higher existence in general are identified
with the increased compounding, multiplicity, and mutual differentiation of
elements of being, then biological observations already point to the genesis
of death out of this very differentiation. Assuming that the cell perishes of

---

5. It should be especially emphasized here that all these conceptual syntheses do not have as their
final aim some sort of significance in reality for the notion of immortality. This metaphysical extreme
has here, rather, only a heuristic meaning: to make transparent the structure of essential and value elements ideally combined in it. At least a very great number of modern people attach scarcely more than
an antiquarian interest to the assertion, demonstration, modification, or controversion of immortality;
it is beside the point here to discuss the justice or injustice of this or the opposite standpoint. Yet even if
immortality itself were a mere fantasy-image, its themes and substructure still lie altogether in the realm
of the real, and these elements are ordered directly, in a manner not otherwise apparent, toward the idea
of immortality. They thus allow derivative analyses and syntheses whose significant illuminating value
lies not in that imaginary flame itself, but in the light that falls from it on the more essential psychic and
metaphysical factors.

its own insufficiently excretable metabolic products, then one-celled creatures have all kinds of means of avoiding it. In multicelled creatures, however, the single cell is surrounded by body fluid that cannot infinitely absorb its meta-bolic products and thus cannot protect it from being overburdened by them. Consequently, only the collective life of cells in a bodily union can arrive at death, which is thus conditioned by the peculiar development of the creature. In other words, only with the combination of cells into a unity—that combi-nation which makes possible an individual character (and the more elements, the greater the chance of morphological individuation!)—is death also given. The corresponding conclusion can also be drawn from the fact that the regen-eration of cells diminishes to the degree that their differentiation progresses. The division of labor among cells, as greatly as it conditions every higher de-velopment, leads ultimately to such a radical specialization of their functions that they physiologically waste away and become atrophied. Among the gan-glia cells, for example, differentiation is conditioned by the fact that cell divi-sion has ceased. Where this is so, however, life is restricted and death is pre-pared. This can be compared to specialization in the most advanced societies, which certainly also brings the individual to an unprecedented differentiation, to a relative uniqueness, but therewith cuts off from him the source of power that flows precisely in the homogeneous, not yet one-sided development of the personality, in the reserve of general vitality not yet brought into specializa-tions. If this does not lead to death, it does lead to the weakening of the whole personality, to its becoming in many ways needy and helpless. Indeed, that exclusively developed special capability of the person often atrophies, or does not even attain its own highest possibility, when it has (so to speak) swallowed the whole person into itself, and is not nourished by any grounding energy flowing from the center, an energy still undifferentiated per se.

This same individuation, which in our general conceptions of value signifies progress and the height of development, is the bearer of transience. In respect to the immortality of the lowliest creature we must say that being able to die is the seal of higher existence—as shown by the fecundity of lower animals that reproduce themselves in identical exemplars, and by the diminishing posterity of the highest human exemplars. If Goethe thus regards immortality to some extent as a prerogative of the psychic aristocracy, this means that man *has need* of immortality—and must justify it on the basis of special claims—to the de-gree that he belongs to this aristocracy, and is incomparable and qualitatively unique. Only these "unique" people die fully and completely, only their death changes the fixity of the world's image—but the death of everyday people as such does not produce this result because their essential quality, extinguished in one place, continues to exist in countless others. Put very generally, this means that the individual is mortal, but the species is not; looking farther, the individual species is mortal, but life is not; life is mortal, but matter is not. Ultimately, matter may disappear as a special case of being, but being will not disappear.[6]

Vis-à-vis the individual entity and to the extent of its individuality, we have the feeling (though only expressible as if from a distance and with fairly inept concepts) that it lives from itself outward; that is, that the world-material of every kind that it assimilates is formed within its own existence by peculiar powers into something relatively unique. The result of this forming—which as practical conduct and theoretical world-persona, creativity and coloring of feeling comprises its ultimate, essential image [schließliche Wesensbild]—lies more remote from that in-streaming world-material, accessible to all others, than is true for the average of these others. Of these average beings, in fact, one has the impression (all this is obviously intended cum grano salis and alto-gether relatively) that the world touching them passes through them in some measure unchanged; they live (i.e., they form the total phenomenon of their life out of the offerings of this material) naturally under the operative a priori of the species. In contrast to this generic life-phenomenon that the world more or less furnishes with its influences and materials and that is thus comprehen-sible on their basis, in individuals the personal a priori, the formative power produced within them from their being and action appears so overwhelming, so centrally defining of the life-phenomenon, that it may even be expressed in the following manner: they live from themselves outwards, they are, figu-ratively speaking, causa sui, not effectus mundi. The nonindividual being lives a life that is not fully his, that does not properly have the form of "his"-ness, for to the possessive pronoun belongs an owner, a person. The world of the average person, in the sense of the persona as of the practical character, is like a security payable to the bearer, while that of the individual is like one issued by name.

6. At least our forms of thinking allow nothing else. We can very well imagine that no world exists initially; but once a being is there, we can as little imagine its disappearance into nothingness as its emer-gence from nothingness. Even the belief that God created the world at a given time does not thereby evade the fact that God also must yet exist. Now if He exists from eternity then there is a nonemergent being that at that point in principle could also likewise be the being of the world; but if one allows Him to "create Himself," then our brash intent to penetrate with our human concepts into the utterly impenetrable is avenged in the absolute inconceivability of this subterfuge, however poetically applicable it may be. No certainty of being can bewitch us; but if somehow being [ein Seiendes] is postulated at all, then the fact we designate with the abstraction "Being" [Sein] is, for every clear-thinking process (granted always only for our thinking), incontrovertibly established upon nonemergence and imperishability. There is no entropy of being.

Therefore if the world is regarded not in the numerical scope of the concepts actualized in it, but in their qualitative specialness, then more is lost with the death of the individual person than with that of the nonindividual one. A more appreciable quantum of the world dies with the former than with the latter, whose essence and inner assets are received from the outset as an inheritance and are left behind as a legacy. He who passes his life in the form and with the contents of the species-type is really immortal, at least insofar as the species is. Only the individual dies completely, and with the absolute individual something would be absolutely at an end. Here we reach the purest and most radical expression of what is intimated at the physiological level: that the complication and differentiation of beings indicates the developmental path, proceeding from the immortality-in-principle of mono-cells, upon which they come to death. As a biologist puts it, death is the price we must pay for the height of differential development.

This may be further portrayed, from the perspective of final categories, as follows. We conceive of material substance as imperishable over time, and each individual bit—purely as matter and altogether ignoring any shaping—is utterly unique; so it would be logically absurd that "the same" bit of matter should exist twice over. The imperishability of form, again seen purely as such and apart from all matter, is of an utterly different kind; it is altogether removed from duration in time, like a concept or a truth, and like these it is also unique. However many identically formed *things* there may be, the repetition of a pure form would be just as absurd as if a concept (which can be *thought* more than once and *realized* more than once) were supposed to exist as a concept more than once. The same indestructible matter can wander through innumerably many forms, the same unalterable form can be realized in innumerably many bits of matter. Because matter and form, each indestructible in itself, can be thus put together, they form destructible particular things, for destruction really means that a linkage between matter and form is dissolved. Now the more firm and solid this linkage was, the more radical, and the greater is the destruction that is its result. Where (as in the reproduction of lower animals) the form migrates so to speak without a tremor to another quantum of matter—that is, where the form from the outset appears not strictly and narrowly linked at all to this definite bit of matter—we do not (as shown above) properly speak of destruction. Vice versa, when the form is so bound to this definite material that it seems to be able to exist in no other, then destruction appears in the fullest degree, because the form, when it has abandoned this *one* actualization, is in this case utterly annihilated. It is therefore not only a value-reflex when we have a more intense feeling of annihilation about a smashed statue than about a smashed flowerpot: in the latter case, the surviving ideal form can be realized again without difficulty in another bit of matter; in the former case, however, this is presumably not true, if we disregard mechanical reproduction (which also presupposes nonsmashedness). The form, even if actualized only once, has its timeless validity; it cannot die since it does not live, but only exists ideally. But we call a form individual when it has (metaphorically speaking) selected a unique bit of material in order to create with it an actuality beyond whose destruction it is granted no further realization. On this account we feel the annihilation of the individual as a loss (to speak Platonically) in the realm of ideas, even though naturally the latter (i.e., form) cannot be lost, but only its sole possibility of being realized; and death is thus more fundamental for an entity the more individual that entity is, since this is the real definition of individuality. The translation to the psychic realm [*das Seelische*] is immediately evident. Here, corresponding to *matter* [*Stoffe*] in its temporally enduring existence is the complex of typical processes or contents of the psychic [*das Psychische*], which offers visualizing agents a common material for the mental life process and the construction of worldviews. Now this material, by means of the psychic [*seelische*] form we call personality, is put into very manifold configurations, and indeed into more or less close connectedness between content and form. Some configurations allow the form into which they bring the material of knowledge and fate, of feeling and will, of fantasy and experience, to be repeated directly in the same material existing in any other personalities. This is a relatively limited "individuality"—that is, the destruction of the whole merely separates elements that were not at all strongly linked. In other cases, however, the destruction cuts through a synthesis that is never found together again in this way; the special personality-form, now no longer clinging to the material of life, can never again descend to it; the construct has really died (i.e., it really was individuality). Even here, form is imperishable in the timeless sense, and matter is imperishable in the temporal sense (relatively). Where they collide, real individuality emerges as the perishable; yet it is less perishable the easier and so to speak the more transient the connection is (i.e., the less it is individuality in the exact sense). Where it is individuality to the absolute degree, where the eternal form is only actualized, temporalized, materialized in this bit of life-matter—there the demise of the entire construct means the irrevocable departure of the form from actuality. Only individuality—that is, the point at which both imperishables so firmly entwine themselves into one another that the one equally inhibits the eternity of the other—can actually die.

Yet since the individualization, irreplaceability, and uniqueness of the image [*Bild*] as which we live are nonetheless valued as a vital maximum, a

tremendous tension arises between life and death through the resulting absoluteness of the indication of death in such beings. The above-mentioned
interpretation of Goethe's idea of immortality rests on this tension. Because
the most elevated and refined life feels itself the most destined for annihilation, it may (reserving all characterological variations) rebel most vehemently
against death and vault over that paradoxical tension by a sought immortality.
We therefore understand—from the strongest threat of death precisely towards the strongest individuality—that Goethe wanted to reserve the greatest
degree of immortality to the utmost significance of personality, and found it
less and less justified as significance decreased. Christianity too has made that
tension effective, although under very different presuppositions. It is unmistakable how strong an individualizing tendency Christianity blazes a trail for,
along with (and even in part on the basis of) all of its leveling tendencies. But
individualizing means not only a qualitative distinction between person and
person, although even this, through "profiting by one's *own* resources" and so
on, did not come off at all badly. It also means, perhaps above all, the person's
responsibility for himself, which he can slough off on nothing else, which no
one can relieve him of, and which in fact can occur only through the strict
cohesion of life's periphery by means of a unitary center, by the true "person."
In the absolute self-responsibility of the soul as it stands naked before God,
and in fact at every hour of life, I see the deepest metaethical core of Christianity. Gone is every legal justification, every tribal or other social solidarity, every blurring of the ultimate personality-point by the opinions of the
world and one's own past life-course: there is only the soul and God. This
utterly undiluted self-responsibility, achieved nowhere else in such intensity
and coincident personality, is nonetheless obviously an unbearable burden for
the majority of souls. First the vicarious and expiatory death of Christ gives
this burden a measure of tolerability and then it is made comfortable to the
shoulders of the average Christian by the Church's interpolation of more familiar intermediaries, all sorts of means of grace, and the declaration of specific paths of salvation. But the fundamental motive—that man is entirely on
his own and is responsible only to his God—could no longer be annihilated
in its immeasurably individualizing, personalizing effect and it has produced
an entirely new configuration and emphasis of the individual ego. Yet with
it the radicalism of death, its immediate proximity to the roots of the sensation of existence, would somehow instinctively increase, as it corresponds to
the developmental maximum of individuality; and it is perhaps to this that
immortality—though now offered in Christianity with an entirely new self-
evidence and security—owes its immense impact. The individual entirely on
his own balances as though on a needlepoint; in the deep sense of threat that is

conjoined with his life situation, he cannot do without his grip on the thought that ultimately death can have no hold on him.

: : :

The idea of immortality brings with it as its condition or its consequence a problem whose close, inner involvement with it has by no means been given full weight in the speculations or dogmatic constructions about it since the Christian era began. The problem proceeds from the (in my opinion) monstrous paradox that a soul which has once come to exist at a definite instant is now supposed to continue existing into eternity. This appears to me as a μεταβασισ εισ αλλο γενοσ,[7] an unjustified claim and encroachment of a merely historical event into the timeless. Randomness in the emergence of a particular human life may not simply be rationalized away—as astrology certainly attempted when its horoscopes interwove the day and hour of birth into the context of the entire cosmos. That the eternal consequence should be coupled without further ado to this merely historical, empirical (one could really say senseless) accident; that from a temporally specifiable, finite human procreation (simply because it is factual) the utterly unempirical realm of the immortal soul, released from all finitude, should ensue—this notion has something incommensurable about it, and something contradictory to the demand for meaning in which such a strong stream of belief in immortality flowed. This contradiction arises both logically and metaphysically as soon as one recognizes the nonemergence of the soul as the correlate of its imperishability.

We must note though that this discrepancy between finite emergence and infinite further existence also arises in a feature of the objective world of the spirit and does no harm whatever to the undeniable actuality of this feature. What we call "immortal" contributions of the human spirit, all the ideas and discoveries, works and manifestations preserved in whatever form (even if only that of oral tradition)—have each arisen in a mind that previously was not there, and again within the latter they flashed up in a historical instant, before which they were perhaps prepared for but nonetheless were not extant. Concerning the immortality of such values I mean here not only their continuation from generation to generation, which is at all events something historical and temporally bounded. Rather—we must so regard it—the world is enriched for all time by and on account of this element appearing in it at some time

---

7. "Transition to another kind" (to apply propositions to matters that lie outside their domain). —Trans.

or other; the world is (as a whole, and whether known by a consciousness or not) thenceforward that much more valuable than before; and if all its forms of existence should collapse tomorrow, the fact that this now actual thing has occurred, been thought, or been created cannot be made not to happen; it remains a transtemporal, incontrovertible value addition to the totality of existence. Expressed somewhat metaphorically or fantastically: by every truly original work of art, every truly creative religious, epistemological thought that imports some kind of meaning to being, the realm of the *idea* is enriched on account of a new content—as, by way of example and symbol, an artistic form may be reproduced through all time, an eternal model, whose spirit and ideal meaning continues to exist even when the original of its tangible matter has long since perished. Here once again we thus have a temporal emergence of the timeless, an infinite extension, relieved of all contingency, and stretching from an undeniably historical and to that degree relatively contingent point of time and departure. One could thus simply declare as settled that irritating antinomy between temporal genesis and transtemporal continuation of life because the exactly analogous formal relationship occurs here as a simple factuality, unbroken by any difficulties of reflection.

Nonetheless the problem is not thereby settled, and particularly not from the viewpoint of this analogy. With respect to its content (considered from what is really the sole matter of concern here), intellectual creation stands in the realm of the timeless *from the outset.* We make a distinction between its contents, spirit, sense, significance (or whatever it may be called) and the psychological-historical act through which, at a particular moment in a particular creature, it is produced for consciousness and for its historical afterlife. To keep apart the content of the idea and its bearer—to separate the intellectual product in its substantive significance and the (presumably) causal process of its production—is a fundamental demand inherent in our mental structure (a demand indifferent to the historical moment in which it is effectively raised by methodological consciousness). The analogy thus appears to break down precisely in the decisive aspect. Immortality would attach the transempirical, transaccidental series of infinitely extended life to the historical-contingent emergence of life, merely because the latter has emerged. The immortality of the objective spiritual world, though, avoids the part of this conception that we sense as somehow inappropriate or inwardly unconnected, because its imperishable substance lies from the outset in the layer of the timeless, of the transhistorical per se, but its genesis lies in the completely different layer of mere occurrence in its causal and temporally determined reality. Thus we do not arrive at a paradox here at all, because the mutual discrepancy is not compressed into *one* series.

But now the thought takes yet another turn. I already indicated that the difficulty in the conception of immortality points to a preexistence of the soul. If the soul exists all along and prior to its manifestation in this human body, then the historical instant of its appearance in the body has no absolute existential significance for it at all; the instant may safely be viewed as accidental, since the soul's current manifestation is only a piece of its continuous life unfolding before and after. Now if the objective spiritual work, brought forth in a specific moment by a specific individual, instantly possesses a significance and validity independent of this moment and this individual, then this noteworthy conjunction—of causal dependence on the historical producer and inner ideal independence from him—has been demolished in this idea: that the great, "eternal" thoughts of mankind actually consist in a kind of ideal eternity, and they are merely actualized by their "creators" in an accidental instant (or rather in the instant corresponding to the spiritual-historical condition); they are merely discovered, not invented. As fantastical as this proposition is, it expresses the strangely actual, incontrovertibly palpable state of affairs, even if it is not something we can precisely grasp. Artists often have the feeling that they are not the real creators of their works at all, but that they only recreate the vision of something somehow ideally existing; Michelangelo expresses it thus, that the statue is already preformed in the marble, and he has nothing to do but to hew it out. Plato's interpretation of knowledge as a remembrance of the preexisting glimpse [Schau] of eternal ideas rests unmistakably on just this basic feeling. Or similarly, the metaphysical puzzle has been given a human-historical turn, as though specifically all of the great thoughts were an ever-existing possession of mankind that is only now called forth from a state of latency into activity and consciousness by a relatively arbitrary individual, by one who has the "mission"; it is the gradually realized inheritance of human essence and its perpetual endowment. Thus we often feel, even concerning deep and essential thoughts that we hear for the very first time, as though we had really known them for a long time and now they are really only articulated. However indistinctly, however brokenly, symbolically, hesitantly—the analogy is again drawn according to the fundamental theme: immortality strives for a correlate from the other side of empirically temporal reality—that is, for nonemergence. Only when life does not rest in principle on the form of empirical boundedness, when it has not emerged temporally [irdisch] as a particular thing, but is a mere excerpt from an eternal existence—only then is its immortality no longer an insupportable leap out of one order of things into a fully different one. The transmigration of souls presents this eternity of life as though in prismatic refraction into innumerable, differently colored, individually bounded existences. Death is then only the end of an individual form of life, but not of the life that has appeared in it.

Spiritual-historical as well as internal-substantive presuppositions and implications of the belief in the transmigration of souls trace back in many ways to decisions within ultimate life-categories. The first and most significant is posed by the question: *which* life ends with death? The personal-individual? If so, it is incomprehensible that the next existence may be considered as that of the same undestroyed subject. Yet particularly if the personality is preserved in all transformations, then it could be difficult to state what is retained in this selfhood when it is born again, now as a prince, then as a tiger, then as a beggar, then as a jackal. Which content of the being or of the consciousness really persists then, that would justify designating all these manifestations as manifestations of the same subject? Historically reported attitudes show these alternatives in polar oppositions. Among very diverse primitive peoples the belief prevails that the newborn child is a reborn person previously deceased. In one African people, small items that have belonged to dead family members are shown to the newborn. If the baby pays particular attention to one of these, then it is the returned owner of this object. "It is Uncle John, he recognizes his pipe!" Among the Maoris the priest tells the newborn the names of his forebears: the one he sneezes or cries at is the one reborn in him. This is obviously the crudest and most extreme form of reincarnation that can scarcely be described as transmigration of souls, because it deals with a repetition of the deceased in his entire corporal-spiritual actuality. It shows, however, the farthest extreme of the *individualism* that constitutes, in many gradations, a form of transmigration of souls. The extreme in the other direction has been brought to full consciousness, especially in recent times, by the deeper teachings of Buddhism. To the ethical consideration of a punishment by which the sins of an earlier ego are visited upon a new one that for its part has not sinned at all, the Buddhist counters: the question is falsely posed in the first place because an ego, whether sinning or punished, does not exist at all. There are only thoughts and deeds, impersonal by nature so to speak, that in a given moment combine into an aggregate; in a later aggregate, connected with the former through causal linkages, appear indeed the ongoing effects of those earlier elements or elemental conditions. Sin and punishment thus do not exist in two separated subjects that are connected by a continuous ego, but behave simply as an occurrence and its perhaps much later effect, played out in two subjectless complexes of physical-psychic elements. Even this highest climax of *impersonality* obviously allows no real transmigration of souls, because a soul that exists beyond its current active and passive contents is denied from the start, and thus cannot persist through multiple corporeal existences linked to a variety of such contents. Between these two extremes lie the possible notions of soul migration whose varieties are dependent upon the respective concept of "personality."

Now it appears clear to me from the start that if one imagines the "soul" as somehow substantial and within the sharp outline of European conceptualization, its migration from a prince into a tiger and from the latter into a beggar is for us an utterly impossible thought (assuming the soul's substantiality should function not in the abandoned sense of former times, but as an abbreviated symbol for the feeling of an ultimately firm, persisting identity of the person). This impossibility arises from very diverse standpoints. From the viewpoint of the physical-metaphysical, organic unity of body and soul, Aristotle scorns the principle of soul migration that would allow any number of souls to enter any number of bodies: the art of carpentry could just as easily go into flutes; in reality a particular soul is united and unitable only with its particular body. From the moral individualism of the eighteenth century, Herder cannot grasp at all how it could be a punishment for the cruel person to be reborn as a tiger, since as such he can live out his bloodthirsty instincts more easily, radically, and so to speak happily than as a human being. But Indian soul migration, even in its ethical sense, may not be based on such personalistically linked characterology. Ethical "retribution" does not attach to the clearly circumscribed identity of the ego at all, as Herder supposed it did. Rather, it is something objective and cosmic, and consists precisely in the fact that such a horror as bloodthirstiness, when it has arisen in the first place, is now realized in an increased, pure, and so to speak absolute degree. The horrible as an occurrence is punished by the fact that it becomes ever more horrible in objectively [sachlich] logical self-development. One could almost say, with an admittedly interpretive turn: it is not the person of the bloodthirsty one who is punished, but the world in which such a thing occurs. The sharply honed question about the subject of the migration from body to body is wrongly posed, and therefore can likewise find no satisfactory answer. The spread of the belief in soul migration among the Greeks shows that with all of the autonomy, autarchy and character-filled definiteness of their personalities—even because of it—their ego-concept did not possess the depth and absoluteness to which the Christian epoch has developed it. Christianity—which for its foundation and its demands required the form of the self-reliant personality, responsible for itself alone, and which left the human soul alone with its God, or unharnessed the world between it and God, or even ecclesiastically mediated the relation—could thus evidently do nothing with soul migration. The latter only appears among the Gnostics and the Albigensians as an inconsequential borrowing from random contacts, and one finds the remark in Origen that one must regard the suffering of human life as punishment for previously committed sins, because otherwise God would be evil. I will furthermore not deny that if one fixes one's eye, beyond its abstruseness and inconceivability, on the principle's ethical core—the gradual purification of the soul until it is ripe and worthy of bliss—the latter occurs more beautifully and satisfyingly in this way than in the corresponding Christian notion of purgation. For however deeply internalized and indescribably moving is the joyful free will with which Dante has the souls in Purgatory bear their penances, the moment of passivity in this infliction of pain cannot be extinguished, and in the more popular, robust images of purgation it is much the predominant one. The contrasting and ethically most significant theme of the higher forms of soul migration—that the soul is always given anew the chance to redeem itself in freedom, and also that this must ultimately succeed, despite the freedom for repeated failure, because infinite time is available—is worthier and deeper than that of being cleansed by sufferings externally inflicted.

If it has been impossible within our contemporary conceptual schemas to find an answer to the question of the so to speak substantive subject migrating from body to body, then—perhaps precisely because of this—the incomprehensibility of the principle may perhaps be somewhat lessened by substituting the legal-functional way of thinking for the substantive one. A sense of individuality might be conceivable which is not tied at all to particular, qualitatively specifiable "character traits," but rather to the special form in which the psychic elements hang together at various times. This could be done perhaps by seeing how a particular one among these emerges as dominant; at what tempo such dominance shifts; whether the other elements are relatively leveled with respect to it or whether a decidedly effective hierarchy operates among them according to grades of importance; whether increasing integration or increasing differentiation, antagonism of essential traits even, determines the development; in what rhythm the concentrations and the emptinesses alternate in the succession of contents of the inner life; in what degree every element is, as it were, determined in its hue by the shadow cast by its surroundings; and countless other things. None of this can be discovered in any singular element or trait of the individual, even pro rata, because it signifies only the formal relationship of the particular elements among themselves, which can present itself uniformly in the most qualitatively and dynamically diverse complexes of contents of living souls.

The relations in question naturally represent only the makeshift and retrospective splitting of a unifically effective, impressive *law of being*. This *law* stands as something purely functional and relational above all phenomena, and lends to the totality of each being an unmistakable cachet—*approximately* as one speaks of a style as of a palpable commonality of human activities that by their concrete characteristics are utterly noncomparable, or of the "habitus" of plants that beyond all particular forms and their possible divergence arises from them as a general impression for which nothing particular in them can be held responsible. This law of being is thus no abstraction from multiple individuals, but comes to the individual as his most personal property and characteristic. For all that, however, it also has the character of *timelessness*, the same timelessness that attaches to natural law, but with the peculiar additional condition that it can only create the law or the form of a unique individual manifestation. It may be repeated, according to the phenomenon, in others not spatially or temporally linked with the first; but this is an extrinsic accident that has nothing to do with the essential of such a law of being; by its sense it is bound throughout to the manifestation that is in fact thereby individualized. The particular identifiable qualitative elements of the individual soul: intelligence or stupidity, fascination or dullness, goodness or evil, religious or worldly tendency, etc.—these very elements have in fact a *universal* nature, they are understandable as general concepts that are realized as relatively similar, yet distributed throughout mankind in infinitely manifold combinations.

What leads more deeply to the point of uniqueness of the individual, by contrast, is only the manner of functional relation of the particular elements, which is the *general* aspect *of this individual, his* law of being, which—precisely in contrast to the particular elements—he can as little share with others as he can have his life in common with others. And now—speculatively—the timelessness of this law, the ideal form of individual reality, would perhaps admit a turn to the idea of migration of souls. Nothing of this reality, that is, but only its form, the essential law of its functioning and its inner structure, would transfer to another being with qualitative contents different in every respect. The latter's existence immediately adjoins the first; and it could be considered with it as *one* individual living through infinite ages, since each later one characterized by the same functional and strictly uniquely individualized form would be the continuation of that earlier one; it would in the deepest sense be "one" with it. What lasts beyond death would then not be the soul -in its historical-real substantiality, but a timeless form of being that presents itself now in this, now in that actuality-complex and would have only the special condition that these complexes comprise only a *single* series, proceeding in time and divided into periods by the death of the particular realities—as even the process of our world as a whole possesses an individuality (with respect to spatiality, causality, conceptual constructions, etc.) that also actualizes itself in the *single* course of a monoserial time. Though this thought may be no less fantastical than other modalities of soul migration, this continuity of mutually detaching individuals—held together by the essential law flowing through them all, independent of their temporal conditions, and passed on one to the next—this continuity seems to me somehow deeper and freer of contradiction. Here a "soul" does not migrate through entirely different bodies while remaining self-identical; instead essential totalities, each weaving all its elements in reciprocation, show a common form (completely independent of temporal determinants) of precisely these reciprocations, a "habitus" of its vital functions palpable for itself. They thus comprise a temporally illimitable and incomparably singular individual whose life episodes are marked by the birth and death of particular individuals, with their unlimited room for the diversification of life-contents, powers, and qualities.

But an analogy of much more realistic character attaches here, an analogy that in fact removes none of the implausibility from the idea of migration of souls, yet removes something of its alienating abstruseness. The individual who owns his unity in the same law of being of infinitely diverse, conjoined individuals finds his likeness to that degree in the life-course of each one of these particular individuals. The soul of each man wanders between birth and death through immeasurably many destinies, dispositions, and drastically opposed epochs which, regarded as to their content, offer each other utterly alien overall features. Only the individuality of the subject allows them to coalesce into a unitary image: just as the sound of a person's voice remains the same and unmistakable, however variable the words he speaks, so there remains a basic coloration, a basic rhythm, a basic proportionality for all that this life ever experiences, an a priori formal law of his action and suffering that survives the demise of every particular content and, as the individuality of the whole, is transferred to the next.

Thus, the soul migrating through many bodies and lives is nothing but the soul of the particular life "writ large"; and soul migration is nothing but a grotesque enlargement, a radicalization and a rendering absolute of certain experiences of daily, relativistic life. If we clarify for ourselves the vicissitudes that its course between birth and death present to us, their range sometimes seems scarcely narrower than as though it existed between some human and some animal existences. No significantly eventful life lacks the occasional feeling that its decisive poles have touched the boundaries not only of human existence but of imaginable existence whatsoever; that it includes not only contradictions (such a life always contains a correlative unity of its sides), but distantiations and intangible indifferences that ultimately are embraced only by a purely formal life-unity, perhaps by that law of being, not immediately graspable, and by the fact that these contents are arranged with respect to each other in a continual flowing, in the temporal continuity of a life process. Even in the intervals of typical development (the stammering child, the man at the height of his creative power, the worn old man): on what basis are these manifestations spoken of as a unity, other than that *one* life-stream flows through each individual, but a life-stream incapable of giving its contents unity and comparability and that (assuming soul migration existed as fact) needs no greater push, as it were, at least none aimed fundamentally otherwise, to assimilate into its formal continuity the still somewhat more disparate contents among humans, even between the human and the animal.

Between the one birth and the one death we feel ourselves on countless occasions to be "someone who has become different"—physically, psychologically, or in fortune—and yet of course we feel the same "soul" that runs through all this without being at all influenced by anything particular coming from its nature as soul; otherwise it would be inconceivable that tomorrow this soul calls exactly the opposite particular into the same psychic life. Something persists in us while we are wise men and then fools, beasts and then saints, happy and then despairing. (Here "persistence" is a very bad, stiff, and makeshift expression for the behavior of living things, which certainly is not done justice to by virtue of our conceptual forced choice between persistence and transformation; living behavior involves a unitary third option, one which may only be experienced, but not characterized.) A mechanically determined structure is certainly a different thing as soon as any one of its determinants is changed, for it possesses no real inner unity that holds these together; if it is still described on conceptual-technical grounds as "one" even when its determinants are no longer the exactly identical ones, then in actuality it is no longer *this* one, but another. But the vital (or, exactly stated, only the sentient) being behaves differently. Of the latter we suppose that it would even have to be able to act, to be determined, even to be otherwise without losing its identity, because all these specifiable elements in it are borne by an enduring ego standing beyond its particular determinants and actions. Thus, perhaps only of a human being can one say that he must be able to be different than he is—as every other being in this case would simply no longer be "him." At this point clearly lies the connection of the idea of freedom with that of the ego; here it becomes conceivable how that polarity and estrangement of diverse temperaments and destinies, decisions and feelings are the divergent swings of a pendulum that ultimately hangs upon *one* fixed point.

If one looks from this image of our actuality towards soul migration, the image only appears in soul migration as if caught in a magnifying glass. The puzzling, basic fact of life, especially of that gathered in the soul—that a being is always something different, yet always the same—is distinguished from soul migration only in a coarser disparity of the moments. Or, from the viewpoint of the belief in soul migration, the particular life is an abbreviation of the soul's existence (which stretches through immeasurable times and forms), roughly as the individual life has been viewed as a cursory representation of the life of the species; or as the single day—with its multiple echoes of desire and suffering, oscillations between feelings of strength and weakness, the fullness and emptiness of the hours, the alternations of productivity and receptivity—is a miniature image of the entirety of life. The various bodies through which the soul passes are only, as it were, materializations and fixations of the various states that the soul, purely as soul, generates and experiences within itself. The fate of the soul between the particular birth and the particular death, and that between the first birth and the final death, as the teachings of soul migration depict them, are mutual symbols of one another—the theme of the relativism of life and death, into which the beginning of these pages transformed the absolutism of their contradiction, leading upwards with this interpretation of the myth to a freely constructed summit.

4

The Law of the Individual

When we call an object "actual," we mean to ascribe to its given content a consistency, a kind of absoluteness, that in itself regards all other ways of conceiving the same content—imaginatively, conceptually, evaluatively, artistically—as subjective, merely derived from its actuality. Yet viewed precisely, the special or predominant position of the object under the category of actuality signifies only that we are used to experiencing this object as chronologically the first and pragmatically the most important and consequential. We must, so to speak, first reach through things in the form of their actuality and extract the content that they offer in this form in order to be able to place that content into other categories. But this is merely a psychological necessity, one which makes or produces no objective rank ordering—no more than we presuppose a ranking among languages when we express a concept in a foreign language and yet must first know its meaning in our mother tongue. Again, actuality is only a *form* (i.e., only *one* form) in which we apprehend content, and has no more intimate or privileged relation to that content than do the categories of science, art, wish, and value.

With *one* object, to be sure, the form of actuality may seem so organically rooted that this object, even when its content appears under another category, cannot be separated from it: namely, the subject's own life. Even he who, purely according to its content, conceives his

life under artistic, religious, or scientific viewpoints, knows it at the same time
to be his actual life, because the conception could not occur at all if it were not
actual, not actually lived. Nevertheless, I believe that there is a second category
with which actuality shares this monopoly position in regards to the sequence
of experience—a category according to which we continually experience our
life, one which is somewhat parallel to actuality, but in no way reducible to it:
the Ought. This "Ought" is not from the outset to be understood merely ethically, but equally as a quite general aggregate condition of life-consciousness in
which both hopes and drives, eudaimonistic and aesthetic demands, religious
ideals, even caprices and anti-ethical desires are to be found, often simultaneously with the ethical and each other. In the definition of logic as the norm
according to which we "ought" to think, Ought acquires even a purely intellectual meaning—for when this logical thinking is used to rationally serve the
most immoral intentions, it surely ought not to be from an ethical standpoint,
even while it continues to correspond to an Ought from an intellectual standpoint. To fully understand the Ought, one must not attach it, even in its ethical meaning, to wish-images and ideals and then construct it from these—any
more than one may regard psychological life, under the category of actuality,
as a succession of individual "representations" that are only logical and periodic
legitimations of *contents* crystallized out of the steadily flowing psychological
life process. Both representations, the ethical and the psychological, ultimately
have the mechanistic tendency of constructing the whole from pieces. With this
tendency, life (precisely a continuous flow) and its Ought become unbridge-
ably opposed, even though the whole of life with its up-and-down–surging
fullness is just as ethical [*gesolltes*]—in the positive or negative sense—as it is
actual. The conventional notion is that life is an unfolding subjective actuality
which is confronted by the ideal demand of the Ought, and that this demand
issues from a different order than that from which life springs. Instead, however, the fundamental view must be this: what stands opposed is not life and
Ought, but life's actuality and its Ought. Actuality and Ought are equally categories into which consciousness puts our life, and in which it is experienced.
Only that prior and apparently more unconditional solidarity of life and actuality deceives us about this. Certainly the subject is always conscious of life as
it actually is—but likewise, and categorically wholly independently, the subject
is always conscious of life as it ought to be. The one is as much a full life as the
other. I am just as aware that my life, characterized in this-or-that way, is the
actual one, as that, characterized thus or in some entirely different way, it is the
one that ought to be. In its steady flow it produces its contents in the latter as
in the former guise. The Ought does not stand altogether above life nor over
against it, but instead is precisely a mode by which life becomes aware of itself,

just as being actual is such a mode. Though we thereby appear to lead two lives, what we sense as the unity of life is in no way destroyed. For the fact that life's stream flows in various branches, that its deepest essence is at all events not exhausted in the logical alternatives of unity and multiplicity, has long been known. Even when we experience the content of the Ought as an imperative, somehow confronting us objectively over and against the subject, the comparison with the category of actuality is still not lost. This is because separation of the subject from an opposing object—a separation which occurs within the subject in the widest sense as something entirely objective—is nonetheless also the form in which our self-consciousness grasps our *actuality*. The "I" that is known and analyzed, approved and resisted, understood and not comprehended as a "Thou" is precisely the one that knows and analyzes, approves and opposes, understands and is puzzling to itself. Existence as simultaneous subject and object, this embrace of its opposite by the life-unity that presents itself only thus—this is the general schema of the conscious Spirit; and within it life as Ought also aligns itself by opposing an objective commandment to its subjective process. This is the particular dualism of life as Ought, just as the consciousness of oneself is the dualism of life as actuality.

Only when we understand the Ought, beyond all of its particular contents, as a primary mode in which individual consciousness experiences a whole life does it become understandable why one can never extract, from the fact of the Ought, *what* we ought, content-wise, to do. All these efforts necessarily fail, for the same reason that one cannot deduce, from the fact of actuality, *what* is genuinely actual. One could as easily insist on inferring from a particular tonality which melodies are possible or necessary in it. These proffered moral laws also are always conceptualizations of contents which are experienced as Ought, but before which life's future lies in all of its unpredictability—yet because the Ought too is a life, its forms [*Gestaltungen*] can therefore no more be predicted than those of life experienced as actual. The subjective character imputed to the Ought in general and to all particular moral principles (and not just by those with cynical and skeptical tendencies) seems to me attributable simply to the fact that the Ought has not been recognized as an absolutely primary category, but instead a source and legal basis was sought behind it: a God and His will, society and its needs, reason and its logical values, the Ego and its well-known interests, etc. In fact a circle lurks here: contents which the category of the Ought first accepts into itself, and which only thereby receive an ethical or ethical-metaphysical character, are for their part supposed of themselves to return the Ought as a whole. Accordingly, none of these substantiations of the Ought has proven to be sufficiently and durably sound. Being-as-Ought is just as irreducible as being-as-actual. For if one expects being-as-actual, insofar as it has this-worldly empirical contents, to emerge from the will of God, then God and His will must surely first be conceived as "actual," so that the problem remains unsolved in principle; and the representation of the fully actual as *causa sui* is ultimately only a clever fallacy, as it attempts to compress being-caused and not-being-caused (which logically exclude one another) into *one* concept. To this the ethical counterpart would be the following: obligation must be obliged.

The difficulties in recognizing the Ought's objectivity occur where one fails to avoid attributing a teleology to its character and thereby ends up sampling, by trial and error, various ways of substantiating its subjective provenance. It must be realized that Ought in general has as little a purpose as actuality in general has a cause. Accordingly, despite the right basic feeling, even the formulation "What is moral ought to happen simply because it is moral, or simply in that it happens, or because it just is obligated" as a formulation is an unhappy one because it brings in the teleological element of which the primary and total essence of the Ought is precisely free. At its deepest the Ought stands beyond all teleologies and their unavoidable subjectivisms. Moreover, there is that fateful limitation of objective value to "actuality" (including the ideal laws of actuality, as well as the mathematical and logical ones). As soon as fundamental and foundational significance is attributed to the Ought as to a categorical *Ur-phenomenon,* all these points of attack on its possible objectivity fall away. It is an indisputable fact that the *contents* of all this Ought are utterly variegated, accidental, determined in each case historically and psychologically, and in no way form a systematic order. Yet this changes nothing in the objectivity that so to speak ideally pervades these contents. For as often as mere wishes and desires may rise into the domain of the Ought, we still distinguish them (as long as they are still presented in their simple subjectivity) very precisely from the Ought-element that partly or completely dominates the elements of that very domain. The world of Ought—at least moral Ought—is that of the required [*Geforderten*], whose required-ness [*Gefordertsein*] possesses objective validity.

In this I am not trying to establish by what arrangement the ethical Ought decisively emerges from the entire sphere of what generally ought to be. What is undertaken here does not aim at a "moral principle" that would offer a yardstick for the moral value or antivalue of human behavior. Rather, whichever behavior someone holds to be duty and morally good, we will attempt here to determine only that metaphysical location in which the source for this decision of last resort is to be sought, so as to do justice to the intrinsic structure and the context in consciousness of the ethical phenomenon. Under the question of "location" I understand the alternatives to be the following: (a) do moral necessities draw their contents and their legitimation from a metaphysical actuality beyond the life of the individual; that is, from a general, self-supporting principle that of itself is not linked to the individual life, but instead confronts it as a law (particularly a law of "reason") or as the moral value of the particular act that should be performed because its content now possesses this materially moral value?; or (b) do the contents of the Ought develop from the life-totality of the individual—so that the act is in no way judged in isolation or required equally of any number of individuals according to a general law, but instead is required and judged according to the coherence of the ideal life-formation that is woven directly into such an individual, as though with ideal lines, following the particular uniqueness of its sense of life—just as his life, as an actual one, is individual and unexchangeable? This is only a very preliminary outline of the problem, which can really only acquire clarity and significance, even as a problem, to the extent that approaches toward its solution succeed.

∷

Now here a difficulty must be remembered that—as these pages have already shown elsewhere—extends far beyond the ethical arena and signifies a typical tragedy of spiritual culture in general. Formulated most succinctly and generally it is this: that as its immediate manifestation life at the level of consciousness [Geist] produces objective creations in which it expresses itself and which for their part, as life's containers and forms, tend to receive its further flows—yet at the same time their ideal and historical determinacy, boundedness and rigidity sooner or later come into opposition and antagonism with ever-variable, boundary-dissolving, continuous life. Life is continually producing something on which it breaks, by which it is violated, something that is necessarily its proper form but yet, by the very fact of being form, in the deepest sense conflicts with the dynamic of life, with life's incapability of any actual pause. Thus it is with Christian dogmatics as against the creative or revealed experience of immediate interaction with God; thus it is with "law and justice," which are inherited like an eternal disease, because though they were originally beneficial and reasonable for life, they become nonsense and a plague in its evolution; thus it is with the forms of production which are suitable to the abilities of an economic level, but in which these abilities develop in such a way that they act as straitjackets to be burst in acute or chronic revolutions—until the new, momentarily correct form of production meets the same fate; thus it is with the artistic style in which the artistic vitality of an epoch is happily formulated, but which, with its inevitable elaboration, comes to be experienced by the younger generation as unendurable academicism and is either replaced by its polar opposite or gives way to an anarchy of artistic production; and thus it is with innumerable other things in the greatest as in the narrowest dimensions of development. But this oppressiveness of existing cultural forms is only the outer phenomenon—long since become trivial—of a deeper fundamental relation. This relation is the utterly fundamental opposition between the principle of life and the principle of form—an opposition which, because life *can* only enact itself in forms, is expressed in each case as the struggle of the form just brought forth by life against the forms that life has previously produced as its character, its language, its specifiable quality. As life consciously defines itself spiritually or culturally, creatively or historically, it is also thereby compelled to exist solely in the form of its own opposite, produced immediately by it—in the form of *forms*. Herein, it seems to me, lies the ultimate reason for the discomfort and unrest that—sooner or later, in fact from its moment of emergence on—turns against every product of life that has become objective and congealed into fixed form, just as soon as this product claims to receive life's flow into itself, to bound it with its own boundaries, to normalize it.

This general fate of creations that life produces, but which already in their very production life has externalized and opposed to itself as independent, occurs also in the norms, principles and imperatives with which creative life consolidates itself as Ought. What is often described as their alienation or sterilizing distance from life—that they don't fit actuality, that they construct ideals that have and can have nothing to do with actuality—this indeed I would not view as the principal difficulty. For this view rests again on the naïve identification of actual life with life in general, whereas the latter, even in its unfolding under the consciousness category of Ought, remains absolutely genuine life. The discrepancy of those principles from the actuality of life affects them, so to speak, not at all; what is obligated is an autonomous construction, rooted in the same peculiar depth that actuality is; neither its internal consistency nor its right to make demands on actuality suffers from the fact that the latter does not fulfill it—any more than actuality becomes more irreal, for its part, in the resulting divergence. That unsatisfying character of moral principles (which makes ethics appear perhaps the most inaccessible of all provinces of philosophy) arises instead from their internal, functional contradiction to the living Ought itself; the contradiction remains wholly on the plane of the Ought and has nothing whatever to do with the relationship to the plane of actuality. The imperative, objective tone that we hear, sharply or mildly, in the contents of our Ought does not prevent us from feeling these contents as waves of our stream of life, born of the continuous coherence of life as it ought to be. Yet if we then hear that we should always keep to the golden mean, or that we should always be able to imagine our actions as a universal law, or that we should judge ourselves according to the greatest good for the greatest number, or that one should in every instant overcome the nature in himself by reason, then perhaps we sense that indeed deep and content-rich ethical experiences have developed these formulations in some measure as their silhouettes—now, though, they stand as fixed structures and attempt by force to assimilate a life that is endlessly dynamic, endlessly differentiated, endlessly obligated, and which nonetheless sometimes overflows these structures and sometimes leaves them unfilled. This contradiction need not always, by any means, affect ethical content. The respective vitality of the Ought will prove instead to be largely in agreement with that content as those norms establish it, though the contradiction of the two aggregate states of the Ought in principle also creates space for a similar contradiction between Ought-contents and gives the Ought that "despotic" character that Goethe deplored in it. This certainly does not have to do with resistances that our other preferences oppose to the moral demand, nor with the fact that psychic actuality will not yield itself to the realization of the Ought—rather, it has to do with the fact that life flowing forth as Ought, precisely because it is spiritual life, cannot escape from the latter's self-contradiction; namely, that the forms it produces and in which alone it can proceed have a supervital meaning and persistence, established by their own logic, against whose demand for regulation of life the steady stream of this same life—its inescapable differentiation, its restless content-exchange—resists. Necessarily and in order to reveal itself at all, life produces form (here as practically indispensable, formulated moral law and supra-individual valuation), and precisely because it is continually producing form, life necessarily feels the principle of form as that which does not fit it. Obviously within empirical processes this contradiction appears only fragmentarily, in more or less obscure strivings and counterstrivings, and in apathy through adaptations [*Anpassungen*] and outward prescriptions.

This inner antinomy is thus no rebuttal, but rather a deepening confirmation that the Ought does not stand over against life, but is instead a mode of its entire fulfillment. Attempting to find this relation of the two concepts in Kant's "autonomy" of the ethical [*Sittlichen*] would be close to the mark: where we "give ourselves" the law, its ego-alien quality appears to be put aside, and it seems to be sunk in the ground of life itself. Actually, however, with Kant it is not at all the individual as a whole, living, and unitary being that gives itself the imperative of duty, but only that part of the individual with which it represents superindividual reason. In this manner Kant could achieve confrontation, the unavoidable relational form of the imperative of duty, only by placing "sensuousness" over against our rational, legislative parts within the individual life as a whole. Ultimately Kant simply could not avoid the conclusion that whatever commands the individual must be something beyond the individual. And because he rejects all heteronomy, he must make this conclusion possible by tearing the individual apart into sensuousness and reason. In fact, heteronomy is not avoided, but only transferred from a relationship with the outer world to an inner one between reason and sensuousness. Only through the undemonstrated, naively dogmatic claim that that rational, universally valid part of us is the "true" I, the essence of our essence, can Kant support the illusion that when reason commands sensuousness we thereby "give ourselves" the duty-imperative. Herein is expressed the moralistic megalomania—which is, by the way, endemic to the history of morals—that sensuousness does not properly belong to the "I." Now these two may perhaps be alien to each other as abstract concepts; but the *measure* of sensuousness (i.e., of sensual seducibility and seduction) that the individual realizes in himself belongs just as much to the ego as any other element of its psychic actuality. Even the will's distinctive value is supposedly upheld by the crude displacement that, because the *object* of sensuousness admittedly lies outside the ego, sensuousness itself does not belong to it either. One might just as well maintain that the lungs do not belong to our body because they can carry out their function only with air from outside the body. As if it is ever an *object* that seduces us, and not exclusively our own urge, breaking forth from our inner self and in this moment representing the ego! If one identifies the actual ego with Reason, with the Good, then it can only follow to write sin off as possession by the devil, who approaches us from without; he is the necessary correlate of that ego from which (as such) only good can come—for otherwise, whence comes the evil that is expatriated from ourselves? Full responsibility for this, the spontaneity of sin, is thus removed from us; and we remain, according to our true nature, always rational and good creatures. The invention of the devil is the greatest moral cowardice of mankind, the expression of the fact that one will not (or will not in full measure) face up to the evil that one does. And sensuousness that does not touch the pure or actual ego, passing for sin, is nothing other than the refined and somewhat weakened devil. Yet only on the basis of this split can Kant proclaim his moral law as one that "we give to ourselves." For since it is a fully rational one and is directed against sensuousness as such, he would never be able to pass it off as one given by ourselves if this self signified anything other than reason divorced in principle from sensuousness, if it really embraced the whole person, conceptualized thus to include his other spiritual energies as well. What I have endeavored to show is that life, proceeding in its totality as Ought, means law for the very same life that proceeds in its totality as actuality; Kant, however, transfers the dualism into the totality of life itself, by splitting this totality between the real or rational ego and the sensuousness that is only peripheral or opposed to it.

The law-based imperative, which in large measure determines the psychological tone of ethical consciousness, doubtless cannot resist the spatial metaphor of opposition, of something confronting us. However, this challenge to be better than oneself, this construction of the other and the opposed, is nonetheless the function of life itself: the exterior from whence objective norms, values, and judgments approach life is a form of the vitality of its interior. And thus it becomes clear that the distance (measured against the Ought) between life's actuality and life's ideality shows infinite gradations—it is as though the strictness of an imperative arises in imperceptible transitions from the unconstrained stream of moral life until it ultimately appears to arrive from a point beyond life. These gradations and intermediate steps would scarcely be understandable if the Ought actually had this origin; I could not imagine how the stark relentlessness of the opposition between life and ideal demands could ever be lost to consciousness, or how this tension could be felt as somehow reconcilable. But exactly this happens continually. If one observes the actual course of life it turns out to be, even in its positive-moral phases, very much less dependent on the consciousness of a law than one would have to believe according to the representations of moral philosophy, even according to the still-haunting normative idea of the Decalogue, as though it were the prototype of all ethical demands. Admittedly, so long as the contents of both fit together, the clearer or obscurer consciousness of what we are and what we ought to do steadily accompanies the actuality of our life without especially obtruding from the mental image of this actuality. Only extremely rarely does this accompaniment occur in the character of a formulated or even formulable "law"—it occurs mostly, rather, in a wholly fluid, intuitive way. Even where, in the course of our activity, we attend completely to what we ought to do, we do not as a rule turn first to the solemnity of a more or less general law—rather, the Ought has the "quality of being known." Only Kant's moral homunculus, constructed from purely conceptual material, continually appeals to the highest instance of a law. What the forms of the Decalogue and moral principles have so to speak balled up into a hard clump is in actuality the continuity of life that flows along under the category of the Ought. As such, the imperative that stands opposed to life seems unable to be "vital." Even Nietzsche gave it life alone for *content*, to be sure, but the ideal form of the Ought still remained the "tablet" that is placed "above life." It is still a question (not posed by Nietzsche himself) whether the Ought, vital in its form, could be an analog of life or a category under which life becomes aware of itself. If we adopt the term "law" for the ethical demand, then at all events it is something much more flexible, runs through many more stages, and is in itself more differentiated than we may assume by its formulations in the former principles; yet not so flexible that the modifications corresponding to its vital character remove from it any of its strictness, its ideality autonomous of all actuality, or its unbending objectivity. The possibility of this unification remains to be shown in detail. From this vital character of the Ought it is understood that even moral actions mostly occur as something internally integrated, something simply emergent—indeed the more surely so the more deeply moral the personality is—as an ever more integrated process develops within it, as life-as-actuality and life-as-Ought. "Good will," especially, does not require obligation to a law; in fact, by definition it knows nothing of such an obligation because it is good from the outset—that is, its life proceeds, so to speak, without discrepancy between the form of its actuality and the form of its Ought. When reflection separates these two, it is not hard in our manner of thinking for the moment of the Ought to congeal around certain chief contents into a tightly circumscribed construction, delineable for itself, of unique spiritual character, namely, into laws. There is a certain analogy to theoretical procedure: many notions [*Vorstellungen*] and views [*Anschauungen*] are given as unitary, as concrete and simple; to these simple ideas reflection subsequently contributes the categories of natural law and of the special case; this produces a dualistic tension in the interior of the immediately existent thing. Or, in another twist, a dualistic tension is produced when cognitions [*Erkenntnisse*] intuitively and in some measure spontaneously arise in us, whose further development and arrangement then requires them to separate into the form of proposed problem and found solution. With all their utterly indisputable significance and indispensability, conceptually formulated moral laws are secondary formations. Life creates a detour over these products of itself, which have become alien to it in form, in order to finally come to itself again. This insight is needed so that one does not believe the Ought to be neglected or negated where it does not conform to such laws or can find no attachment to them. I would like to say, in an admittedly very cursory way, that our actions always require lawfulness, but not always laws.

Perhaps a religious analogy will clarify what is meant here. Many people today have declared themselves fully rid of religion and religions in the traditionally formulated sense, yet they defend themselves most decidedly against being viewed as irreligious. They distinguish so precisely between religion and religiosity that they believe they can unreservedly break with the former even as they unreservedly affirm the latter. It even sometimes happens that they extend the Kantian dictum that he had to set aside knowing to secure a place for faith: they have abolished faith in order to retain faithfulness. They understand religiosity or faithfulness as an attitude, determined entirely from within, that requires no characteristic contents or objects whatever, but is a way to live an entire life and to color every moment of its steady unfolding. To them religious dogmas are only particular hypostatized constructions (situated beyond life) whose conceptual fixity ultimately assigns only particular life-moments to them—they are determinations that come to the soul from outside, while the soul's continuing totality can only receive a truly uninterrupted character from an inner source. Thus, if one imagines a completely moral person—one in whom the ideal law of the Ought that accompanies life is one with his psychological-practical actuality from the outset—every instant of his volition and action would certainly be lawful, though in the endless variability and unpredictability of life itself, and he would tend not to ask whether each of these instants belongs under a law formed beyond himself. Certainly, that one resists temptations toward pecuniary or sexual hazards, helps those in need, and cultivates oneself in the cultural, patriotic, and humanitarian sense—all of this is derived from formulated moral principles. But the attitude of the moral soul, obedient to its Ought, is not exhausted or exhaustible with this. In fact this continuous morality is not oriented according to some externally established value point (even when a partial interest of the soul, rational or charitable, aesthetic or religious, furnishes this external point); rather it is, as it were, the rhythm in which life pours forth from its deepest wellspring; it is the tone not only of what are called actions, perhaps not even only of the will, but of the whole being, and resides in every thought and the manner of its utterance, in glances and words, in the feeling of joy and the bearing of grief, and even in relation to the indifferences of the day. This entire coherence of life is different for the person who is moral (and not only does the moral thing) than for the person who is otherwise qualified. The rhythm of life that makes no leap, but steadily brings forth situation from situation is also characteristic of the life of the Ought. It is what Goethe called the demand of the day: not the one that the day, in the sense of the outer milieu, brings to us, but instead the one proceeding from the deepest inner [eigen-innersten] life which hour for hour prescribes the next step; the next-but-one lies in darkness and only becomes clear when the next is done. For this conception moral life is not cut up into a number of individual "actions," each measured against a law constituted once-and-for-all; instead, the entire life-continuity of everything insignificant and fleeting—words, moods, and relations—from which only in exceptional cases a peak emerges suitable for particular mention is accompanied by the ideal line of the Ought, whose strictness and absoluteness, however, is not thereby diminished in the least. Yet it is a *supple* absoluteness, the counterpart to what Goethe once, with admittedly highly mysterious significance, called the "eternal, supple laws" of nature. Against this stands only the mere prejudice that the worth and force of the ethical demand would not be maintained if its contents were subject to development, evolution, change, in short to the pulls of *life*—one of the false conceptual deformities within a gradually foundering worldview.

Binding morality throughout to preexisting laws, as though these were in some measure the goals whose attainment alone would satisfy the Ought, is reminiscent of how the concept of evolution used to be understood narrowly to imply the apparent necessity of a definable evolutionary goal. In such a view, only when a definite direction came to characterize a series of events would it make a mere succession into an evolution. For as many cases as this fits, it does not exhaust the concept of evolution that instead, when applied to the life process of organic existence, signifies an immanent quality of just this process, independent of any goal—whether the goal be the "summit of evolution," an idea to be realized, or the like. In the relationship of life's moments to one another, in the manner that one proceeds from the other, in the tone with which the earlier is echoed in the present and the next is anticipated, we feel our life as an evolving one. Whether it is evolving *toward* something or other does not arise at all and is at best a minor addition of reflection; to make the entire concept of evolution dependent on it is a rather crude transfer of our practical teleology onto the quite differently organized natural evolution of organisms. The same thing happens with ethical life when one tries to bind it to previously given laws (whether of reason or religion), such that it is ethical only to the extent that these laws are realized. Though linguistic expression may always bind us to the dualism of law versus the obliged action particularized by situation and individuality, in fact we feel it quite simply as one quality—as the inner, unitary manner of certain actions—that they are as they ought to be; just as we often have a qualitatively quite simple feeling that we are evolving, that we are progressing, without being conscious in the least of a goal toward which we strive.

Now the regulation of an action by a law is conditioned by the fact that the action's content corresponds to a *concept* whose overall positive or negative value the law establishes; otherwise the action would become indistinct from steadily unfolding occurrence and would present no secure application of the law. This conceptual character of action is a decisive element of all ethics that establish norms according to principles, especially Kantian ethics. However, precisely because of its apparent obviousness, we must investigate what the concept does for the definition of a content—namely and above all, it causes a thing to become a thing in the first place. Our eidetic image [*Anschauungsbild*] at any moment lies spread before us, to begin with, as a color complex from which certain parts must first be separated out in order to be recognized as belonging together (i.e., as a thing). Likewise we must represent the world objectively as a continuum with absolute interaction of all elements, whose purely natural-law concatenations and sequences know nothing of division into individual "things." The forging of such a "thing" seems to be the result of a very primitive spiritual function that for lack of immediate description we call the collaboration of differences and connections. This function, however, operates on the immediately sensory and objectively natural-law continuum such that any concept (however it originates, however obscure, incomplete, or precarious) exists when within its outline a complex of elements of that continuum combines into a unity. In the language of conventional wisdom: only by becoming recognized as an exemplar of a particular concept can a complex of elements become a "thing" for us. Or yet again: it must be *a* thing in order to be a *thing*; but it can only become *a* thing in that it is recognized as numerically *one* representation of a concept. Kant's assertion that we perceive an object when in the manifold we have produced unity of its intuition can only be carried out in this way. For I have no idea how this unity could be produced (since unity in general, as a fully undifferentiated schema, is a thing entirely without effect), except as a preexisting concept determines: this segment of intuition is this one, unitary thing. This observation holds not only for proper, thing-like objects: an action too is only *one* action in that, by means of a concept, it is carved out from the steady flow of our willing and our activity, and only thus does it obtain definition and can it be depicted as this particular action, whence it can become for itself alone the object of a moral judgment. This is a most highly remarkable thing in the structure of our world-image [*Weltbild*]: that only through the concept—a construction lying in the category of the thoroughly general, a form legislating for innumerable contents—is every particular phenomenon produced as such; that our perception and thinking have available only this supra-individual means of organizing and forming into individual objects the continuity and the eternal flow of what is given in primary objectivity. In that primary objectivity there is in fact no unity, thus also no "object," except the totality of being. The fact that the material of an exploded bit of rock hangs tightly together even as it is movable against its neighbors in space signifies only a relative difference in the interactions among the material elements. A magnet is *one* thing, and a piece of iron that clings to it is also *one* thing, although its coherence with the magnet may be much stronger than that which binds the other material elements into *one* thing—because the latter stand for themselves under *one* concept. By what fashion such a thing-creating concept emerges psychologically is a question of another order.

Now there does exist a domain of objects for which this necessity does not hold, or holds only in a diluted fashion, mixed with other formative principles. We do not conceive of organic beings as among those that find their unity only through selection out of the continuity of being, as can only happen under the control of a concept. They have, rather, an objective unity immanent to themselves, they find their formative boundary through their own characteristic entelechy; they have a center within themselves that frees them from the (so to speak) indifferent stream of being as a whole, a stream that gathers everything into a continuum. For this reason the living being for us has never submitted as completely as the inorganic entity to the domination of the concept. Admittedly, one belongs under the concept "lion," another under the concept "man," and each other one under as many other concepts. But we feel that its essence is not exhaustible by the concept; it is not comparable to the inorganic, which awaits from the concept its definition as this specific thing—that is, as a thing at all. Since the organism presents itself from the outset as a unity, first and most decidedly in the consciousness of its own personality, its concept arises out of its actuality, while by contrast in the inorganic case the unity is formed by the concept. The relative freedom—deriving from the variability of our concept-formation—to determine which complex of elements will serve for us as *one* object probably does not exist here at all; the organism itself determines the defining form that is to serve as unity, and sets very defined limits to the fluctuating combinations that are possible in lifeless matter. And this now also modifies the earlier preliminary definition concerning "the act," as if it too were something unitary and characterizable only through conceptually legislated delimitation. The act, regarded as the pulse-beat of immediate life, cannot be introduced at all adequately into a preexisting schema; it determines its essence from the interior of life, and its interminglings with what precedes and follows and with the whole psychic complex of this life make its delimitation by an extrinsic concept—however necessary this may be in practice—something accidental and external. The act is *one*, because life rises out of itself to a certain intensity of will and application of power, sharpening to a crest with which it projects above its leveled, unpunctuated gliding through the course of the day. This concentration and accentuation out of the rhythm of volitional life itself, which yet does not break continuity with life's total course, is this life's scene-form which we sometimes call "an action," and which for this designation need not be fenced in by a concept that isolates the action content. The intent of the entire discussion is to establish this: that the object of ethical normalization be freed above all from that bondage to concept which is definitive for all rational ethics, from Socrates to Kant and beyond, and for its ultimate foundation on a "moral principle."

Here we must first pursue the most important attribute of law, its universality, in its ethical significance. One could generally develop the principal points of Kantian moral philosophy from the proposition that the *universality* of the moral law amounts to its essence. The meaning of law as such appears to be that the concretely living individual is determined by it; thus, the law cannot for its part be determined by the individual, but precisely by the nonindividual; it must be universally valid in order to confront the individual as its concept demands. Nonetheless the basis for this confrontation with the law appears to lie primarily, not in the form of individuality as such, but in the fact that this form is seen as coupled with the concept of actuality. Since each being can only exist once at all (its form, its qualities, its movements can repeat themselves in other bits of being, but the multiplicity of the being as being is an absurdity), and since being has ontological individuality, this individuality comes toward psychic existence as existence itself. In this sense then (not in the qualitative or differential sense), every actuality is individual. On this metaphysical basis the following reversal seems to me to arise: that everything individual is only *actual*—this reversal is admittedly not logically binding, but nevertheless could apply in practice. Its ethical significance is found in its correlate: the nonactual, the demanded, the ideal, cannot be anything individual, and must thus be something universal. Here, as already indicated, lies the fulcrum of Kantian ethics; it is even the general element in the decisive proposition that sets the tone of this ethic: one is never commanded to do what he himself already certainly wants. This is surely intended against eudaimonism, which identifies ethical demand with the pursuit of happiness. In principle though, the viewpoint is as follows: that which is actual at all lies outside the sphere of the ethically demanded. Actuality as given (and not only as formal fact of existence, but also as content) cannot at the same time be the "commanded," because this would nonsensically set as one the actual and the ideal (which is always only *supposed* to become actual). If everything actual is individual, then the ideal must be universal; if everything individual is only actual, then it cannot at the same time be more than actual, the ideal demand of a law. The law cannot have any source in the individuality of the person for whom it is valid; it resides in the region of the superactual. In fact, the law does not even really apply to the individually actual person—in whose sensual-egotistic, accidentally determined nature (as Kant depicts it) it would find no point of entry—but rather to the reason in us, to our "pure ego"; and in the process of morality Fichte can attribute no other role to the empirical-individual ego than that it enters and merges with the pure ego and is thus dissolved: to the degree that it still exists, moral law in fact does not rule. The pure ego however is one in which all differences from person to person disappear, and is constituted only out of the general concept of man—out of that humanness in man that Kant calls holy even when man is unholy enough. "If all people could become perfect," so says Fichte of morality (admittedly unattainable on earth), "if they could achieve their highest and ultimate goal, then they would all be fully the same as each other; they would be only one, a single subject." But this ingenuous proposition of Kant and Fichte (which still survives in many modifications)—that the pure or fundamental ego is the general one, while the empirical by contrast is individualized, differentiated in its qualities by perhaps unmistakable particularity—seems very debatable to me. The opposite phenomenon cannot be completely rejected. Precisely as empirical beings we are determined by a thousand influences that affect others similarly, we are graded by social institutions and stratifications, and colored by general historical conditions; precisely as empirical beings we are governed by natural law with its deindividualizing general validity, just as we also submit, as empirical beings, to the universal laws of justice. The superempirical ego, however—the one we bring along into empirical relationships as an a priori element to form them with—might very well be something qualitatively unique, metaphysically solitary and indifferent to all others. At least, I see nothing that excludes this possibility. Regarding the equality of natural conditions in which (purely as natural beings) we are placed, we could even ask whether all empirical individualizations of a social, historical, or personal kind do not ultimately originate in the *variability* of that factor which is only carried into the empirical and first constitutes it in its particularity: the transcendental personality, the founding "I." In the ultimate—or original—sense man makes "circumstances" [*Verhältnisse*], even if circumstances subsequently make man, and it thus seems to me rather problematic when Kant-Fichtean idealism tries to give an absolute substructure of similar, quite generally determined personalities to those individualizations that, precisely on the ground of their empirical character, it must derive from the given circumstances of the moment. Once it does so, however, the expatriation of morality from individual actuality and its transfer (as regards both *terminus a quo* and *terminus ad quem*) into the sphere of the universal is sealed.

However one consideration, leveled against a dogma of rationalistic morality not yet properly discussed, seems to me at once to loosen this seal in at least one place. The Socratic principle—that virtue is *one*, not differentiated (e.g., for man and wife) or in the expression of the man of Megara: that the plurality of virtues are only different names for this one—is highly characteristic of the entire direction criticized here, right down to its ultimate internalization with Kant. The principle would acknowledge without further ado that there are many different *vices*, individualizations of evil, but in the good as such there

are no divergences of direction. As satisfying as this picture—so to speak, of
the aesthetics of morality—appears, a cooler eye might perhaps perceive the
opposite. If one wants to stretch a unifying concept over specific spheres of the
ethical at all, then sinfulness seems to me to suit much better than moral values. While the proposition that sin consists in a domination of the sensuous
over the deeper and more central in us may be utterly cockeyed and erroneous, it still has some kind of connection to the true state of affairs; doubtless
though, sensuousness is the broader layer, the more consistently universal of
humanity. It is the greatest error to assert that egoism, with which we associ-
ate the sensual-sinful, bears the character of the individual; on the contrary,
because egoism is always directed towards *having*, because it leads the person
out of his center towards objects that ultimately others could or would also
want to have, there is always in it a deindividualization, an intention toward
some kind of impersonal universal. Only superficial features, the techniques
of sin so to speak, lead to a belief in its individualistic character: the exclusivity
of egoistic enjoyment, the necessary secrecies, the antisocial tendency. In its
deeper essence, sin much more than good is really a universal thing into which
we sink, and indeed in its ultimate meaning it is fairly indifferent whether it
adopts this specific context or another—and this is in no way true for our
positive life-values. It cannot be without significance that on countless occasions moral behavior is described by a "Become what you are!" as a return to
the most characteristic and genuine self. Now if one does not go along with
Kant's act of violence in declaring this central ego, producing moral life from
itself, as identical with universal reason, but instead apprehends it in the inner
uniqueness or solitude in which it is experienced, then morality itself originates from the point where the person is alone with himself, and to which he
finds his way back from the "broad way of sin"—whose breadth signifies not
merely its alluring ease, but also its accessibility for all.

Declaring the moral as a universal, hence as a unitary thing, and its opposite as an individualized, essentially isolated one, belongs to a persistent type
of valuation: of regarding the positive qualities of a particular value area as
unitary and its negative qualities as differentiated, in fact accidental from case
to case. An old Jewish saying puts it this way: "it is remarkable that God made
so many illnesses but only a single health." This seems to me an abstraction
drawn in the wrong direction. Health in fact means that the normal functional
capability of the organism extends all the way into its most subtle characteristics; each is healthy only in precisely his own way. In principle the corresponding point naturally also holds true for illness, yet just the same, circumstances
of illness not only permit the combination of typical groups; but also, while
health deals with the respective individual life in its limitless particularities,

illness is by definition oriented toward death, which is the utter universal, extinguishing all differences. Thus Tolstoy observes in one passage: "all happy people are as such similar to one another"—as though there were ultimately only *one* happiness, which is also Kant's view—"but the unhappy are each unhappy in their special way." This can only hold if one confuses happiness with its typical *causes*, with riches, social position, successes, "possession" of a beloved person; then it is admittedly something everywhere pretty much the same: these goods can be brought under a few very general and qualitatively ratable concepts. However if one asks, not about the external causes of happiness, but rather about happiness itself, about its subjective actuality [*Tatsächlichkeit*], then it is just as individual and incomparable as life itself, whose momentary excitement and beauty it forms. Simply because suffering often cannot be traced back to any such visible external causes—because it often consists only in a lack, a disappointment, a decline—it seems to flow more from the inner, specific essence of the individual than does the happiness that in actuality abides there to no less an extent. To the contrary, happiness is for the most part something so much more delicate, indefinable, and dependent on the favorability of unusual combinations, that it strikes me in much greater measure as something special, individual, and so to speak accidental than does unhappiness, which can be brought about by much more frequent elements always existing, so to speak, in the air.

The universality of the moral—in particular when this is emphasized as its form of unity—thus seems to me to have a root also in this typical tendency toward *harmony of values*, which is nonetheless only psychological-optimistic. With a more realistic view we can scarcely conceal from ourselves that our sins bear a much more general, typical character than our deepest and best elements. Setting this aside as parenthetical, however, we ask: what then is the real meaning of such universality; where in the entire ethical situation is the law's point of attack that it determines; what is the object for whose sake it requires emphasis at all?

The all-decisive element here seems to me to be the concept of the "act," which (I must again use what was established above) must be seen as something precisely circumscribed—finding its meaning in its own center and its closed periphery, and sufficiently described by a concept—if action is to come under universal laws at all. When Kant demands of the ethical act that its principle be capable of being always and everywhere a valid law, it is assumed that the act can be recognized as exactly the same act within the most diverse life courses. So long as individual life-moments, impulses, decisions, etc., are woven into the unity of a continuous existence, they have significance only in relation to the center and course of the latter, they exist at all only as the breaths of such an individual life. They must first be released from this context if they are supposed to be the substance of a lawfulness reaching beyond the individual. Only when they become independent from this individual and no longer draw their nourishment from his bloodstream can they be brought into other combinations, and can a normative form appear in them for as many other individuals as may be desired. At all events a motif often appears in Kant that appears to place the act into the uninterruptedness of the life context: he emphasizes the "progress of morality" that the individual exhibits in the course of his life right to the end. In the first place, however, this holds only with those for whom such a perpetual progress actually occurs, which experience seems not to show all too often and which was most doubtful to Goethe, for example: a man, he says, surely becomes a different one with age, but it cannot be said that he becomes a better one. Yet even disregarding this, for Kant this progress is quite obviously a succession of individual acts that mark an ascending series through the rising quantum of morality contained in each. The isolated act, therefore, as it belongs to a fixed concept, is the object of moral judgment. And thus it is with all general principles, not only with the categorical imperative. Even the divine commandment or the Aristotelian "mean" or the optimum of social evolution does not seize the act as it emerges from the center of the individual life, but as it is delimited as though from above by a concept. It makes no difference here whether the act is regarded only as an external *opus operatum* or as purely psychic content of the will independent of outward success or failure; for even in the latter case it comes into play for a universal law only through its precipitation [*Herauslösung*] out of life's entirety and through restriction of its meaning to that expressible by a concept. Life, regarded morally, consists here in a sum of mutually connected individual acts, such that the first act ends with a definite boundary legible from its conceptual domain, and the next act begins with a corresponding boundary. The kinship with the psychology of perception should not be ignored. Out of the stream of consciousness, whose contents continually slide into one another, this psychological method carves out, one at a time, each content that allows a somehow logically self-supporting expression, or better: it seizes in each case the logical kernels of these flowing contents and clothes them with a kind of psychic body, with which each content then appears as a "perception." Perceptions, thus delimited into units, then produce the idea of the psychic life in which they rise and fall, join together or separate, reproduce or inhibit each other, by turns dominate the area of consciousness or even waste away, etc.—in fact, as though each were supplied for itself with a special power that makes it know nothing, so to speak, of the common individual life source of all. Beyond its now essentially largely abandoned standing as scientific principle, this mechanistic image of the "play of perceptions" in wide measure determines the popular manner of speaking about psychic occurrence. Now the ideality of the Ought has also seized this manner of representing inner actuality by means of "universal ethical laws." The universal law cannot attach itself at all to inner processes insofar as these processes stand within an individual life-context, are only possible in this context, and are only the currently unfolding scene of the entire unitary life-drama. It embraces vital substance, not in the form of its becoming lived, but rather in the form of a conceptualized content [Inhaltlichkeit] that can recur as universal in every life-course and finds in each the same judgment deduced from moral law. The mechanistic way of thinking unmistakably dominates altogether in ethical reflections—and even here, deep into the realm of popular thought, law and obedience, egoism and selflessness, happiness and virtue, sensuousness and reason, and many others appear within this domain as securely defined magnitudes. How much this corresponds precisely to a certain unhelpfulness of intellectual formation as opposed to the living actuality (which is only accessible to a more supple conceptualization) may be seen in medieval ethics. In this whole literature there are schematizations of virtues and vices where these confront one another as fully and firmly defined personifications—down to the bizarre symbolism where animals often represent the individual vices. In this hierarchy of ethical qualities their functional character largely withdraws in the face of a closed substantiality. Yet even setting this extreme aside, they endlessly often pass for those firmly defined magnitudes precisely on account of their objective idea, even when one admits fluctuations and contradictions in their subjective elaboration—and they proceed in relations of mixing, of comparison, of attraction and repulsion, above all of quantitative definability, as though they were the elements of a physical system. And just as such elements can only submit to a natural law because each is exactly and constantly determined according to the definitions in question, there exists in ethical conceptions a correlation between the universality of the laws and the isolating circumscription with which the individual acts are set off from the life-stream. And that is possible so long as the Ought is seen as removed from life and opposed to it in principle; then admittedly no impediment exists to rational calculation with self-contained constructs, exhaustible by their concept, that submit to a universal principle on the strength of this concept. But as soon as the form of life itself is recognized in the Ought, such discontinuity is excluded; the stream of the Ought accompanies (though flowing on an entirely different level) that of the actual life, whose steadiness does not take refuge in precisely cut concepts and rejects the logical hierarchy of such concepts.

Excursus

In the relation of contents of consciousness as experienced to those consisting in detached ideality there lies a paradox which—because this relation forms the principal problem of these pages—I want to examine for its most universal (here, its theoretical) validity. However, if one has grasped the Ought as a life process to which its contents nonetheless stand opposed in more or less imperative form (up until the metaphysical reconciliation that comprehends this transcendence as most deeply immanent to life), one will have no difficulty in placing ethical values and questions meaningfully, as a general form, into the theoretical relations now to be discussed.

We must regard our psychic life in each waking period as a continuously unfolding process and our consciousness of it as a fact comparable to no other, for it has not yet split apart into the knowing subject and the known, somehow objective content. As soon as we think of this consciousness as objective, we do so under some sort of image: of a movement, of a flowing, of an unwinding thread or the like. We know very well, however, that its essence is not grasped by that, and in fact it eludes us in the instant that it is supposedly *grasped* (i.e., made into an object): knowledge of uninterrupted life is perhaps the only intuitive knowledge (in the absolute sense) we possess. But even in this sense we in fact never have this knowledge purely for itself; where we have it in this way, it is always already abstracted and objectified. It consists only in whatever contents it is connected to in a fully indispensable way; we always know, hope, believe, feel a something; all observation and reflection fills itself with *contents*. However, as we envisage these contents and thereby have life in them, life's continuity is fractured—just as we assemble "history" (which is a continuous life) scientifically and intellectually out of individual "events." The fact that perceptual contents, taken purely psychologically, replace each other without hiatus is not thereby dismissed. As soon as we become aware of them as contents, and not only have them psychologically, but *assert* something with this having, then what is asserted is a construct of discontinuous validity all its own. When I conceive of any something, a star or a war, a gadget or a fundamental metaphysical concept, then this, as perceptual content, is something entirely fixed and immutable. I can think of it, or could think something else in its place— something, perhaps, that deviates only in a miniscule way from it—but this would in fact be something else, and not the original thing that had changed "itself." This is the character of thought-content: its objective matter in space and time is, like everything cosmic, in continual, restless change; so too is the subjective process with which it is thought. But the content itself can only be exactly what it is, and if common parlance allows it to change, this is only an anthropomorphic transference of the ego-consciousness that is felt to persist amid all fluctuation in its process. Granted, if the thing is in outer or inner motion, I can also perceive the latter, which is a change; but then this change is itself a fixed thing in the ideal realm of contents, its concept is something timelessly persistent in its thus-ness [So-Sein]. It is close to the mark to say metaphorically that the living consciousness runs through that realm, glancing at or picking up now this one, now that one of its contents, only to fill itself in the next moment with another. This happens perhaps most clearly in the forms of the visual arts. Everything that was or is reality in the Venus de Milo, for instance, shows uninterrupted movement: the creative process in the soul of the artist and his working hand; the stone itself, at which atmospheric and other influences continuously gnaw, but in which molecular processes likewise occur continuously; the sensory absorption by the viewer; and the psychic significance of her image for him. There is nothing stable in the absolute sense here. Nonetheless, the artistic phenomenon that we mean when we say "Venus de Milo" has just this stability, its form is not vulnerable to temporally actual physical or psychic powers, it is timelessly utterly unchanging—the same even if a piece of marble falls in the Louvre and even if at some point no one thinks of her anymore. In this eternity of the once-thought form each objective content of consciousness as such has its place. Physically or psychically actualized, it stands in the παντα ρει[1] of the cosmos—yet in the form of its own meaning (there, where thought seeks it) it is untouchable by any flux, and its periphery is so bound together by its center that it opens upon nothing else. The purest illustration of this is again the work of art, an island within its frame, into which nothing else, no being or movement of the entire rest of the world, can penetrate. Yet we never have consciousness in its own living purity, instead we always have only contents, images, a this and that, in short, that unmoving-discontinuousness that is held together not in itself, but only in the consciousness that steadily flows through it. So above all there remains this bizarre circumstance: that psychic life, the ego, is surely a continuous process, limitless in itself—yet we hold this process exclusively in contents of consciousness whose essential meaning is in fact not process, but rather discontinuity and timeless permanence-in-itself; they may exist or not exist, but motion and process do not inhabit them. When we think, we are only a vessel of contents or, more accurately, the existence [Dasein] of contents; we cannot grasp the gestative or generative process because it is already content in the moment when it is grasped. And yet we know it—with a consciousness sui generis, existing only

1. "Continuous flow" (Heraclitus).—Trans.

for it and nothing else—as the ultimate reality of this very thinking, as against the ideal, conceptually expressible contents.

Of course, a metaphysical consideration approaching from the other direction could bring a certain relief here, if it had a chance—which I will not assert—of translating its simple logical structure into living-psychic reality. It may be most simply represented in the process of logical deduction. In the syllogism S is M; M is P; S is P—the expression that the conclusion S is P results or follows from the two premises conceals an extraordinary difficulty. To begin with, each of the three statements is a self-contained truth, valid for itself, without requiring anything further or extending to anything further. And then the successive arrangement in which they unite into a syllogism has nothing whatever to do with the statements themselves, for all three are equally timeless. It is not their own material content that the thinking consciousness *asserts*—but only this consciousness itself grasping them in psychological form, which brings them into the conclusive order and allows each of them to break through its constraints so that its connection with the others may be completed. We may think of each individual premise and likewise the concluding proposition as something that exists and is valid independently of this thinking—the conclusion itself, that very "deduction" of the third from the first two, occurs only in this thinking, only through this thinking; the propositions themselves remain in their fixed and sterile juxtaposition from which the flowing between them and their unification cannot be squeezed out. Thus, since only the continuous flow of the thought process brings the latter about, it is clear that the thought process transcends the limits that isolate each proposition as logical in itself. In fact since it is continuous—and thus is not set aside after the "S is M," only to reappear after a hiatus in the "S is P"—it weakens the boundaries of the individual contents, so to speak, and places something between them, something not expressed in the logical deductive form of the syllogism, that makes them linkable. The content of this logical form is thus only a *part* of what the psychic process, the sole conclusion-forming process, contains; the three propositions are here only stations or transitional points that admittedly establish the psychic development of the syllogism in its direction but do not constitute it or fill it in. What makes the conclusion a conclusion, the movement, the execution, the connective impetus—is not contained at all in the propositions that appear to present it fully.

Yet this must not be accepted simply at face value. The three propositions have (by assumption) that timeless validity which is independent of their psychic realization and which even brings it about that this realization has truth-value. Whether one understands the concept of truth realistically or idealistically or howsoever, in every case it is for us the correspondence of psychic reality with something ideally predetermined: because of this, truth is discovered, not invented, and this correspondence is the essence of its "necessity," since every deviation from that predetermination allows it to veer into error. If we call this supposedly timelessly preexistent counterpart to the true perception the "Idea," then there naturally exists for the syllogism-forming psychic process a corresponding idea with which it accords as truth: for the whole process—not only for the conceptually named stations, the premises and the conclusion, but also for all of that which lies between, the whole movement, transition, synthesis, that alone forms the isolated members into a conclusion. The spiritual life process of its execution must, like every individual truth, have its legitimating counterpart, its idea, which moves in the same rhythm, in the same continuity between the individual members, the same dissolving of their fixed being-for-themselves [Fürsichseins]. Even the strict logician who only recognizes the psychologically executed conclusion when it is exclusively the exact recapitulation of the ideal construct of the conclusion, cannot escape the consequence: because the psychological process of deduction always contains more than just the three propositions standing in their respective isolation, so likewise its ideal counterpart must contain, from the outset, more than just these three bounded elements if it is to satisfy that prerequisite of correspondence. The "idea" must thus have the same form of animation [Bewegtheitsform] as life itself; we could say: the idea lives—if we are willing, not to understand "life" as the empirical actuality of a physical or physical-spiritual organism, but to understand it in the wholly general or symbolic sense where it can be expressed by the purely ideal-spiritual, merely valid construct that gives content and truth to our cognition.

The logically ideal construct must even contain an analog of the form of time, to which life as such is bound. Within it, each of the three propositions, as long as it corresponds to truth, is of timeless validity. Because the relation with which the first two pass over into the third lies on the same logical level, it too is therefore timeless. This relation, though, is nothing other than the movement that grasps the premises or flows through them into a conclusion—the movement that corresponds to the succession of the psychic process of realization. Since this succession is formally inevitable because a series of life-moments is present, it is also inevitable in the determinacy of its contents because both premises produce the psychic constellation that then releases the conclusion as its result. Yet as timeless and thus concurrently valid as all those components of the purely logical domain are, their sequential order is determined exactly as is their temporal order, because the syllogism only comes about with the premises preceding and the conclusion following. Now while the psychic temporal order may be determined as inwardly meaningful by this ideal sequential order, the latter is nonetheless the projection of the former onto the logical plane; and we have here the peculiar phenomenon that can only be called timeless movement—the timeless is the full analog, the adequate symbol of the movement produced by and characteristic of life as such!

This proceeds according to principle and no less visibly, even in the linguistic expression of the individual sentence. In the proposition "life means suffering," each of the three words has a comprehensible meaning, a corresponding inner vision, though without truth-value in isolation. The words then lose this isolation inside the sentence structure, though this structure does not bind them to one another externally or catch these formerly homeless, fluttering words in a common net. Instead, the supposed meaning of the proposition is something thoroughly unitary in itself, so unitary that it cannot at all accurately be called a synthesis. The thought that has creatively arisen in the person who thinks in this way is actually only *one*, and does not first occur through a synthesis. The latter, on the contrary, is only the taking apart of its unity for the purpose of its logical and linguistic expression—as the organic germ unfolds into functional and spatial differentiation of its members—the three words are not even its "parts," and none of them contain it pro rata. Only when they stand next to one another do they require, when seen as discontinuous, a synthesis; but when the listener has accomplished this, there has thereby emerged in him the fully new, trans-synthetic construction of that absolutely unitary thought, a thought which is nonetheless not expressible as a unity. Thus as long as the three words are presented discontinuously, in mere succession, they have absolutely nothing to do with the sense of the sentence, as little as brush strokes seen in their juxtaposition make a painting. They are thus something entirely different inside the sentence than outside it; they have completely lost the demarcation of their separate meanings. Nonetheless these separate meanings themselves have not simply disappeared, since they still offer the possibility of expressing that unitary, internally seamless thought comprehensively and immediately in the form of the three-term sentence. This remarkable and still by no means fully clarified relationship should here only reveal the insight that if the individual sentence is to have any meaning at all (let alone a truth-claim), its utterable elements must step out of their conceptual closure and isolation into that symbiosis with which they can become the symbol of the integration of the sentence's unified idea, an integration only achievable by psychically productive *life*. For that is the decisive point, that the thought, absolutely not consisting of parts, can be engendered only in psychic vitality, not out of its rigidly enclosed elements or its external objects. Thus, it is not only the truth of the syllogism (assuming the truth of the premises) that has a transvital, ideal correlate, possessing nonetheless within itself life's

steady flow and denial of boundaries so that correspondence can govern between it and the psychic process, thereby allowing the latter to be "true." Even
the individual sentence (from which we provisionally require as yet no truth
at all, but only a meaning) can only realize this process in the form of an objectively disclosed proposition when it takes from the individual components
their logically fixed delimitations. Even the transvital meanings of words must
undergo the fusion process dictated by life, for they have a sentence-meaning
[Satzsinn] only as a symbolizing development of that unconditional unity of
thought that has no locus outside of generative life. Once again, incidentally,
the earlier claim is confirmed here: life is in no way banished to the exclusive
form of the concrete actuality of being. If the Ought means that conscious life,
life as spiritual occurrence, also proceeds as the irreality of a mere demand
[Forderung], then one can describe the ideal content of this demand, released
from the life that bears it, as idea. And now it becomes evident that even this
abstract idea is able to recapitulate in itself the form of life, that even in this
release it need not be anything dead, in the discontinuous fixity of individual
pieces. Just as cognition acquires truth-value in that it agrees with the idea, and
therefore the idea, in all its timelessness and independence from vital realization, must nonetheless show as its archetype (in a way not further describable)
the entire movement, the smooth transitions, the wealth of nuance of thinking life—so too action attains ethical value through its agreement with that
idea, the content of the ethical demand, which thus, if its vitalization is not to
fragment into value-emptiness, must likewise recapitulate the inner form and
steadiness of life.

:::

Here we have now arrived at the decisive theme of our whole train of thought.
It is this: universal law can address itself only to the individual (and individually identifiable) acts that are carved out of the individual life context. The
individualization of the act, achieved by its subordination to a concept (by
which its subordination to a universal law is determined), contradicts the individualization that it possesses as the scene or pulse of the whole life of its
subject, and in which alone—this is certainly my fundamental axiom—its full
and ultimate ethical significance can declare itself. If the law standing over
action should actually demand this significance of it, then that law can only
stem from the life unity of the individual unfolding as obligation—or more
precisely, the law must be the instantaneous arrangement of it. As long as the
particular act is demanded on account of its conceptually isolated meaning
(always even presupposing that it is meant as moral intention, not as extrinsi-

cally good work), it lacks that full, ideal-genetic connection with the whole life of its executor; and responsibility does not find a unitary foundation—since for that the law would have to come out of the same ultimate life-source from which its attainment is demanded. Moreover with the rooting of duty in the totality of the particular life, a much more radical objectivity is produced than rational moralism can attain. That is, the notion in rational moralism—that each person absolutely knows his duty and that nothing else is duty than that which he knows as such—is consistent with the proposition that he knows no other obligation than what is realizable through the will. To this view it would be unthinkable that we should *be* in a particular way, or should feel in a particular way, etc.; in short, that something or other should happen that cannot be purposively willed. But if one grasps the Ought as the ideal sequence of life, it is self-evident that every being and occurrence of this life has an ideal above it, a manner of how it should be within this life. All of existence *should* be thus, regardless of how its actuality is, and only by a tearing-out (admittedly unavoidable in practice and reflection) of individual pieces can one confront a particular element of the series of actualities with a particular element of the series of ideals and say the former should be like the latter. The *whole* should, as I have said, be thus, once a definite individuality is given. Clearly duty possesses a much more decided objectivity, determined through a much richer coordinate system, when even its purely will-related meaning is determined not only within its particular domain, but according to its connection with the ideal sphere of the entire personal life.

Only out of such an inwardly unitary creation of norms within a total life (even if this norm creation surely cannot be formulated in a unique concept or even a concept at all) *can* those obligations [*Sollungen*] also arise which defy inclusion under the categorical imperative, let alone under the more material universal laws—all those obligations that relate to the sliding, fluctuating, floating life-contents or life-situations for which there are no concepts; that in their totality or in their nuancing can only be experienced, not formulated; and for whose ethical adjudication the generalization to a universal law breaks down entirely. All such things, which cannot be formed into a universal maxim at all, remain outside the realm of the categorical imperative, and fall into the very problematic category of αδιαφορα[2] or into an anarchy. I cannot deny that I have often felt the reverse of Kantian moral rigorism to be a quite anarchic helplessness in the face of elements of life that cannot be logically schematized, that is, in the face of the entirety of life. However, we never live simply as such "creatures of reason" [*Vernunftwesen*], but rather as a somehow unitary totality

2. "Indifference."—Trans.

that we only analyze *retrospectively* into reason, sense, etc., according to scientific, practical, teleological viewpoints. But these elements have other laws and developments in their isolation than within that entirety of life—just as an organic subprocess under experiment in the chemistry laboratory by no means allows per se the conclusion that it proceeds exactly the same way in the living body. But how may the relation of unity and multiplicity among these "powers of the psyche" [*Seelenvermögen*] be determined—with what right do we shut out the innumerable other elements of our being [*Wesen*] from it, in order to form an Ought-ideal for it alone or out of it alone? For example, may the sensuous in our existence actually only remain in its pure factuality? Is there not also for it a manner in which, purely as the sensuous, it *ought* to proceed, an ideal immanent to it, toward which it can approach and from which it can distance itself? And is it not thus with fantasy, with the formation of ethically indifferent elements of life, with religious belief regarded really only as belief? Only the law of the individual—developing from the same root from which his (perhaps utterly diverging) reality springs—captures every analytically or synthetically attainable piece of life, because it is nothing other than the totality or centrality of life itself, unfolding as obligation. For this reason the principle intended here cannot even be formulated by saying that what is sin or virtue for the one person is not yet so for the other. This is only superficiality or consequence. For already this "what" is even at the outset something different in the one case than in the other (and not only because it is retrospectively evaluated as sin). Only the external effect, not the internal, the ethical, is "the same." *Si duo faciunt idem*[3] is already in itself so false an assumption that the subsequent clause is superfluous.

For Kant, the indifference of the law towards the individual to whom it applies arises from the fact that he draws the prototype of the concept of law generally from natural science and jurisprudence. In both of these contexts "law" applies absolutely, without allowing the individual situation it addresses to unfold somehow as a source of determinations separate from the universal. In natural science, this is the case because law here means only the formulation of the factual course (wherever and however often realized) of particular occurrences; in civil law this is the case because it ordains, from itself and for the sake of a social order, how the particular action should proceed. The categorical imperative has on one hand the logical structure of a natural law of mechanistic provenance (as Kant himself notes); on the other hand, it has that of a legal proposition. Thus for the categorical imperative, the circularity

---

3. "If two do the same thing," from the Latin proverb "Si duo faciunt idem, non est idem" (If two do the same thing, it is not the same thing).—Trans.

that threatens every a priori universal moral law appears not to exist: namely, that a law should obligate me because it is or can be universally valid, but how can I maintain its universal validity before I know that it is also valid for me and applies to me? This is obviously the well-known difficulty of the syllogism with the universal premise. How may I conclude, from the mortality of all men and the manhood of Caius, that he too will die, for the former premise is only valid when I am already certain of the mortality of Caius? In nature, the law is immanent in the individual fact; here nothing exists to confront both that would allow the question of applicability or nonapplicability to arise. For its part, civil law commands the individual from the outside; it imposes only a partial demand in fundamental indifference to the totality of the subject—the question of applicability to the subject is thus not even raised, though admittedly nonapplicability is possible in unlimited measure. Yet here already appears the inadequacy that enters into "universal law" from both of those sources. For ethical law is neither appropriate in principle to the individual case like natural law, nor is it absolutely opposed like the command issuing from persons; rather, since opposition here signifies also the deepest connectedness, the problem of application now emerges indeed—if it does not apply, it is also not valid—and therewith its "universality" resides within the above-mentioned circularity.

However, precisely because of the latitude I have demanded here in the conception and meaning of individuality, one can justly maintain the concept of "universality" which prescribes to each particular act its law: yet this is not the universality of all men, but that of this specific individual instead. The universal of the individual is not an abstraction from his particular qualities and actions. Indeed, the notion that there are such particulars (in the exact sense of particularity) is an artificial abstraction that does not at all touch the inner form of action within the real constancy of life, but only the circumscribed visibility of its outward result or its outward stimulus. Seen from within, the "particular" act is only a relatively legitimate, retrospectively subjective extraction out of an absolute continuity; the singularity of an act exists indeed only for praxis, for others, for the external world, but not for its welling up out of the deepest ground of life and essence from which ethics nonetheless wants to originate. This is the real reason why a purely ethical judgment on man is so difficult. It is not the difficulty of knowledge—located in the theoretical imperfection of the judging subject—but rather the structure of the object itself, which really forbids the distillation [Herauslösung] of a particular object of judgment. The universality of the individual does not stand above his actions as an abstraction, but under them as a root. It is every "part" of an individual pervaded by the life of the whole; within the plane of life, no part has a meaning exclusive to itself. But because of this, the unity of the parts is an even more absolute one: whoever cannot grasp the individual as a whole is thereby incapable of absolutely grasping anything of him at all. The individual can only be imagined through a kind of intellectual conception, insofar as this means the apprehension of a whole through an integrative function. I do not claim that one may not also grasp one element after another in the individual; but then comes an instant in which they combine into a totality that is not juxtaposition—mere combination—but an entirely new construction. At once the order is now reversed: this unity does not come from the combined parts, but the parts from the whole. That a man lies or sacrifices himself for his conviction, that he is hard-hearted or beneficent, that he behaves licentiously or ascetically—this is absolutely entwined as momentary actuality in the continuity of his life; in fact, even the expression of entwinement is wide of the mark, for it appears to assume a somehow independent existence or genesis of the act as though it were one tightly circumscribed by a concept, and as though it is injected into the life process only with this proper characterization, retroactively as it were, or as though of itself. On the contrary, it is a piece extracted from this process by an imported concept, and it belongs just as much to the continuity of this process as every other part occurring between two arbitrary moments in time. Though the external aspects of our behavior may show relatively sharp boundaries with respect to one another, life is not assembled inwardly from a lie, then a courageous decision, then a licentious act, then an act of beneficence, etc.—rather, it is a steady gliding where every instant represents [darstellt] the perpetually self-creating, transforming whole, where no part has sharp boundaries with another and where each reveals its meaning only within that whole and seen from its viewpoint. That the act occurs in this instant means that life in its continuous process has momentarily assumed just this form; it is, so to speak, not defined by the fact that it is a lie or a good deed; rather, it is the present reality of this life process, just as the form of a jellyfish, continually changing its outline, is not determined now by the idea of a circle, now of an ellipse, now of an approximate square, but only by the inner life process of the animal (in conjunction with external conditions)—regardless of whether the circle or the ellipse in themselves, as objective forms, have laws or necessities quite indifferent to the vital process putting them forth as the form of this creature. Now if a universal norm exists in regard to the lie or to the act of beneficence, it does not yet directly find a point of attack in the continuously arranged life process—for this, the contents of this life process must instead be set off from it in a way foreign to itself, and then subordinated from outside (albeit from an ideal outside) to an already existing concept. If the Ought is centered on such universal concepts as lie, beneficence, etc., then it cannot grasp the act from its inner source at all, but only after life, flowing steadily out of this source, is brought into the form of discontinuity—or not actually life itself, but its contents which are expressible and isolable by a conceptual system. The lie or the act of beneficence, as the current vitality of its subjects, possesses the uniqueness of everything actual and, from this direction, is in no way a representation of the universal lie or the universal act of beneficence of which the universal law speaks—instead, it is subordinated to the latter only after it is removed from its organic context and placed into a conceptual one that can only employ it as singularized, stripped of its vital dynamic, and as the sum of ideally preexisting, fixed features. The Kantian imperative is in principle oriented in such a way that it expresses only the most universal formal abstraction among all possible particular universal laws. As a regulator of action it must be immediately transformed into a content-specific (i.e., a singular) norm that can be (relative to its pure consequence at all events) in each instance only an empirically valid one, perhaps to be contradicted in the next case. Yet the categorical imperative is decomposed into the possible sum of these relative universals as soon as it seeks to become practical. Granted, its formula seems even then to be wide enough to decide on the ethicality of an act by means of its "possible universalization," if our action is understood as it *actually* is in life: seamlessly enmeshed in its wholeness, merely the directly observed wave in life's continual flux. But in fact the act thus conceived cannot be universalized at all, for this would mean nothing other than thinking of the entire life of this individual as a universal law. The question would then be as follows: can you desire that all men behave, from their first to their last minute, as you do?—for, as must always be reiterated, the particular act reveals its inner, truly authentic meaning only in the totality of the life-context. But disregarding the inconceivability or absurdity of this consequence, under some circumstances it can doubtless be valuable (even by the highest criteria under which the categorical imperative decides the desirability of an act) that *one* person of this particular kind should exist, yet not that more (even just a few) such persons exist. We cannot at all avoid the question of how the ethical fault of that one person is supposed to result from this latter constellation. Thus, if the contexts given with each particular act are not to be arbitrarily cut away, the ultimate consequence to which the categorical imperative leads is the following: can you desire that you exist at all, or that a world in which you exist (for this one, as it exists, is the unremitting condition of your whole life and thus of your particular action) should exist infinitely often? In this way the Kantian formula, consistently developed to its full meaning, leads to the Eternal Return, and hence the question of universalizing obviously can no longer find a purely logical answer (as it itself demands), but requires one based on decisions springing from will or emotion. If all this is to be avoided, if the particular act is to be conceived as universalized so as to answer the legitimation question, then nothing is left but to isolate it out of the entire context of life, to set it into external boundedness: the universalization of its full reality within our existence invalidates itself, or at least invalidates the claim to an objectively logical decision by the Kantian formula—the very universalization presupposes an artificial individualizing of the particular act. The Kantian formula governs at most from case to case; the *whole* it cannot govern, for this whole (vitally speaking, as little an assemblage of particular cases as the actuality of an organism is an assemblage of particular pieces), when conceived as "universal," produces all that absurdity. Individualizing the particular act, as I have already emphasized, directly opposes personal individuality, that is, the unity and wholeness that is experienced consistently through all of the multiplicity of particular acts, or more exactly, that lives *as* this multiplicity. The immediate Ought is a function of the total life of the individual personality. This is perhaps the deeper meaning of the mystical notion that every person has his special angel or genius guiding him from circumstance to circumstance, that to a certain extent represents the "idea" of his life.

With this it also becomes clear (I note this as more of a side effect) in what sense the "consequence" of action can apply as value. Consequence is usually understood in an objective sense: as though the situation, the task, the prior development from its logical content allows that manner of conduct to be deduced which is now consequent, and thus to be demanded of the subject as ethical. Yet whether this is always the consequence for precisely this individual remains altogether doubtful in many cases. Indeed the consistency of *his* nature perhaps leads (by the same or a similarly individual logic) to an entirely different action, without prejudice to the fact that those objective sequences may be elements of his being and their consequence may come to be his. In that popular concept of consequence lies the erroneous application of logic (advancing by pure conceptual content) to an area not subject to it, an error that the assumption of perceptual psychology also produces—for it too can be led in its associations, etc., ultimately by a more or less hidden *logic* in the relation of elements. We have now freed logic from the falsifications with which the interference of psychology threatened it. But we have not yet become sufficiently attentive to the dangers that conversely approach psychology, and therewith a large part of ethics, from usurpations of logic.

As though in an imaginary partisan conflict, the actions of life—each of which we perceive as a particular, somehow bounded unit describable by its content—seemed up to now to oppose the entire stream of life, whose all-embracing unity is not about to give way to any special unities, any particulars with their known boundaries. The particular act—which is oriented in its emphasis towards conceptual, and if not extravital then at least extra-individual content, and which assembles the life-series by connecting one content to another—and individual life welling up from within, which like a fluid substance obtains only its continuously changing form in all those phenomena: these two understandings of life are obviously among the most separated in principle. But we cannot content ourselves with this antinomy or foreignness between the meaning of the particular and the meaning of the whole. A view must be sought in which both of those understandings are united by a functional relationship and inner necessity. This view unfolds from a fundamental motif which seems to have attained its full right in ethics neither by its depth nor by its breadth, and which is again initially characterized in opposition to rational morality. For the latter (and here I am really only adopting a notion of popular ethics) derives ethically relevant actions either from the pure, sense-free ego or from the sensual ego. In contrast, I most decidedly maintain (at first in a wholly aphoristic formulation) that in every human behavior the *whole* human being is productive. Though rational morality may even put "disposition" into what is valuable in the outward act, so to speak as the shortest line between the act and the absolute ego-point—the entire realm of the empirical personality, which this line does not affect, is here excluded from every factual and ethical relation to the act. Here the person is judged insofar as he has committed this very act, not the act insofar as it is committed by this very person. Indeed, the isolated normalization of the particular act (i.e., to a universal law concerning its content) can occur only through such an exclusion of the whole person. And vice versa, this extraction and particularization of the act leads to the construction of the pure, absolute, and transcendental or transcendent ego that is its correlate. In actuality, however, this applies only to the logicized and mechanized notion of the psyche, and utterly collapses when each particular behavior is allowed to serve as a new enriching possibility with which the totality of existence can be presented. Then the relationship—hard to grasp in rational morality—between the absolute, really nonvital ego and alternating singular acts becomes at once an organically unitary one. For now the singular act does not exclude, but includes, that totality; and though our knowledge does not suffice to demonstrate it in detail, the basic metaphysical feeling here is this: that every existential particularity expresses exhaustively and in its particular idiom the entirety of the individual existence [*Dasein*] out of which it comes. Thus, every instant of life, every behavior [*Sich-Verhalten*] and action is the whole life; and life is not a totality for itself that stands opposite to the particular act in ideal detachment. Rather, this is the peculiar form of life, not exhaustible by any mechanistic metaphor: that in each of its moments it is still this entire life, however multifarious and mutually opposed the contents of those moments may be. Not a piece of it, but the whole appears in the particular act. In the instant of its occurrence, as in every other, this individual life has within itself all the consequences of its past and all the energies of its future. Thus this psychic instant is actually the whole life, because right now there is no life outside of it (where would it really be?) and because life has at its disposal no other character [*Gestalt*] at all than a continuous one, occasionally rising to a crest, however variable. Naturally, a single moment is not the entire life if the latter is understood as the sum of content-determined experiences. But life as process—as that which bears and produces all contents, and which these contents symbolize (in a manner not further explicable)—is not a sum at all; rather, it is entirely actual in each of its instants. These instants are utterly diverse in strength, intention, and value. But this diversity is the immediate essence of life; it *is* sometimes weak, sometimes strong, now inwardly balanced, now in acute excitation, sometimes intensive, sometimes empty—none of these instants, except through the vital lawfulness of "reaction," points from itself towards another so as to combine with it into the entire life (this could occur only under utterly differently oriented conceptual systems). I am *actually and wholly* strong in the one instant, weak in the other; that is, my being has this quality now, regardless of whether it had another at a different time—though naturally, these sketchy examples are much too simple; the whole-status of the instant, though unitary in the vital sense, is infinitely complicated in its content-wise conceptuality and at best incompletely analyzable. Throughout, we must rule out the notion that any valuation or relation of contents or even of intensities of life determines whether the whole and "full" life exists in a moment. For the concept of a "full" life here would have a value or subjective feeling-sense [*Gefühlssinn*], one entirely different from that of the objective vital process. Even if one understands life in the sense of a measurable quantity, so that an individual course of existence shows more or less life, the genuine and entire life is nonetheless present in each of these different situations: it *is* indeed by turns a fuller and an emptier one, and only by a concept or a yearning does the latter stretch out ideal arms toward an ideal abundance [*Mehr*] with which it seeks to be fulfilled; in the truly vital and metaphysical sense there is only *one* life, of which sometimes abundance, sometimes poverty is its truth and totality. Thus it is also wrong to say that, if I desire and accomplish good in one hour of my life and evil in another, the latter or the former is my true nature, and the other a temporary, so to speak accidental, deviation. Who claims to recognize surely where the truth of my nature lies? Perhaps it becomes visible only in one single hour of my existence. This whole distinction is most highly problematic. The person is at one time thus and at another otherwise, and only optimism or pessimism about our own value moves us to conclude merely from the more frequent appearance of a specific quality that one resides in principle in a different characterological or metaphysical layer than the other. That this possibility of life, to be really entirely good or really entirely bad, exists; that we are not inwardly divided into layers of different ethical-metaphysical depths of being [*Wesenstiefe*] so that the one act falls unalterably into the fundamental, the other into the superficial—this is human freedom. Transcendental "character" sets in freedom's place a fate that is only fantastically concealed by the principle of metaphysical choice of character. Furthermore, regardless of the related problematic of freedom, the uniform legitimacy (in the sense of representing life) of our most heterogeneously valued actions is by no means incompatible with "innate character." For it is a truly peculiar constriction and rigidity that innateness of character is equated with a qualitative uniformity of behavior describable with *one* concept (even if, perhaps, a complicated one): that the individual would be born as a moral or an amoral, a sanguine or a melancholy, a pedantic or a broad-minded character, and either he could never behave in a deviating sense at all or, if this were to happen, he would be deflected by ego-alien forces, or a (truly inconceivable) contingency would produce this rare and ephemeral, superficial phenomenon. But even if we allow that there is a character of such invariant, persisting nature, I do not see why it could not be "innate" in an individual to take on a particular inner attitude in one epoch of his life, and an utterly divergent one in another—and so on in infinite possible variants. Why should this be otherwise than with innate physical characteristics? That our beard grows in the second decade of life, that it is first sparse and then heavy, that it later grays and finally becomes white—is this change not unalterably allotted to us by the original blastoderm? Why should not the change of essential color in the course of development of life be just as much an innate feature as the supposed monochromaticism of character? The mere prejudice that its predefinition is joined to its conceptual-qualitative conformity has doubtless arisen only from the fact that, for our incomplete knowledge, the likelihood that a thoroughly predetermined character exists certainly very significantly increases with a consistently observed qualitative equivalence of conduct. But in the material itself, whether diagnosable or not, there is not the slightest reason to believe a temporally variable characterological conduct to be less predetermined—nor is there a reason to see a more limited connection with the innate root of being [*Wesenswurzel*] in the one phase than in the other.

Life is contained in a rather differential arrangement in the cross-section of the life-stream we call its present (so that each cross-section, whether very narrow or very wide in content, signifies a full phase of the life-totality)—and this fact naturally is presented in multifarious empirical modifications. Even in regard to particular energies functioning apparently independently, we should never forget that it is the whole person who thinks, feels, desires, and that each particular sense is only a canalization of the life-entirety through which the life-entirety deals with the external world. We easily deceive ourselves insofar as we can often ascertain no connection or determination between one partic-ular energy and another and thereby forget (as is typical, by the way, for count-less psychic and practical situations) that an element of a whole can very well be determined by the whole as a unity, even if we cannot discover the influence of any other single element upon the element in question. Thus, the Christian believer not infrequently forgets that he lives in the absolute embrace of the divine One when divine good, divine wisdom, or even divine justice and divine wrath do not intervene in his life as he had expected.

The form-type (by no means easy to understand theoretically) in which in-dividual life always rises only as a whole towards the developments that we call particular acts or experiences has a certain logical analogy in our formation of concepts. Of the concrete material that a concept describes, it includes only certain parts, sides, and definitions, but leaves many others—the material's individual configuration, everything in the material that either belongs under other concepts or is not conceptually expressible at all—outside of its content. Nonetheless it is taken for the totality, for the unity of the material, inclusive of all those qualities not touched by it. When I call a plant a tree, this con-cept does not determine whether the plant has needles or leaves; yet it applies, not for a part of the needle-bearing one and a corresponding part of the leaf-bearing one, but for the whole structure (unitary in itself) that bears needles, and for the whole that bears leaves: tree-ness in some measure permeates each one without being constrained by individual variations. Or, if one calls some-one an idiot—this concept does not include all of the countless characteristics of the person that have nothing at all to do with idiocy or cleverness, and for which the latter do not even form a prejudice. Nonetheless, *with* all of these, with his goodheartedness or wickedness, his normal or abnormal sex life, his talkativeness or reserve, and all the rest, he *is* an idiot—this concept, under which he is brought according to an only partial characteristic, nonetheless embraces or dominates his entirety, which also includes all those intellect-alien determinants in its unity. This structural relation between particularity and life-entirety brings about a peculiar problematic precisely in ethical value judgments. For Dante, sinners generally suffer their condemnation on account of single deeds. If one may extract the deeper meaning here, that the person does something once in his life that concentrates in itself the entire sense, the entire tendency of that life, then the ethical value of such a representative deed—how it is measured against a system of preexisting norms—is nonetheless determined by its particularity of content. And even if *characteristics* underlie the judgment, they are nonetheless only partial: the envious, the lustful, the wrathful can have truly splendid characteristics otherwise, and Dante does not deny this; in fact, he even points it out occasionally. Where have these gone? Why do they disappear absolutely in the face of the negative values? And how does this reconcile as a formal principle with the fact that the whole of Sodom should be spared for the sake of *one* righteous person? And if this one thing should really serve as the authoritative value-point of existence (as for Kant it could appear to be the purest manifestation of intelligible character), here as there the deed is judged, not according to its organic-continuous coalescence into life, but rather according to its self-declared content, or for Kant according to the mere intention of this content. In both cases, however, it requires isolation (however laden with inwardness) of the deed, because it is supposed to find its value in a norm standing *opposite* to the whole life of the individual and in principle indifferent to it. Here it is not uninteresting to observe that when the deed is pursued in the opposite direction, towards those effects turned back on the doer, its isolation with respect to the whole of life is at once removed. The judge may punish only the defined transgression, to him the person may only be its bearer, to all else he is indifferent; but the punishment—its immediate pain, as also perhaps the social degradation—factually affects the entire person. Our deeds are in no way so localized in respect to their repercussions on us as is (according to the ethical propositions criticized here) their origination from us. Certainly this hundredfold experience should have managed to bring this origin, too, into closer connection with the whole of life. This fundamental relationship even applies more intimately than the layers indicated. We would more easily exonerate ourselves from the guilt over an action that we perhaps feel is relatively isolated and due to a psychic eddy, were it not clouded over by a stifling feeling: you are therefore capable, and for all time to come, of doing something like this! The really oppressive thing is the quality within us (even if this is so to speak a provincial one)—its lasting possibility, now no longer deniable, and thus something extending beyond the act as singular and onto the entire life-course. Thus it should also be noted psychologically that when a radical inner change makes it utterly unthinkable for us to repeat a regretted act, the suffering of regret is significantly assuaged. It should also by no means be overlooked that we in fact do not feel fully responsible for many actions; that they suddenly appear as strangers of unknown origin in our inner landscape, something peripheral, not joined to our life-center. But such descriptors of these phenomena seem fallacious to me. As discussed above, we are always (and thus also in such moments of action) our whole life, and the division (here offered easily) of life into our actuality and our potentiality, in very unequal proportions, is a thoroughly problematical makeshift expression, because only the indissoluble interweaving of the so-called actual and the so-called potential constitutes the actual and effective life-moment. Life, by its essence, fluctuates in an ongoing up and down, strong and weak, light and dark, without thereby giving up in any moment its totality as this one life. It is thus not mere "parts," it is no extraterritorial "somewhere" that allows actions of that kind to escape; rather it is our entire life-unity that in such moments only passes through the stage of atrophy, of alienation from self, of abandonment of the otherwise habitual. Yet even this condition described as being-other is not a contingent thing wafted in from somewhere or other, but a mode of life itself—the outside is a form of its inside.

In more detailed elaboration—and opposing the mechanistic view on the one hand and the Platonic on the other—the decisive theme for us here is shown perhaps most significantly where we aggregate our behavior into persistent characteristic traits. I will proceed from the points just discussed. When we call a person greedy, it is not his greed that is greedy but the whole person, who is likewise brave, sensual, clever, melancholic, and all else possible—*he* is greedy. Therefore this whole person is contained in every action we designate as a greedy one, just as he is contained in every other action that appears a clever or a brave or a sensually determined one. It is an utter misunderstanding of the essence of life when one will only see its unitary wholeness insofar as one observes qualitative uniformity in it—a uniformity one then tries to achieve through a kind of blending of all differences in its moments' contents, through taking an average of them, or in a "pure" ego, that is, in an abstraction of all differences of content in general. The category of whole and part, as it applies for the inanimate, is not applicable to life at all, especially not to the individual psychic life. Here there is an inner connectedness of life that not only affects before and after in the sense that one can reach from one point to another only through all those points lying between them; but beyond this, elements of the past so to speak reach over the head of everything lying between and affect the present, combining with it into a steadily changing unity—as in a painting each fleck of color stands in relation not only to its neighbors, but to every other fleck on the same canvas; and thus emerges the network of oppositions, syntheses, and comparisons that we express as the "necessity" in the artwork (i.e., as the indispensability of each particular part, because *every* other is this specific one, and vice versa): every part of the artwork in its place is what it is only through the fact that every other is what it is. The significance of each in a certain sense includes the entire work of art.

But ultimately even this comparison only very incompletely and, so to speak, only disjointedly approaches what the authentic form of life accomplishes in principle completely and in unity: that it actually *wholly* exists in every respective present. The fact that these present conditions—since they mutually exclude one another, on the one hand as temporally separate "pieces," on the other hand through the contradictions in their contents—bristle from time to time at being a whole life, goes back to the effectiveness of the viewpoints that are imported into life from outside. Thus the schema of whole and piece possibly holds for *time* in life (i.e., for the empty, linear time-schema that one gets when one so to speak erases the life from life). Within this there are certainly "pieces," parts that are snipped out by sharp, punctual boundaries and therefore cannot even be a symbol of life that proceeds in absolute, unbroken continuity. Granted, a "piece" of my life occurs between 6 and 7 o'clock, another attaches to it between 7 and 8 o'clock, so that each of them contains my life only pro rata, the whole is summed from them. But seen from life itself, this piecing out is certainly not something objective, something prescribed in its own structure; its continuity can be expressed only by saying that each examined moment is the whole life—because the form of this entirety, and its unity, is to live itself out in what we must call, under the outward temporal aspect, multiplicity. It is no different with respect to the qualitative variability of pieces of life. That I divide my activity into now a miserly or a spendthrift, now a courageous or a cowardly, now a clever or a foolish aspect occurs on the basis of conceptual categories that confront the life process in objective systematic fashion and completely disconnectedly. Naturally it is upon differences in content within this life process itself that the process allows the application first of one category, then of another. But this circumstance draws its true essence and susceptibility to ethical judgment [*Beurteilbarkeit*], not from the concepts of greed or prodigality, of courage or foolishness, but from the continuous and continually changing life-stream. Here again, the distinction between the conceptual-universal and the vital-individual outlooks reveals itself most sharply. From the Platonizing standpoint (which here also forms the presupposition for the ethic of the "universal law"), the courageous act is an exemplifying realization of the concept of courage; only by being clothed with this or another concept is it an action at all, so to speak; it receives its essence from that concept, not from the life whose pulse-beat it comprises. Even if one rejects Plato's transcendent-substantializing expressions according to which the person, by acting so, participates in the idea of courage, nonetheless the basic motif is still operative. Relative to its meaning, its valuation, its placement, the act still appears, not as the whole life of the individual now realizing itself just *so*, but rather as a realization of the concept of courage. From the perspective of these

paraphrases of the conceptually expressible contents of action, the current element in life is admittedly a mere piece within it, one that forms the whole life
only together with others (thus, e.g., rational with sensory, practical with theoretical, individualistic with social). This manner of reflection is doubtless necessary and useful, since for us life tends to be of significance (as much for action as for knowledge) only through its connections to such real and ideal
series and values, and to its consequences that stretch from these to itself. But
seen from the source point where the act actually is formed, it is not an "act of
courage" (this half-poetic manner of speaking nonetheless has for rationalism
a somehow realistically intended basis), but rather it is the present actuality of
this total life and thus, when it comes to ethical responsibility, it may only be
judged and evaluated on the basis of what the entire Ought of this life indicates at this position. As an unfolding of the single life, the Ought is just as
amenable to firm (even if dissimilar) qualitative polarities as those I earlier
emphasized, concerning the actuality-form of life, in arguing against the superstition that the innateness of character constrains us within an essentially
always homogeneous attitude. Precisely on this account, the Ought, directed
towards the point of responsibility, cannot be determined according to a universal law. Certainly courage is good as such, and greed is evil as such, and as a
universal law one could only wish that the one should be and the other not.
But what the actions so named signify in the series of an individual life—or,
more exactly, what they signify *as* this life (for they are still only the momentary representations of its totality and thus only judgeable from its whole
Ought)—is not yet thereby determined. With this point, the ethical significance of this very detailed discussion emerges: that in every action it is the entire person who is productive, not an ever-so-rarified "psychic capacity" that
ultimately leads to the circle in which our greedy behavior proceeds from our
greed and our courageous behavior from our courage. Universal law that must,
even as formal, always translate itself into a material one for praxis defines the
entire person by the transvital, transindividual significance of a rationalized
action-content; as is now properly shown, it *cannot* do otherwise at all, but it
applies an unsuitable means to the task because it imposes its demand from
the conceptualization of an isolated content rather than from the lived totality
of the person. Our thinking sketched here proceeds contrariwise: that the person, in the totality of his life conceived as a unitary continuity, should be something, that he has an ideal given with this life to actualize himself, an ideal
whose essence (like that of life itself) is to develop as ceaselessly changing,
often perhaps logically mutually contradictory actions. This demand does not,
as might be supposed, have to do with the universal "good conscience," which

always requires further norms for its individually practical development. Here, from the principle that in every action the entire person is productive, the individual action is now morally determined by the whole person—not by the actual, but by the obliged, which is given with the individual life just as the actual is. An action must create its obligatory quality from this and not from a life-transcending abstraction of the action into the universal; logically it must do so, because the ideal continuity of life (since it is *life*), has its existence exclusively in elevating its totality into (admittedly singularly *namable*) contents of action.

Naturally in every given instant it always comes down only to some particular ethically demanded act. Yet such an act is ethically required only on account of its belonging to an entire, ideally prescribed life. For to the Ought belongs the possibility (however understood) that we conform or do not conform to it with our actuality. Now we can well imagine an entire life, bursting forth from the same point of germination, otherwise than the actual one. However, it seems truly absurd that a particular act could be "otherwise" than as it has occurred; for then it is another, and not the same that is nonetheless different. At best, if one ignores the hard autonomy of its content (which can only be as it is, or not at all), places life purely under the viewpoint of process that has dissolved the content into its fluidity, and now grasps the particular act as the immediate actual configuration of this life-entirety—only then could one demand of it that it ought to be otherwise than it is. For that is the incomparable quality in organic existence, highest of all in the soul, which lives as a whole—that it can be changed and yet be the same. The usual illustration of this fundamental phenomenon—the somehow substantial, fixed ego, or even the ego that persists only in identity of form or function—is surely utterly incommensurate with the actual state of things; this inner knowledge of the identity of the individual amid full variability evidently extending into the deepest level is a fundamental fact in the face of which, for the present, all analytic conceptualizations fail. Thus, only if this character of life stays bound to the motif that the particular act is the present, full expression of this entire life can this act have any part at all in that "capacity to be otherwise." But this motif is nonetheless also connected with the ever-reappearing proposition that we are certainly free in the whole of life, yet the particular is determined. And this is only an expression for the fact that the Ought is also a totality from which the particular act cannot be lifted out into a circumscribed self-responsibility.

If the relation of each conceptual, temporal, and phenomenal boundedness to the totality of an individual life process is grasped in this sense, then it is obviously valid for each of the categories under which the unity of this process can proceed: as the actuality of an individual life in general rises to its respective present reality, so too the Ought likewise rises to its respective duty.

:::

We thus oppose all efforts to derive the Ought from the material or the formal relationships of its contents. Naturally, every Ought exists in these, if they are obligations. The difference pertains only to this: *on what basis* they are prescribed, from what authority they receive their ethical selection and their ethical accents. While the solution is sought here in a uniquely determined concept of life, we should not consider the significance of the contents as thereby excluded. Rather, this Ought—when it is recognized as a form of each individual life coordinated with its actuality-form—accepts all possible linkages external to itself, remaining by its breadth far less prejudicial than the moralism of the categorical imperative with its tie to the demand for universality; for all ties, demands, impulses—whether social or fateful, rational or religious, or stemming from the thousand conditions of the environment—surely influence this life itself; duty is determined according to the filling and forming that life experiences from these. Because life is fulfilled only in individuals, the creation of moral norms is in principle an individual process. Yet therefore the establishment of law and universal law, as it dominates ethics and is developed to the purest abstraction in the Kantian view, perhaps does not possess the logical or self-evident necessity claimed for it. And further—though I may deduce what I have to do ever so precisely from the material relations of things and from laws that arise outside of me—ultimately or primarily *I* have it to do, it belongs to *my* circle of duties, and *my* life-image [*Daseinsbild*] is a more or less valuable one by its completion or neglect. If we do not admit this sense of individuality (which by the way does not mean unique incomparability)—the emergence of duty out of the irreplaceable, unmistakable point of unity or, what is here the same thing, the totality of the living ego as the present moment of the ideal life thus determined—then I do not see how we can get to real responsibility, and hence to the innermost area of the ethical problem.

To deepen and clarify, we must reiterate above all that the Ought does not derive from a purpose at all. We are obliged, not from such a purpose, but from ourselves; the Ought as such is no teleological process. This naturally does not apply to the *content* of the Ought, which in fact continually presents itself under the category of purpose: on innumerable occasions we ought to make ourselves simply into means for ends [*Zwecke*] that supersede minimal individual existence and in respect to which, as ends in themselves, we do not matter in the least. But *that* we should do this, that it claims us under the category of duty—this again is not itself dependent on the purpose we serve with the actuality [*Tatsächlichkeit*] of such action [*Handelns*]. Admittedly, when seen from the viewpoint of the external forces that surround us, this too is not an autonomous, but a teleological event: society, the State, the church, the vocational or family circle enjoin on us those duties toward altruistic, selfless actions as means for the purposes of these institutions. Yet on that account, because it is *demanded* of us, it is still far from being ethically obligated, since as a *demand* we cannot distinguish the ethically acknowledged from the unjustified. Accordingly, the decision that the one should serve as duty for us, and the other should not, cannot come from the purposes its content serves without a vicious circle; rather, it can only be established as an immediate fact, developed from the interior of life itself, though absolutely surpassing its reality. The ethical in action cannot as such be a means (however much its content may make us into a mere "means"-element of social, cultural, spiritual, religious series) without being separated from its essential root and decomposed into the linking of particular, objective occurrences.[4]

We may even, with full justice, recognize any number of sanctions of a rational, objective, social kind: the act becomes *my* duty only by incorporation into the duty-series determined by my entire life-image [*Daseinsbild*]. For no one can name a single action, a single universal law, to which we are not compelled under certain circumstances, as *our* duty, to refuse recognition—in other words, there is none whose *material content* does not have above it as the ultimate authority the following question: is it then *my* duty, does it belong to the objective-ideal configuration of *my* life? The decision remains reserved

4. Kant has very well understood the impossibility of sanctioning the Ought through the content of duty. But he is nonetheless so thoroughly caught in the category of ends that he then attempts the clever twist of making morality, or obligation as a whole, the ultimate end of life. But the fact that he then reties it to the rationalism of the "universal" law again makes illusory the liberation of the moral from any character as means. For at this point it is once again a mere means to the end of helping into existence a logicized, rational-legal world. Seen from this last motif, even the categorical imperative is not really categorical but instead dependent on whether we want or should have a logical world, because the imperative is legitimated only as a means to this end of a logical world—just as the truth value of Kant's theoretical a priori is conditioned by the fact that we recognize the validity of experiential knowledge, and it is lost in the instant in which we deny it recognition on some ground or other, or on no ground at all. Even here, the fact that action by its individual moral *content* turns us on countless occasions toward higher, more universal purposes tempts one to subordinate even the Ought as Ought to that broader ideal purpose, and to base its existence on this subordination (i.e., on something transcendent to it). Principles of ethics divide on the question of whether the Ought as ethical emerges from or comes to life—and "rational morality" also maintains the latter view. For with the concept of "autonomy," rational morality only conceals its assumption that judgment of ourself [*die Vernunft unseres Selbst*] is content-based logic somehow transformed into us and represented by us, but is at the same time on *its* side ideally or metaphysically autonomous—in other words, that self-judgment exists outside of the self to which it prescribes its "ultimate purpose."

to the sense and constellations of my whole life even when it demands the sacrifice of this very life; for even death can take only the living unto itself. Yet this means that even if all particular duty-contents were to come to us from those domains, the decision concerning them cannot be composed from them themselves, or from any number of *particular* purposes and norms, but rather remains reserved to the unity and continuity of life. I mean only that this very combination is here not simply empirical actuality—for only actualities can ever be derived from actualities as such, never, without μεταβασισ εισ αλλο γενοσ,[5] a *demand*. The form of the demand must instead subsist beforehand (i.e., life must already originally proceed under the category of the Ought)—regardless at which point this appears in the chronology of empirical consciousness. Or otherwise expressed, the respective Ought is a function of the total life of the individual personality.

To see how far removed this basic theme is from all subjectivism, all arbitrariness, and all contingency, everything depends upon the differentiation of otherwise fused concepts. Up to now the moral demand seemed to be referred for its sanction to this decision: either it is that which presents itself as obligatory in subjective consciousness, in a decision based on personal conscience, or it comes from the objective, from a superindividual precept drawing its validity from its material-conceptual consequences. In contrast to this choice, I believe a third way exists: the objective Ought of this very individual, the demand imposed from *his* life onto *his* life and in principle independent of whether he really recognizes it or not. Again, a new distinction, and a new synthesis of concepts, is required here: the individual does not have to be subjective, nor the objective transindividual. The decisive concept is rather the following: the objectivity of the individual. Once a firmly individualized life exists as an objective fact in the full sense, then its ideal Ought is there also as an objectively valid thing, in such a fashion that true and false notions about it can be formed, both by its subject and by other subjects.

I will illustrate this with the analysis of a simple example. Let us imagine an antimilitarist who is convinced that war and military service are utterly condemnable and evil, and who avoids patriotic military duty, not only with a peaceful conscience, but also with the sacred conviction of thereby doing the ethically right and unconditionally required thing. Now, when his conduct is nonetheless judged, when the fulfillment of that patriotic claim is demanded precisely as ethical although it may be wholly irrelevant how he thinks about it subjectively—then I do not know how one who denies an "erring conscience"

---

5. "Transition to another kind" (to apply propositions to matters that lie outside their domain).—Trans.

can reconcile this situation. But it is also not at all sufficient simply to introduce state authority and *salus publica* as sanction. The fact that the latter exists
as a power for which the issue is only the fulfillment of its demand, not the
inner perspective of the performing subject—this fact in itself signifies not yet
an *ethical* claim on this subject. And if all objective earthly and supernal orders
surrounded the person and presented their claims to him, still *he* has to fulfill
them; and if it is to be an *ethical* act, then they must come out of him as claims,
must represent the Ought located in *his* being—what comes to him as a demand from outside, from however ideal and value-filled an outside, can only
be material of the authentic ethical Ought, and must first be legitimated by the
latter as ethical for this person. On this basis, which tolerates no compromise
or concession, I certainly believe nonetheless that the antimilitarist really is
ethically obligated to armed service, although his subjective moral consciousness condemns it. For the individuality that lives in the form of the Ought is
not something ahistorical, nonmaterial, or only consisting of so-called character. It is much more determined by, or includes as an ineluctable element,
that this person is (we would suppose) a citizen of a specific state. Everything
that surrounds him and that he has ever experienced, the strongest drives of
his temperament along with the most ephemeral impressions—all this forms
the personality in that flowing life and from all of it there grows, just like an
actuality, an Ought. "Not only the innate, but also the acquired, is the person"
(Goethe). By all means, from outside only the *demand* for armed service can
approach this person; that its fulfillment is his duty, regardless whether he
agrees to it or not, stems from the quite boundless, indissoluble interweaving
of nation-state powers and values into his individual existence; and from this
therefore the duty of his armed service can arise, as a thoroughly objective
superstructure or neighboring structure to his reality. Now, whether he knows
this duty, recognizes or fails to recognize it is just as irrelevant for this sphere
as it is for the reality of his existence whether he judges correctly or wrongly
about it. Naturally it is sufficient for the abbreviated manner of expression of
habitual practice if one declares armed service morally obligatory "because the
State demands it." But for the ultimate ethical question, which comes from
the person's real point of responsibility, it is not sufficient. Here that demand
of the State operates only insofar as belonging to the State is woven into the
actual being or life of the individual, such that the Ought (as which this life
fulfils itself ideal-ethically) includes the fulfillment of that demand—but at
that point the demand is utterly independent of everything subjective.

The decisive element, however, is that the individual life is not anything
subjective, but rather—without somehow losing its limitation to this individual—is thoroughly objective as an ethical Ought. The false fusion between

individuality and subjectivity must be dissolved, just like that between universality and lawfulness. The concepts will thereby become free to form new
syntheses between individuality and lawfulness. If a universal-lawfulness sta-
bilized beyond life and its individual process were merely removed, without its
replacement bearing the full character of objective lawfulness, then we would
glimpse in the latter no corresponding expression of ideal or real ethical actuality. Rather, only an individual *law* can come into the question, a law that
stands as far from all subjectivism and all anarchy as the universal, deduced
from conceptual Right, asserts of itself. The discrepancy that exists here can be
illustrated in the obviously very widely cited characters of Russian life. In Russian novels, from *Hero of Our Time*[6] through *Ssanin*,[7] we encounter innumerable people who refuse everything objective, every material obligation, every
subordination under a higher universal, and whose life from beginning to end
is a purely individual one; but the consciousness and will of these people very
seldom stand under the individual *law* of that life. Because they feel somehow
entitled to reject the validity of all matters outside their individuality, they fall
on the other side of that alternative which is asserted ultimately even by Kant
and the whole universal-rational morality: into the instability of individuality,
once it is allowed to operate merely as subjectivity.

I have previously argued that a universal ethical law, even in its highest
formal acuity in the categorical imperative, can only ever be directed toward
the individual act firmly circumscribed by its content. The act receives its conceptually demonstrable valuation from the applicable law according to this
content (which by nature need not be carried out, but only intended by good
or evil will). The notable and decidedly suggestive element of this course of
judgment is the objectivity it seems to give to the ethical domain, which itself
is easily felt to be precarious and questionable, and only subjectively determined. While its regulations do not come from the unobservable interior of
the subject and correspondingly so to speak do not become involved at all
with the sliding, scarcely conceptually definable flux of life, here a *materiality*
[*Sachlichkeit*] of moral determination decidedly and decisively comes to the
fore. As in the theoretical realm the universal validity of a perception only
means that it is *materially* true, so here moral universality of validity and
recognition goes back to the *material* meaning and configuration of the life-
contents. By "material" I naturally understand not a connection to something
external but, rather, that the factors of ethical conduct—impulses and maxims, inner emotions and tangible consequences—figure as objective elements

6. Novel by Mikhail Lermontov, 1839.—Trans.
7. Or *Sanin*. Novel by Mikhail Artsybashev, 1904.—Trans.

representing a material content [*Sachgehalt*] from which then the connection to the highest compulsory norm logically follows. The meaning and relation of practical contents, freed ideally from the individual in whom they are realized, release from themselves the moral necessity of definite kinds of conduct. Because this holds with conceptual necessity for each case in which the conditions apply, the conclusion appears justified: where the universal validity of a law is immediately felt or proposed as logically possible or actual, this is a sign that it has drawn that necessity out of the material contents of the practical world. While the linkage of practical law to possible or actual universality at first glance heralds a violation of the one by the many, a leveling of the special by the typical, there certainly need not here be any social (or, as Schleiermacher calls it in Kant, political) motivation; rather, only the conditions and content of praxis are elevated into an ideal, conceptually expressible autonomy beyond their individual bearer, and from them the logic of morality develops those formations in which these contents *ought* to take place. Thus regarded, the universal validity that the categorical imperative demands for the maxim of the particular act is only the symptom or distinguishing sign for the fact that the act is "right" in the pure material sense of its content. That is the sense in which Kant declares his formula valid not only for all people but for all imaginable rational beings. In ultimate metaphysical absoluteness, an imperative that is valid for all men would nevertheless have only individual meaning, because mankind is an individual construct. Only when it applies materially [*sachlich*] is it really superindividual. But it remains admittedly problematic whether the Kantian insertion of materiality [*Sachlichkeit*] and reasonableness rightly holds its own, and whether this reason, supposedly not conditioned by humans, is not perhaps a very human-historic product. Regardless of this, however, it is perfectly clear that this ethical determination by a superindividual, extravital, material content of the act belongs to the essential, practical outlook (which is one of the greatest, infinitely significant partisan choices of the spirit). Sketched from the viewpoint of its similarly essential opposition, it is the way of thinking that punishes the deed because it belongs by its content to those that are in principle punishable but not the doer who is merely the *in se* indifferent bearer of the *in se* punishable action; the attitude that in pedagogy places all value on the learning material to be implanted, on the notion that the pupil possess a certain sum of objective knowledge, while his "education"—as fulfillment of the spiritual life process to which all learning (beyond its technical necessity) is ultimately only means—remains out of consideration; the attitude in medicine that treats illness (with dogmatically prescribed means) in a way as a fixed construct abstracted from the continuous living context of the entire body, but does not treat the entire organism in whose holistic function the illness is embedded (treating the illness, in other words, and not the patient). Doubtless this isolating objectification of life-contents which makes of them a meaningful, self-sufficient materiality per se is a stage of cultural development that cannot be leapt over. It makes possible a knowledge perhaps not attainable by other paths, and allows specialized cultivation of important domains. But just as unavoidable is the further stage: the redissolution of these rigid, so to speak substantializing objectifications into the flowing relations, the functional, holistic linkages of the life-unity to which they belong. But here follows the task: to discern or work out (in this much more fluctuating, problem-rich way of thinking, implicating genuinely immense factors) the pure and firm objectivity that in historical development can perhaps only be demanded and achieved with the individualizing framing and conceptual fixing of those objective contents—obviously one of the most all-embracing and deepest themes in the world-history of the Spirit.

This now determines the entire transition, expounded here, from the morality of the rational-universal law to that of the individual law. I do not ignore the vastness, power, and historical necessity of the ethical valuation that subordinates purely practical, material content to an objective law (as this presents itself to infinitely many persons and indifferently toward their individual life-context, as a timeless element within or opposing the temporality of the latter), a material particular to a material universal. The issue here is not even progress from a theoretically incomplete knowledge to a theoretically more adequate one—rather, in accord with the essence of philosophy and especially of ethics, a certain spiritual-historical stage has been reached for whose basic inclination and central attitude one interpretation of the genetic meaning and home of the ethical is the more appropriate, the "truer" expression, than the other. Whether the extension of objective value to the Ought, as to a form in which individual life flows, can be logically proven does not enter into the matter. Likewise, though, I can hardly see a logical reason why full objectivity should *not* befit a law that is born from the authentic and total life of him for whom it is valid. The givenness of this individual life is the premise for just as strict a demand of the Ought, dominant over all subjective arbitrariness; yet the quantitative expression of this objectivity exists, not in its validity for as many as may be, but only for this individual life.

As a kind of analogy, we observe an individual law in the so-to-speak morphological coherence of the human exterior and interior. We know no universal law, not even problematically, on whose basis the necessity of a specific interior may be deduced from some given exterior as a function of the latter. Nonetheless, we have the sure feeling that the two are not bound together by chance, but rather that the being thus-and-so of the one is bound inevitably to the being thus-and-so of the other—even if empirically neither body nor soul are formed purely according to this personal law, because impersonal forces often mightily and unevenly influence them. It belongs in a certain sense to those laws of which Goethe says that in occurrence only their exceptions are to be found; the deepest task of individualizing portraiture is to make this law meaningfully felt beyond these exceptions, even if it is not actually formulable. Yet in every case the law is obviously as individual as man himself is, and holds this body together with this soul just as necessarily as if these inner-outer qualities in their relatedness were calculable according to a formula valid for all.

Now the concept of the individual law requires the most decisive statement that the sense of individuality that first presents itself—being-other and being-special, the qualitative incomparability of the particular—is *not* in question here. We are concerned not with uniqueness, but with the true character in whose form every organic life, and above all psychic life, proceeds—with growth from one's own root. So much that is erroneous and inadequate attaches to the concept of the individual precisely because we often see its content only in the specific *difference* by which the individual is distinguished from the universal, from what is shared with other individuals. But this distinction does not pertain to the individual in his essential reality; the latter is instead a living unity, to and in which the comparable and noncomparable elements coordinate fully and to this extent intermingle and work together without inner differences of rank. The individual is the *whole* person, not the remainder left over when one takes away from this person everything that also falls to others. Admittedly, in a certain sense qualitative uniqueness may not be denied, especially because we maintain that each particular Ought represents the entire personality, and that an entire life, however much it may have in common with others, really experiences a double incomparability: first, in the deepest level of personality which each person feels, unprovably yet incontrovertibly, he cannot share with anyone or impart to anyone (the qualitative loneliness of personal life, whose isolation is felt to the degree of one's self-awareness); and second—alongside this so-to-speak localized individuality, withdrawn into the nonextensive aspect of life—the whole embrace of our existence. Though individuals may agree in many particular segments of the latter, the totality of a life-course with really *all* external and internal qualifications and experiences surely does not repeat itself a second time. The comparable areas, whose contents alone can provide room for universal laws of reality and of demand, lie as it were in the middle layers of the personality; its most inward center and its phenomenal totality both have the cachet of the incomparable, of that which exists only once. Yet however this occurs, the autonomy of the

Ought identified here does not affect this incomparability, because inequality with others can condition this autonomy as little as (so Kant would have it) equality with others can condition it. Both reside to this extent at the same level, because the Ought that arches over the individual life—or, rather, *as* this life—stands in its inner meaning beyond every comparison, no matter to which result it may lead. The qualitative differentiation of ethical conduct is by no means so utterly opposed to the principle of universal law as it appears. Of course, it can be considered even a *universal* law that each should behave absolutely differently than every other. (The ethics of Schleiermacher and that of the Romantics in general lies in this direction.) However, because it would thereby prescribe a defined (if only *in abstracto*) *content* of action originating externally, it would in principle be a different law than that individual one which, entirely unprejudiced in relation to action's contents, confronts their entire immensity of similarity and difference. The distinction must thus be made elsewhere than is usually done: not between uniformity or universality and individuality in the sense of particularity, but rather between content and individuality in the sense of life. For the whole question is whether the norm should be determined by where action originates, by life, or by where action is headed, by an ideal exterior of life, by content. And the whole third element set forth here is this: that determination by a terminus a quo, by life, does not restrict it to a naturalistically real causality; instead, this life itself, otherwise than as actual or as ideal, proceeds as Ought; and it tends not to draw the ethical claim from a source outside itself (even "reason" has shown itself to be such an external source as against the life totality), but encompasses it as its own developmental process, though indifferent to that process in its unfolding as actuality.

This principle is thus of equal validity for the sort of uniformity of beings that determines the universal law and for the sort of diversity of them which makes the law inapplicable. It therefore entirely excludes the motif by which the individual so often loves to extricate himself (rightly or wrongly from a substantive viewpoint) from the following universal law: that he is different from others, that he does not belong in the general scheme, that what applies for all other cases does not apply for him, etc. This cannot serve any longer. If you are otherwise than all others, then on that account an ideally prescribed Ought exists no less for you than for all others, for it comes from your own life, not from a content that is determined by the possibility of being universalized (and thus perhaps does not include your case at all). Where individuality and law pull against one another, the individual can always say the following: the law doesn't apply to me, it is not *my* law. But the arbitrariness possible here is immediately excluded by the individual law, which rests entirely on the basis that individuality is nothing less than subjectivity or arbitrariness: if actuality—the one form in which individuality lives—possesses objectivity, then the other form, the Ought, possesses it no less.

Now rationalistic ethics could still try to produce the valuation of the act as an admittedly individual one in such a way that a universal law is sought for the entire abundance of its partial contents, for all its determinations from its individual life-contexts; the relevant definitive normalization would then result from the combined effects or balancing out of all these laws. The categorical imperative itself—whose height of abstraction at least in principle rises above every a priori *particular* stipulation of ethics, in that, when it becomes concrete, it must be detailed in special maxims—appears to make imaginable such an envelopment that would allow no element of the act outside itself. This would be an exact analogy to theoretical science, which obtains the factual behavior of an object as the sum or resultant of the effects of all laws that apply for each of its particular determinants. Now, it has been shown that a complete, all-encompassing determination of even the simplest real object in this fashion is not possible at all—for every such object contains such an infinity of characteristics and connections that we can assemble no sequence of concepts, and thus no sequence of laws, that could exhaust them; we must content ourselves with one-sided, particular definitions of things that omit infinitely much. Above all, this certainly also holds true against the attempt to assemble the moral claim on a moment of life—in all its complexity—from universal laws that hold for each particular one of its factors. But it is more important that knowledge-critical [*erkenntnis-kritische*] thought does not yet go far enough. The *quantum* of determinants of a reality may *in fact* suffice to thwart the attempt for a conceptually lawful stipulation of its complete totality; *in principle* the number of these totality-factors could nonetheless always correspond to a similar one of concepts and laws. On the contrary, however, there exists between the *mode* of actuality and that of our concepts a discrepancy, in consequence of which the latter can never so to speak catch up with the former. The determinants of a real thing have a continuity among themselves, a flowing gradation of transition into one another, that makes them utterly ungraspable for our firmly circumscribed concepts and their extension to natural laws. The artificial procedure that nonetheless creates the bridge between the two is not only an omission with respect to degree, but also a transformation with respect to kind and form. If we want to master the real with concepts, we must (on a justification not examined here) allow the gliding and the uninterrupted interrelationships [*Korrelativitäten*] in and between things to congeal into sharply separated pluralities, we must make the continuous discontinuous, and on all sides dam up the endless flow of connections to the next thing, up to the most distant. And obviously this transposition drives its factors farthest from each other when it deals with the application of concepts to, and the recognition of laws of, the living thing. For while the latter is conceived as a subject that somehow congeals among the transformations occurring with it, these transformations achieve an especially complete continuity, and the determinants of the (in this sense unitary) being reveal a fullness and a closeness of their relations that seem not to occur in mere mechanisms. Because of this, extracting and fixing particular determinants of the form of real organic being and occurrence is inadequate in the highest degree. Now, natural science may account for this inadequacy for itself, perhaps with the response that its intention and apriorities pertain to the self-sufficient realm of concepts and laws that require only a symbolic relation to reality. Since ethics stands much nearer to life in its immediacy, however, it becomes clear, even through the medium of this theoretical analogy, how foreign the essential form of the "universal law," which postulates a particular content, is to the essential form of life, which nevertheless *ought* to adapt its reality closely to it; how little an ever-so-vast accumulation of such laws of the motivation and multiplicity of life can fulfill—not from quantitative insufficiency, but on account of the discrepancy in the essential form of both.

Old-style objectivity is therefore not maintainable in this manner with respect to those claims which arise with the recognition of the Ought as a categorically proper and total form of the psychic life in general. But while this form likewise claims all objectivity for itself, it repels from itself not only all arbitrariness and unreliability, but also the popularly and dogmatically predominant meaning of practical subjectivism: eudaimonistic self-interest as ultimate telos. For the ethical life thus defined does not recoil upon the subject itself whatsoever. If it has always been asserted that such a life could not be based on its own happiness, this is in fact certainly true because happiness here is always thought of as the *aim* of the deed, and the fundamental ethical motivation [*Bewegtheit*] is determined, not by an aim at all, but by life growing from its own root (even if the specifiable *contents* of the motivation should always present themselves in the form of an aim). But even if it is otherwise correct—because this happiness represents a reflection of the act backwards into the subject, while the ethical act never runs in this reverse direction, but in the forward-striving direction of life as such—the exclusion of the eudaimonistic motive is yet only a fractional part of this very much larger definition in principle. Because of this, it would even be misleading to designate as perhaps the "perfection of the true personality" the demand—growing from the individual life and ideally building upon its reality, yet proceeding from it—that proves to be the opposite of the "universal" legitimation of life's particular content considered for itself. For as surely as this "perfection" is an objective value, even it is not simply an Ought-content beside which (because it is a particular, a priori specifiable one) others stand on the same level of justification, but that same naive lack of differentiation we have previously censured is implied in the fact that the ideal formation *issuing* from the individual life must also *return* to it with its contents. Instead, without denying its sources, and driven by them, it can pour itself into social, altruistic, spiritual, and artistic formations and see its respective final-purpose in these; on countless occasions life itself fulfils what is originally its own ideal, nourished only by its individual root, by distancing itself from itself, by giving itself up. If one wants to call this throughout a perfection of one's own personality, this can only be a label, not the ethically definitive final-purpose, because the sanction here in question can come, not from a terminus ad quem at all, but only from a terminus a quo, from the ideal of itself that advances with life itself.

This vitalizing and individualizing of ethicality is so foreign to all egoism and subjectivism (though this directly contradicts all of the amalgamations of thought whose justification I am directly challenging, and their naive dogmatism) that it not only brings with it no easing of the moral claim, but on the contrary tends to narrow the domain of "mitigating circumstances." Many of our acts, pardonable sins examined in isolation, only attain their full weight when we make clear to ourselves that our entire existence has pushed toward them, and that they will define our existence perhaps for the entire future—a criterion, however, that can only be valid for this individual life, and would be utterly senseless if generalized to any others who are not absolutely identical to me. Furthermore, we are now not only responsible for the question of whether we obey an existing law or not, but also even for the question of whether this law is valid for us; for it is valid for us only because we are these specific people whose being is somehow modified by every completed deed, and therewith the Ought-ideal steadily flowing from it is modified in the same instant. Instead of the truly bleak Nietzschean thought—"Can you desire that this action of yours recur infinitely often?"—I propose: "Can you desire that this action of yours should define your entire life?" For the fact that it does so is not even a question, once the tearing of life into discontinuous "acts" is given up. This development of the Ought behaves like that of theoretical values. Whether something is valid as truth for us depends on the entire complex of principles, methods, and experiential contents known by us at that moment, whose association with the new cognition legitimates the latter. But once this has occurred, the added element alters the situation in some manner that will seldom remain purely quantitative; instead it is apt to contain some set of determinants alongside those that led to its acceptance

under those former criteria, and because it is accepted as a whole, these determinants too are valid as truth and thus somehow or other further develop
or modify the totality of truths. The next proposition seeking legitimation
thus discovers an altered criteria-field. That is, in a more general formulation:
every recognized truth alters the conditions by which it itself is recognized
as truth. Now this holds likewise for the development of our life in terms of
the Ought. Because something arises as an ethical demand in the flow of our
life—formed by its prior course, standards, contents—this life is thereafter no
longer the same, but now offers the next element of this ethical life different
emergence- and validity-conditions than the ones under which the modifying element emerged and achieved validity. This naturally makes evident the
difficulties of ethical choice; by contrast, the domination of a universally valid
law, legislating inflexibly once and for all, makes this choice as easy as is the
orientation of life under a patriarchal despotism compared to that under the
autonomy of the free person. Because the flowing formation of life proceeds
as Ought, because the absolute of the demand becomes in this sense a historical one—but this historical demand is an absolute one—the normative
strictness goes deep below the level on which alone ethics previously sought
the responsibility of man, namely whether he actually acts according to the
existing Ought. But now this is not sufficient, because the Ought is already
our own life (under the category of ideality) and, as is correspondingly the
case under the category of reality, every moment of life lived to that point has
jointly formed, jointly conditioned each actual Ought. In Kant's ethics of duty,
the person is responsible only for his action. Duty is given to him, he discovers
it as an inflexible thing which he follows or not, but whose content is removed
from his decision. The infinitely more difficult responsibility—for setting up
this particular thing as a duty at all—seems thereby lifted from him. The logic
of the categorical imperative, with which one only has to go along, spares him
the creative aspect of the ethical realm, with its dangers and responsibilities.
Since Kant regards the act only on the value of its self-contained, purely self-
focused content (for even his exclusive valuation of conscience takes place in
an atomizing condensation to the respective act), the whole of life becomes
the sum of discontinuous particulars. Now because this nevertheless does not
satisfy life's felt actuality, because its unbroken unity somehow must have its
say, it unavoidably withdraws to a "pure ego," to a singularity or function with
respect to content, beyond change and multiplicity. The pure ego is the correlate of the image of life as a mere succession of particular acts, each forming
a self-accountable totality. In contrast to this stands my view, which does not
decompose life into ego as an empty process versus particular acts filled with

content but sees the form of its unity immediately in the fact that it expresses itself in changing contents or, more correctly, that it consists in their being lived and done. Thus the whole life is responsible for every act, and every act for the whole life, the contents as experienced are continuous because each one is only the respective height to which life rises. Alongside the *operari sequitur esse*[8] it is also true that *Esse sequitur operari.*[9] Every act works back upon the ground (not definable further) from which our action arises at all. *Thus the responsibility for our entire history already lies in the fact that every particular deed becomes obligatory [Gesolltwerden].*

Thus concludes the depiction of the continuity of life in both of its forms, here asserted to be coordinated. If, as I *believe*, life has such a character as to be—as a whole—its respective moment at any given time, and if the incomparable manner of its oneness consists of the very fact that the full contrariety of these moments in terms of content does not hinder it from presenting a personal life in its entirety, that every behavior is "life"—then the conditioning inclusion of the entire past in the current Ought is only another expression for this. And again it is only another expression, extending along another dimension, when in every particular obligation that confronts us as a formulable law we feel that so should we behave in this particular case, because we should conduct ourselves as whole people in a specific (if not in a similarly formulable) way. Even in the Ought, the whole determines the part, the whole lives in the part. Probably this respective individual-universal law may not be fixed conceptually; instead this is attained only by those more singular precepts that arise in its collisions with particular givens and situations. But this law of individual ethical holism is not on that account less valid and effective than its counterpart in the domain of actuality: that indescribable style and rhythm of a personality, its fundamental gestures, which make each of its expressions—called forth by situational factors—into something unmistakably belonging to it. Although we can never grasp this law purely, but only within a materially particular behavior as its formative power, we nonetheless know that the deepest determination of the individual being is experienced here. The fact that, correspondingly, the entirety of the individual personality's Ought without exception determines its current obligation is only the ethical elaboration of the fact that life in every moment is its totality. In this manner, account is taken of all the multiplicity of ethical situations and evolutions, and yet likewise of the unity, steadiness, and consequence of the ethical claim, which the ethic of

8. "Action follows being."—Trans.
9. "Being follows action."—Trans.

the universal laws thinks to achieve only in the mechanical, temporally enduring constancy of some set of *contents* of the moral value-domain (and even
the mere *form* of the universal law is in this sense still a content and must be
converted into such a content.)

Thus, on the basis that the "law of the individual" (regardless, by the way,
of whether we label what is meant here with this or another slogan) completely reverses the direction of the Ought, and that it is generated by the life
process instead of the life contents, it broadens the normative demand simultaneously along two dimensions beyond the domain that Kant and really all
of moral philosophy had allotted to it. Everything varying, or by definition
unique, or gliding in the continuity of life without assignable boundaries; everything that eludes any subordination under a preexisting law and likewise
eludes conceptual sublimation to a universal law—all this now finds an Ought
over it, because the latter itself is a life and retains its continuing form. And
indeed because the demand does not confront life as a rigid once-and-for-all,
everything we have ever done and everything we have ever been obligated to
is the condition under which our ethical-ideal life rises to the crest of what
is currently obligated. Just as each pulse-beat of a living being is determined
by all its past pulse-beats, likewise nothing can be lost in this process, which
makes not only the act but also the Ought of every moment into the heir
and the bearer of responsibility of all that we have ever been, done, and been
obligated to. Thus is finally completed the differentiation—the freeing, so to
speak—of the elements of whose amalgamation in Kant's ethics these pages
have so often spoken: that only the *actual*, but not the ideal-normative, can be
individual, and only the universal, not the individual, can be lawful—these are
the linkages whose undoing has been accomplished on this long path, so that
the linkage of individuality and lawfulness could be accomplished.

Journal Aphorisms, with an Introduction

Georg Simmel

Translated by John A. Y. Andrews

German text published as "Fragmente aus dem nachgelassenen Tagebuche" in *Georg Simmel Gesamtausgabe*, vol. 20, ed. Torge Karlsruhen and Otthein Rammstedt (Frankfurt: Suhrkamp, 2004), 261–301.

Introduction

Beyond his strenuous efforts to review the proofs of *The View of Life* in the weeks leading up to his death on September 26, 1918, Simmel prepared instructions for the management of his literary estate. Rights to previously published works passed to his wife Gertrud Simmel (née Kinel), but the disposition of unpublished manuscripts was entrusted to his pupil and former secret lover, Gertrud Kantorowicz.[1] Simmel requested that she prepare two of these—a collection of aphorisms and a brief essay on love—for publication in *Logos*, a journal for the philosophy of culture he had been involved with since its founding in 1910.

At his bedside during his last weeks of life, Kantorowicz began compiling—from Simmel's "large journal bound in brown leather"—the short entries translated here. Conditions associated with the end of World War I delayed the work, but the "Journal Aphorisms" went to press the following summer and was published in December (Simmel 1919). (Further difficulties delayed "On Love," which appeared two years later [Simmel 1921, 116–75; Levine 1971, 235–48].) The "Journal Aphorisms" generated so much public interest that *Logos* sought permission from Kantorowicz—unsuccessfully—to publish the Simmel journal in its entirety or else to publish a special reprint of the Simmel aphorisms. In lieu of this, in 1923 Kantorowicz published independently an anthology that included these and other previously unpublished manuscripts under the title *Fragmente und*

---

1. For further details on these matters, see Rammstedt and Karlsruhen (2004).

Aufsätze: Aus dem Nachlaß und Veröffentlichungen der letzten Jahre (*Fragments and Essays: From the Estate and Publications of the Last Years*).[2]

A number of threads connect "Journal Aphorisms" and *The View of Life*. For one thing, some evidence indicates that the material in the journal evolved over the same years that Simmel developed his earlier *Logos* essays into his mature work on *View*, between 1912 and 1918. In a collection of sixteen aphorisms in 1915 Simmel had published material that reappeared in the "Journal Aphorisms." As to the journal itself, Simmel's son Hans recollected in 1941 certain passages from 1912 through the war years that could have come from the journal.[3]

What is more, a number of the "Journal Aphorisms" express in condensed form the themes found in *View* or its antecedents. Thus, aphorism 7 points clearly to the project of chapter 4 of *View*, in particular toward that part of the project that drove the addition of new material in 1918, as against the earlier version in *Logos* (Simmel 1913); namely, how to provide the law of the individual with a grounding beyond mere subjective caprice. Likewise, the segue in aphorism 7 to "the eternal significance of the temporal" points to the relationship of ephemeral and fixed aspects of objects of consciousness detailed in the excursus of chapter 4. Aphorisms 21 and 22 touch poignantly on the question of what traces one leaves behind—whether in the form of species survival (more-life), created thought (more-than-life), or (interestingly, in view of Simmel's foundational contrast between more-life and more-than-life) a third group of traces that propagate the effects of one's existence and actions. Aphorisms 20, 21, 45, and others pick up the theme advanced in chapter 1 of *View* that situates human life (and, along with it, human freedom) in a middle position between boundaries or contrasting ideals: Ego and Idea, subject and object, person and cosmos, and the like. Elements of "turning to the idea" and of the "worlds" of objective culture found in chapter 2 of *View* appear in aphorisms 39 and 47 among others. Aphorisms 83 and 84 again pick up, this time from the direction of guilt, chapter 4's discussion that guilt and sin cannot attach or be restricted to abstracted acts torn out of the fabric of ongoing life, as Kant would have it, but must needs embody and refer back to the entire life as fully lived.

On the other hand, certain aphorisms offer positions somewhat at odds with those of *View*. For instance, aphorism 96 appears not fully to reflect Simmel's move in *View* to understand life as the overarching framework within which to understand the various "worlds" of which art is one—a later formulation might have contrasted art with Ought, perhaps, rather than art with life.

2. Ibid.

3. Alternately, Hans's recollections may have referred merely to loose notations that were also among the unpublished materials and that, along with the journal, disappeared without a trace into the rapacious hands of the Gestapo in the early 1940s (Rammstedt and Karlsruhen 2004, 523n77).

Beyond the connections with *View*, however, it is worth noting in these a diversity of themes less prominent or not represented in *View*, but reminiscent of earlier discussions in Simmel's work. Aphorism 60 offers a defense of "superficiality" as a necessary protection against the irreconcilability of competing demands—and in doing so, reflects Simmel's lifelong interest in taking the superficial seriously. Aphorisms 126 and 166 briefly reprise his earlier work on subordination/superordination and conflict (Simmel 1908, 160–283). Aphorism 154 contains a curious echo of *The Philosophy of Money* (Simmel 1900; trans. Simmel 1978) when it associates the modern shift from "use-value" to "scarcity-value" with the notion of "mystery"—and aphorism 160 reechoes, in reference to war, some of the same work's connections between means/ends and their relation to value.

It is indeed a curious and delightful paradox that in contrast to his essays, some of whose sentences and paragraphs seem to spill endlessly from point to point, these polished nuggets with their compact forms often lead to insights nearly as deep as those of the four metaphysical chapters.

REFERENCES

Kantorowicz, Gertrud, ed. 1923. Vorwort. In *Fragmente und Aufsätze: Aus dem Nachlaß und Veröffentlichungen der letzten Jahre*, by Georg Simmel, v–x. München: Drei-Masken-Verlag.

Levine, Donald N. 1971. *Georg Simmel on individuality and social forms*. Chicago: University of Chicago Press.

Rammstedt, Otthein, and Torge Karlsruhen, eds. 2004. Editorischer Bericht. In vol. 20 of *Georg Simmel Gesamtausgabe*. Frankfurt: Suhrkamp, 481–553.

Simmel, Georg. 1900. Philosophie des Geldes. In vol. 6 of *Georg Simmel Gesamtausgabe*, ed. David P. Frisby and Klaus Christian Köhnke. Frankfurt: Suhrkamp.

———. 1908. Soziologie: Untersuchungen über die Formen der Vergesellschaftung. In vol. 11 of *Georg Simmel Gesamtausgabe*, ed. Otthein Rammstedt. Frankfurt: Suhrkamp.

———. 1913. Das individuelle Gesetz: Ein Versuch über das Prinzip der Ethik. In vol. 12 of *Georg Simmel Gesamtausgabe*, ed. Rüdiger Kramme und Angela Rammstedt. Frankfurt: Suhrkamp.

———. 1915. Aus einer Aphorismensammlung. In vol. 17 of *Georg Simmel Gesamtausgabe*, ed. Klaus Christian Köhnke, 132–35. Frankfurt: Suhrkamp.

———. 1919. Fragmente aus dem nachgelassenen Tagebuche. In vol. 20 of *Georg Simmel Gesamtausgabe*, ed. Torge Karlsruhen and Otthein Rammstedt, 261–301. Frankfurt: Suhrkamp.

———. 1921. Über die Liebe. In vol. 20 of *Georg Simmel Gesamtausgabe*, ed. Torge Karlsruhen and Otthein Rammstedt, 116–75. Frankfurt: Suhrkamp.

———. 1978. *The philosophy of money*. Trans. Tom Bottomore and David Frisby. London: Routledge & Kegan Paul.

Journal Aphorisms

I know that I shall die without spiritual heirs (and that is as it should be). Mine is like a cash legacy divided among many heirs, and each converts his share into whatever business suits *his* nature, in which the provenance from that legacy cannot be seen.

1   The usual notion is as follows: here is the natural world, there the transcendent, we belong to one of the two. But no, we belong to a third one beyond words, of which both the natural and the transcendent are reflections, projections, forgeries, and interpretations.

2   We feel the empirical, historically contingent Ego as less than our self, and the pure, absolute Ego as more than our self. Therefore there must be, so to speak, still a third Ego that holds them both. Roughly as we consist of body and soul, and yet we are something that *has* a body and *has* a soul.

3   It is only possible for the conceptual world and the thing-in-itself to confront one another through the fact that the concept—taken absolutely—embraces both. But perhaps one can say exactly the same of the thing-in-itself.

4   The phenomena of nature are conceived to be in restless mutation and transience, but thought retains its conceptual form. Nature is the ever-constant, undeviating One; but thoughts are manifold, alternating, playing around it in opposites and pure relativity.

5   The indispensable condition on its own does not suffice to produce concrete reality—and sufficient conditions are not indispensable.

6   The richness of form is that it can adopt an infinity of contents—the richness of content, that it can enter into an infinity of forms. Where both infinities meet, the finite construct emerges—and that is why they hover around every being that is viewed as formed content, and make each into a symbol of the infinite.

7   My problem is: the objectification of the subject or rather the desubjectification of the individual (the former is more a matter for Kant and Goethe); and likewise it is: the eternal significance of the temporal.

8   There are three categories of philosophers: the first listen to the heartbeat of things, the second only to that of men, the third only to that of concepts; and a fourth (professors of philosophy) who listen only to the heart of literature.

9   The philosopher is supposed to be the one who says what everyone knows—but sometimes he is the one who *knows* what everyone only says.

10   Everything that is proven can be disputed. Only the unprovable is indisputable.

11   That there is something which is beyond belief and which we really know—*that* we can only believe. But that there is something which is beyond knowing and which we can only believe—*that* we really know.

12   We only really believe we understand things when we have traced them back to that which we do not and cannot understand—to causality, to axioms, to God, to character.

13   What is beyond knowledge is not what lies *behind* the scientific image of things (the obscure, the in-itself, the ungraspable)—on the contrary, it is

precisely the immediate, the fully sensual image [*Bild*], the attractive surface of things. Knowledge ends not on the far side of science, but on its near side. The fact that we cannot express in concepts what we can see, touch, experience—that we cannot indifferently shape them into forms of knowledge—we construe this fact so erroneously as though something mysterious and unknowable lurks behind the contents of precisely these forms.

14   There probably is an absolutely necessary and valid Apriori, but we can never know what it is—for the criterion that would permit us to know it would itself already have to possess the absoluteness to which it was only supposed to lead us. Similarly, it probably requires authority for life in general to achieve a maximum of ethical, aesthetic, and other values. But what that authority is supposed to be, we do not know—for in order to know it with the same confidence as we seek from it, we would either require a further authority with respect to which the question is repeated, or we must already have precisely that knowledge that, by assumption, we cannot have without that authority.

15   We proceed and arrive at a goal—but given the relativity of all motion, who knows whether we aren't standing still as the goal comes to us? This would presuppose a movement of the objective world of ideas. But on this ambiguity rests much of religious belief.

16   The process of the world seems to me like the rotation of an enormous wheel, at least as the postulate of the Eternal Return would have it. But not with the same result that what is identical actually repeats itself some time or other—for the wheel has an infinitely large radius. Only when an infinite amount of time has passed—in other words, never—can the same element arrive at the same place—and yet it is a wheel that turns, that proceeds ideally towards the exhaustion of qualitative variety, without ever exhausting it in actuality.

17   Bergson's difficulty—how can the intellect conceive of life, given that it is an emanation of life—is solved through the fact that this retrospectiveness, this understanding of itself, is the essence of living consciousness.

18   "Everything perfect in its class [*Art*] surpasses its class"[4]—this is true of intellectuality above all.

4. Goethe.—Trans.

19   Self-consciousness—the subject that makes itself its own object—is a symbol or real self-expression of life.

20   I locate myself in the concept of life as though in the center—from there the path goes in one direction towards soul and Ego, in the other towards the Idea, the cosmos, the absolute. The question of the Ego-principle must be dealt with. And yet the knowledge we achieve with it—that we cannot simply philosophize or form a worldview out of absolute objectivity—cannot be simply set aside. Life seems to be the most extreme objectivity towards which we can immediately advance as spiritual subjects—the broadest and firmest objectification of the subject. With life we stand in the middle position between Ego and Idea, subject and object, person and cosmos. And this is granted to us—we are neither the masters nor the slaves of existence, and precisely on that account we are free. Admittedly this awareness appears to arise only within the most extreme intensification of life, with spiritual consciousness—though already at lower levels, the scientific inexplicability of life already points towards freedom. Still, it might possibly be that life could reach a yet higher level than that of consciousness—we would then be yet more free. Perhaps in our life these days there is on the one hand too much "I," and on the other too much mechanical. It is not yet pure life.

21   I feel in myself a life that is impelled towards death—that in every instant and every content, it will die. And I feel another life that is not headed for death. I do not know which one carries its true properties, its process and its fate—I know only that death is not included in its meaning. This dual life is visible in two forms: in the species-life that flows through me and in which posterity is propagated into eternity; and in the timeless significance of created thought—in the world's becoming more valuable or more evil through the presence of our ethical goodness and ethical badness in that thought. The *effects* that our being and doing leave behind in the world, and whose propagation is imperishable, emerge as a third form. But these three forms nonetheless do not completely express that dual life—any more than does immortality, commonly understood.

22   Perhaps one has to have placed life in the center of one's worldview and valued it as much as I have in order to know that one may not keep it, but must yield it up.

23   Natural science deals with possible necessity—religion with necessary possibility.

24   The Church wants to introduce the Beyond into the world—philosophy aims to lead the world into the Beyond.

25   Natural science seeks to trace obscure facts back to clear ones—metaphysics, contrariwise, seeks to trace clear facts back to obscure ones.

26   So far, there is no timeless religion—religious eternity is only infinite duration. Granted, Eckhart's "Divine" [*Gottheit*] is timeless (as distinct from God, whose source it constitutes). But this no longer enters into historical religion.

27   Art and religion have this in common—that they move their object into the greatest distance in order to pull it into greatest proximity.

28   The artist can do what the logician cannot: widen the embrace of a concept without having it lose its content.

29   Music has something insular and sterile about it—there is no path, either objective or subjective, that leads from it into the world or into life. One is either completely within it or completely outside it. It does not influence life, yet life has influenced it. The world no longer receives it because it has already received the world.

30   Music and love are the only activities of mankind that need not be described in the absolute sense as endeavors with unsuitable means.

31   Art is our thanks to the world and to life. After both have fashioned the sensory and spiritual forms of our comprehension, we thank them for it as we now create a world and a life with their help.

32   Not only philosophy's reputation but also its actual significance feeds generally on that which it has not yet attained.

33   Perhaps it is not only at the stage of humanity we know that humanity arrives at the highest problems, if not the highest solutions. Perhaps it is its inner necessity, the essence of the human type. The apple of the tree of knowledge was unripe.

34   Man is the creature who arrives simply at problems, but not simply at solutions. This is related to the fact that he is expected to act as though he knew the future reliably, and yet he does not know reliably even one step of it.

35   Man's possibilities are unlimited, but so too, in seeming contradiction, are his impossibilities. Between these two—the infinity of what he can do and the infinity of what he cannot do—lies his homeland.

36   When man says of himself that he is a fragment, he means not only that he does not have a *whole* life—but also, more deeply, that he does not have a whole *life*.

37   Only the whole of the world and of life—as it is knowable, lived by and given to us—is a fragment. Each individual detail of fate and achievement, though, is often complete in itself—harmonious and unbroken. Only the whole is a part, and the part can be a whole.

38   One does not fulfill his destiny as it is prefigured and as it could and should potentially be—this also is a manner of fulfilling one's destiny.

39   The dreadful conflict between whole and part is solved in principle for the consciousness by the fact that it can represent the whole in conscious form. Art, science, and imagination in general are only actual in man, this tiny fragment of being, but each of these has the remarkable power to have the whole of being as its content—whether or not this possibility is actualized completely or only approximately.

40   How deeply the destiny of humanity is embedded in the fact that both of its highest ideas—infinity and freedom—are in a direct sense only negations, only the removal of constraints!

41   Man inherently is an inadequate, error-prone, restless being: as a rational being he has too much "nature," while as a natural being he has too much reason—what is that supposed to amount to?

42   It may be important that man is the "goal-setting creature"—but then he is likewise the creature of the "unfit means." We have wonderful, highly perfected means for truly indifferent ends, and utterly unfit means for

our chief ends. Similarly, for things we know, certainty and importance tend to vary in inverse proportion to one another.

43   The human soul is the greatest cosmic endeavor with unsuitable means.

44   Man is not a microcosm, but a macrocosm—a megistocosm—for at least in idea and possibility, everything in him is complete, ripe, and conscious that in the rest of nature is *necessarily* incomplete, fragmentary, merely begun and unsolved.

45   *Man as middle-being.* Man can exist only in a middle region between spiritual constriction and spiritual breadth, with neither too little nor too much knowing. That is why an old person finds it so difficult—even impossible—to live any longer: he knows too much. Illusion is a middle ground between knowing and not-knowing, an as-if for the practical. Indeed, even error is a similar middle ground, utterly different from not-knowing-at-all. However, to know that one *could* know more than he knows—that is something characteristically human. Man's doubt is what makes him human.

46   Most people's lives proceed in dullness. The more highly developed person lives in dark and light. Dullness is the dreary, undeveloped, mixed position between darkness and light.

47   The great turning of the more advanced person is that for him the whole passionately palpable fullness of life is not, as for the historical species, the basis of the spiritual, metaphysical existence evolved from it. Quite the opposite: this spiritual existence is its foundation—for him the tree of life grows in this spiritual soil, and bears its edible fruits.

48   Height is only something that has something higher over it. In the sense of not having something higher over it, only lowness is absolute.

49   What always divides the highest-souled person from the lower is that he does not find it necessary to believe in reality or in the foreseeable real-ization of ideals. Even without this belief he keeps faith in them and in the strength of his striving for them, while the person standing lower, the weaker, loses his faith as soon as he is compelled to recognize the ideal actually as something *infinitely* distant. Thus one can say that people are

ranked according to the varying significance that the concept of infinity has for them.

50   With every sort of life activity addressed towards the whole of life, the decisive difference is this: Does it function as an ideally limited one, such that the subject is free and unobligated when it ends? Or does it become interminable, such that no completed amount of achievement unbinds the subject from further investment of resources, so that he must continue to act so long as he has resources left at all? And correspondingly from the side of the subject: if he invests with a limited capital, do his resources exhaust themselves in their application, or do they continually renew themselves—does he live on interest instead of capital? Does the life-sense of the individual, subjectively and objectively, proceed into the infinite, or is it—however large—something terminable?

51   Among the great categorical distinctions that divide people into two principal groups is the question of whether one is immobile [*starr*] or vital. Fichte's identification of inertia [*Trägheit*] as the radical evil of humans lies entirely within this sense: for fixity [*Starrheit*] seems more and more to me the decisive negation of our life-value. But Fichte narrows the fixity-concept so moralistically because he relates it only to the will. Inertia of the will, though, is itself only a symptom or consequence of the deeper nature of the entire person. Sequitur esse.[5]

52   These are the poles of humanity, insofar as it is noble: those for whom nothing real is without value—and those for whom nothing without value is real.

53   Man is the seeking being par excellence. This is more than "will." We seek also when we "understand," when we ask, and when we answer. Among the practical forms of life of which life-wisdom speaks, "seeking" scarcely appears. Its enormous role in life, from highest to lowest, is typically overlooked. How much "seeking" is in all our activity, yet different from "chance," "probability," etc.

54   Man is the hungry creature par excellence. The animal is satisfied when it has eaten.

---

5. "To be continued."—Trans.

55   Most people first experience through suffering that life is something serious—without this personally emphatic impact, life cannot convey its seriousness to them. It is really appalling to hear of a person who has met with a hard fate for the first time—"Now he understands the seriousness of life!"—as though no one could conceive of the seriousness of beauty, happiness, gaiety, or the overall form of life.

56   Perhaps the most horrifying symptoms of life are the things—manners of behavior, joys, beliefs—with which people make life bearable for themselves. Nothing reveals so much the depths of the human level as what man reaches for in order to be able to continue his life.

57   The decisive and indicative element of a man is where his despairs are.

58   Life's senselessness and constriction astonishes one often as something so radical and inescapable that one must utterly despair—the only alleviation is that one recognizes it and despairs about it.

59   Our deepest shock is the growing emotional awareness of treasures that lie within us as in a locked chest, over which we have neither the key nor the power of decision, and which we therefore take with us to the grave.

60   For the deeper person there is only one possibility of enduring life at all: a certain measure of superficiality. For if he were to ponder all the conflicting, irreconcilable impulses, duties, strivings, and yearnings as deeply, to feel them all as absolutely and ultimately as their nature and his properly require—then he would have to explode, go crazy, or run out on life. Beyond a certain boundary of depth, the lines of being, willing, and obligation collide so radically and violently that they necessarily tear us apart. Only by preventing them from reaching below that limit can we hold them far enough apart for life to be possible. The truth is thus precisely reversed from how monistic optimism would have it: that one only has to follow the contradictions far enough down in order to come to their resolution. Or should the latter apply in its content-objective sense, and the former in its subjectively lived sense?

61   All the thoughts and destinies that make us suffer are really only the triggers that actualize a piece of the limitless possibility of suffering that resides within us. Thoughts and destinies (what are these in themselves?) could not *elicit* all these terrors if they were not already present and

waiting in us in some form. It is the most uncanny thing that on such occasions we get the intimation of a measureless stock of suffering that we carry around with us as though in a closed container—a dark existence that is not yet actuality but is somehow nonetheless there—from which Fate continually extracts pieces of one sort or another, but leaves ever so much more behind. Mostly this container remains still in us, but sometimes, when a particular misery or shock opens it up, it is set in motion in a heavy shaking and we sense (we ourselves don't know where and what it signifies) the fearful stock of possibilities of suffering that we carry around with us, and that is our dowry, never quite realized, and never exhausted by any actually experienced misery. Even having the certainty that our latent suffering never becomes fully actual is no consolation, but is the most fearful thing. For we own it all, even though we do not have it.

62   Seen biologically, pain seems to be exclusively a warning signal, something teleological. Yet we feel sufferings spiritually that are purely causal and have no teleological significance whatever—this seems to me one of the most decisive characteristics of human beings, a counterpart of "pointless" thought.

63   It is astounding how little of the pain of humanity has passed over into its philosophy.

64   The concept of consolation has a much broader, deeper significance than is consciously ascribed to it. Man is a consolation-seeking creature. Consolation is something other than help—even an animal seeks help—but consolation is the remarkable experience that not only allows one to withstand suffering, but so to speak elevates suffering into suffering. It pertains not to the misfortune itself, but to its reflection in the deepest level of the soul. Man by and large cannot be helped. Therefore he has cultivated the wonderful category of consolation that not only comes to him from the words that people speak for that purpose, but which he also draws from a hundred factors in the world.

65   It is an unutterable happiness to be at home somewhere abroad—for it is a synthesis of our two longings: toward wandering and toward home—a synthesis of becoming and being.

66   By my existence I am nothing more than an empty place, an outline, that
      is reserved within being in general. Given with it, though, is the duty to
      fill in this empty place. That is my life.

67   We should treat life as though every instant were an end—and likewise
      as though none were an end, but that each single one were only a means
      to a higher, to the highest end.

68   The connection of people and things to pure individuality always con-
      tains something definitive, and life runs into a dead end with it. In the
      relation of the individual in us to the individual outside us, our great-
      est—perhaps insoluble—task is not to lose fruitfulness and process to
      endlessness.

69   Essential life task: to begin life anew each day as though this day were
      the first—but yet to gather into it all of the past with all its results and
      unforgotten occurrences and to have them as prologue.

70   One can assert but not prove the ultimate, highest, objective values—one
      must prove but not assert one's own value.

71   What a spiritual person, striving to be a higher one, needs to avoid above
      all is accepting things as obvious and making do.

72   The highest art of living: adapting oneself without making concessions.
      The unhappiest natural condition: always making concessions and yet
      never reaching adaptation.

73   To keep from losing objectivity for the sake of passion, one ultimately
      only needs to be a steady person. But to keep from losing passion for the
      sake of objectivity—that is something that the ethical will cannot do for
      itself.

74   In human history, the "precursor" assumes a distinctive place. Insofar
      as the idea of evolution dominates, each person is a precursor, but really
      also a fulfiller. In the form of ethical principles each exists beside the
      other—one should behave as though he were the precursor of all ful-
      fillers, and as though he were the fulfiller of all precursors.

75 One can elevate the man to the idea, but one cannot lower the idea to the man.

76 One needs to properly possess only a couple of great thoughts—they shed light on many stretches whose illumination one would never have believed in.

77 Freedom of the spirit is subjection by the spirit—because every freedom immediately means domination.

78 What better thing can a man wish himself than a great task and a fortitude for it that no longer depends on the hope of its solution?

79 What man can say this highest thing of himself—that he is about his father's business?

80 Ultimately all of our paths are determined by whether we are going away from home by them or coming home upon them.

81 To treat not just every person, but even every thing, as if it were an end in itself—that would be a cosmic ethic.

82 The truly great tragic element of ethics—when one does not have the right to that towards which one has a duty.

83 True guilt can never be expiated—it expresses an utterly indissoluble relation between a temporally fixed moment and the metaphysically atemporal whole of life, and it cannot be affected at all by any later moment. To say that sin is always sin against God is a dubious evasion—created in order to have someone who can forgive it. Expiation through pain is something quite external and mechanistic, where two utterly incommensurable elements are counterbalanced with one another—a superficial self-deception.

84 "Guilt" in the religious-ethical sense means that a particular moment is torn out of the whole, continuous flowing of life—the infinitely diverse and at once infinitely unitary life—and brought to fixity. Guilt and sin emerge from this devitalizing of moments that have an entirely different character within life. Because of this, they are understood as sins *against* something outside of life, against God, and absolution likewise could

come only from outside of life. The same applies with virtue and reward. But life should not on that account be placed into a value-indifferent realm beyond good and evil. Regarded from life, however, the essence of values is something completely different than when they are attached to their crystallizations.

85   We are often moral behind our backs. That is, we make and realize a moral decision that then contains greater power, greater sacrifice, than we had actually imagined. We are not more responsible because of this—although we do the moral thing, we have no greater reward because of this part that it mysteriously contains. Just as our uttered thoughts often have objective contents of which we had not thought in producing them, so too our actions have moral quanta that did not lie within our decision. After we have, so to speak, taken the first step with rashness and an auto-suggestive act of violence on ourselves, we no longer *will*—we *must*.

86   Perhaps justice is a faute de mieux, a mechanical means of compensation, because we can never or only rarely know the individual *right thing*. An inkling of this lies in Dante's notion that divine justice often produces what are, according to human concepts, injustices. We even distinguish a mechanical from a higher justice. It could be that this higher justice also stands in a corresponding relation to a completely perfect justice.

87   Truthfulness, taken logically, appears to apply only for the relation of the thought to its utterance. But it has another, deeper sense independent of this dualistic relation—the intrinsically calm, unitary nature of the soul that expresses itself necessarily and without alternative in that actuality of thoughts and words.

88   The specifically human trait is objectivity, an interest for the object [*Sache*] rather than for the subject (in whatever low or high sense). Objectivity means that one wants to know how things behave such that this objective element may be in consciousness; that one acts such that a certain situation may be realized without touching anything personally; that one serves God without thought of reward, purely from the logic of our relation to the absolute; that one seeks to give his own life a value such that this value may be something objective, without any real or ideal connection back to the Ego. This is the practical application of the purely spiritual fact that man can make himself into his own object. When we first regard ourselves objectively, we reach the bridge by which to extin-

guish the Ego altogether and to exist only for the object. The highest intensification of this is creativity. Here, the Ego has not only repressed and forgotten itself in order to exist in and live from the object, but it is metamorphosed into an object. Its powers have themselves become the object—it is now no longer Ego and yet has left nothing of itself behind. In creative achievement, spiritual objectivity has overcome its opposition to the subject—it has absorbed the subject into itself.

89   Genius appears to us the most impersonal and at the same time the most personal thing—this fact points to its close derivation from a level of being in which the personal and the impersonal are not yet separated.

90   Here, relativity and absoluteness of the same concept exist on both sides (as with male and female)—the personal in the absolute sense embraces personal and impersonal elements, and so does the impersonal in the highest sense.

91   Individuality disintegrates (as it were, dialectically) as individuality when it attains its highest level—for that occurs as it becomes the counterpart of totality—as it broadens to totality.

92   The manifestation of genius is the leaping over of intermediate levels— it is immediately, inherently, at its goal, and its labor occurs more on the footing of the goal itself than in bringing something extrinsic to it. Among intellectuals this is quite clear—genius knows what it has not learnt, and it does not need the bridge to experience which can occasionally bring the nongenius to the same cognition. In practical matters it is perhaps sovereignty in contrast to *resources*. The practical genius squanders resources, subdues them, and exceeds them, even as they demand their due from the nongenius. For this reason, art is correctly a matter of genius; it does not have the intermediate levels of other human pursuits—it is "always at the goal."

93   Wherever we have to deal historically and interpretively with something given, a multiplicity of attitudes is always possible—things are always ambiguous, and no particular statement about them is dictated by the fact that the core of our attitude towards them derives from the things themselves. Only when we *create* is our attitude strictly necessary, established in a particular direction, and incapable of being otherwise—

though when we *speak* of what is created, such speech can still be yet otherwise.

94   Creation is the comparative form of affirmation—just as equal entitlement already contains a desire for domination.

95   It is the wonderful thing about the evolution of the living being that the struggle for mere existence is already unavoidably the struggle for more-being [*Mehr-Sein*]—rather than the simple coordination that the concept of existence seems to indicate but attains only through victory, feeling, and superiority.

96   It is nonsense to say that life should be made into a work of art. Life has its own norms, ideal demands, that are only to be realized as and in the form of life—and cannot be borrowed from art, which has its own.

97   Life comes into its own only in what we call creative. With everything reproductive, merely combinatoric, or overburdened by historically objectified contents, life is already no longer entirely vital—firm crystals float in its stream, constrict its current, and obstruct it perhaps even to a complete blockage. And yet the creative element consists of life's attitude towards contents—it signifies life insofar as contents *immediately proceed* from it. But here is the hesitation: Can novelty decide? If it is after all only a historical social category? It is only the *ratio cognoscendi* through which one is *sure* that a creative act has occurred. Certainly that too is a life process that operates with already existing contents; yet these contents themselves are no longer *intrinsically* vital any more—the life process no longer flows through them, but around them. The opposition of objective spirit and subjective life becomes flagrant in the concept of the creative.

98   In practice the worst mistakes are often those that come quite close to the truth. Just where our notion is almost correct, where our knowledge lacks only a final, often minimal step—just there, the act built on that basis entangles us in the most fearful blunders. Radical errors are more easily corrected.

99   In all human work there is a double measure of shortcoming: subjectively, in that the energies available and dedicated to the effort do not fully find accommodation in it, flow along with it, or exhaust themselves

before they have entered its form; and objectively, in that its idea—that which it is supposed to be—is not completely accommodated, a bit remains on this side of it that is not covered by the work. Not just the sum but the ratio of these two kinds of shortcoming determines the fate of every creative product. And metaphysically a relation can be established between them.

100   It is pure assumption that there is preestablished harmony in which a person's highest performance, measured objectively, is also the point at which his personality as such has attained a peak of its powers, its individuality, and its fulfillment. In fact, the height of the performance curve (always in the objective sense) and that of the existence curve do not correlate at all. Granted, belief in this notion rests on a very deep metaphysical conviction about the relation of subjective and objective value.

101   It is prejudice to deduce the negative value or reprehensibility of a situation or a quality simply from the fact that the subject is led by these into destruction (e.g., declining number of children in a collectivity, emancipation of women, anarchic freedom of individuals, predominance of intellectual over physiological powers, etc.). It may be that societies fail through these occurrences. Now even if these in fact do fail, the life of humankind is not bound to the eternal continuation of precisely these forms—and out of the death of societies new ones have always arisen. Yet these ruinous moments still have their *own significances* that can be utterly independent of their resulting consequences for the life-situation of their bearer—just like the formal-aesthetic meaning of a structure as against its utilitarian meaning. It is just so with the individual, for whom it is more important to live decently than to live at all. And when once it is determined that decent life kills life—then this tragedy must fulfill itself.

102   It is undeniable: living for the objective element, for the creation of practical structures that carry their value purely in themselves, is an evasion of the problem of life—as when one lives exclusively "for his children," when he disregards his own mastery of this problem and only provides the best for the children, so that they will now be done with it. In order for something we do to become as perfect as possible, we often release ourselves as much as possible from our duty to ourselves—while we solve the problem of the object, we avoid solving our own problem. This is a characteristic compensation for the fact that we very often beat our

heads against the object. We bypass the hard demand of our subjective life, which needs to be met despite all opposition from things, when we induce things, through good treatment as it were, to step into the place of that demand.

103   Among the many people who work at their work, there are few on whom their work works.

104   The idea of man requires that the things around him not correspond completely to their idea. In practice, a sort of jealousy has arisen between us and things in the theoretical and artistic realms—the deepest relation between man and the world.

105   Between the free particularity of the Ego and the closed lawfulness of natural occurrence there are two connections—from the former, action and the act; from the latter, fate.

106   I find it utterly regrettable that modern man adopts the *critical* standpoint—as self-evidently the first and only standpoint—towards his reading (and one could perhaps say toward all works of art). One should gratefully accept from a book whatever appeals to us and simply pass over the rest. One should only sit in judgment when that is necessary for reasons that lie outside of the immediate relation of book and reader. Why must one always have a *judgment* about everything? After all, because judging is no easy matter, this leads to disparaging, denigrating pronouncements about everything that are always the easier ones. Furthermore, our whole tendency towards criticism correlates with the currently common mechanical point of view, for which a whole is merely an assemblage of individual parts. That is, it is common to condemn *particulars*—objections to these become a condemnation of the whole. The assumption of the typical critic is utterly opposite to that of every *artistic* person—that the whole is assembled out of parts that are judgeable for themselves.

107   It is among the deepest intellectual detriments that objections to works of art, religions, metaphysical worldviews, etc. pass for "refutations." Though they may have a thousand mistakes, weaknesses, contradictions—these need not alter their value at all, which rests much more exclusively upon the positive elements of their meaning; and why should this not persist alongside of all those defects? The applicable objection is

fatal only for purely theoretical statements, because such statements can only be either true or false.

108   What is right is conceivable from itself and from the context of objectivities. What is wrong is only conceivable from the subject. Therein lies the fruitfulness of the criticism (so materially irrelevant and, in cultural life, so immeasurably overvalued) that the error in a precept is often the channel through which one can discern its spiritual origin, and the basis for what is correct in it.

109   Childrearing tends to be imperfect because with each of its particular acts it must serve two opposed tendencies: freeing and binding.

110   Youth as a rule has it wrong in *what* it proclaims—but right in *that* it proclaims.

111   Youth possesses the wonderful *presence* of the whole person in each individual utterance. Because everything in it presses towards the *future*, nothing from the past holds enough weight to be fixed in its place—and because this entry into the future is only possible through the present, the whole of life is always gathered on it as if on a single point.

112   Dogmatism, upon which age relies, is often in fact a now unavoidable foothold—for with advancing age life becomes ever more problematic, more confused, more incomprehensible. From a certain age on, this tendency becomes so heightened that it is no longer bearable—our adaptability does not reach so far. We either lose ourselves in it, succumb to it—or save ourselves in the artificial fixity of dogmatism.

113   More and more I come to feel as though every older person goes around under the pressure of some fearful secret or another—an act that nobody knows, but that cannot be atoned for, and that no God nor the person himself can absolve him of; an opinion upon his nearest and dearest that never passes his lips; a sinful desire to which he never allows himself the slightest expression. Youth also has such secrets, but either changes their content (now this, now that other entirely different secret burdens the young person) or they are not in the strict sense *secrets*—they are confided to another. In that moment when the *secret becomes definitive of our life*, youth has perished.

114   Granted, we no longer believe that dead persons become ghosts. But
        dead love, the dead ideal, the dead belief—these become ghosts; in fact,
        one feels their life more than before, when their *content* was more impor-
        tant for us and filled our consciousness more than the fact of their *life*.

115   The unique character of the older Goethe is that his works flow no
        longer from immediate, but from a reproduced life. And indeed it was an
        entire life that he saw in himself, and confronted—not, as for almost all
        other poets, one still incomplete in which they continued to live. For that
        reason, every detail of the great works of that period is surrounded by a
        totality of life. To him alone was it given at once still to live a full, current
        life, and at the same time to have another one filled to the brim behind
        him.

116   Perhaps no one lived so symbolic a life as Goethe—because he gave to
        each only a piece or side of his personality, and yet, at the same time,
        "Only the whole must be."[6] As for the pantheists, all of God is present in
        each piece of the world. To live symbolically in this manner is the only
        way not to be a clown and wearer of masks.

117   Difference between wisdom and simple knowledge of the truth: the lat-
        ter is merely directed at the matter at hand and therefore—viewed from
        its position in the continuity and totality of life—is something singular.
        Wisdom, however, is knowledge that—although it may touch only on
        something particular—stands in relationship to the whole of life. It is
        always a summit around whose feet lie the vast plains of life. Perfect wis-
        dom about human existence makes us certain that there is no particular
        knowledge beyond it that would not be achievable out of its entirety.

118   Life in the higher and spiritual pursuits is the only thing that can de-
        fend us in advancing age against deadly boredom and fatigue with life.
        Everything lower, routine, or sensual becomes, through decades-long
        repetition, a despair-filled wasteland. Life in the spirit, actually created
        from the spirit, has a variation and inexhaustibility quite beyond its im-
        mediate qualitative value. Even a higher, more spiritually inclined person
        can spend long years in the lower spheres until their monotony—the
        astoundingly narrow variation that the external and the sensual funda-
        mentally possess—finally gets to him. Once he becomes aware of that,

6. "Allein muß das Ganze geben."—Trans.

however, he must fall into despair—from which, in longer life, only the limitless contents and self-creating continuous variation in a truly spiritual existence can protect him.

119   If our existence coalesces from the two categories of life-process and its contents, then the difference between youth and age is that in youth the process has predominance over the contents—in age, the contents over the process. The real ripeness of life is this: that enough life is present to make the contents vital, and enough content to entirely fill the process. The empty, dull drive and longing of youth, and the fixed wisdom of age, are the extremes.

120   In periods when a heavier, more objectively caused pressure more or less burdens us, we can ascertain a rhythm in us of despair and alleviating hope—a rhythm not at all grounded in the objective situation, but called forth purely subjectively. The one voice exhausts itself and, as though automatically, the other takes its place. One must conclude from this that even hopelessness or depression contains or is a positive force that only holds out for a certain time.

121   Sensing, thinking, feeling, happiness, and suffering are each an act of the soul. Underlying them first, therefore, are the general laws of activity as such. Once one grasps them, all of the characteristics and developments of those particular domains become very much more transparent. The general functional phenomena of stimulus, exhaustion, power and weakness, inertia, rhythm, etc., describe at first roughly the problem of activity in its fundamental significance, carrying all psychological life.

122   The judge of a person intuitively grasps the totality of the individual, from which he deduces the particulars of his behavior. The psychologist, as a scientist, cannot grasp this unity, but only the particular elements into which they divide for him, and which he then analyzes or synthesizes further with the special logic of psychology. That is why good psychologists are so often bad judges of people. Because he looks to the whole, the judge of persons always has only the individual for his object—for a psychic totality always has the form of an individual. Only when it is analyzed into its elements can each of these serve as a cross section through many individuals and become a universal. The judge of persons thus has a quite different object from the psychologist.

123   Modern, sensitive people—who live entirely in the nuances and stimula-
       tion of the superficial and sensuous, in the most delicate appearance and
       shimmer affecting us only—nonetheless often have the feeling of pro-
       ceeding into the transcendent realm and of living in metaphysical depths
       and supernatural significances. The basis or apparent justification for this
       is that the merely sensual surface of things stands just as far from their
       full, unalloyed reality—from the given totality of their existence—as
       their transcendent basis does. The domain of such people merely lies as
       far on this side of simple (but complete) actuality as the metaphysical
       lies beyond it. Yet the similarity of the distance conceals the difference of
       direction in which it extends.

124   Everything is allowed except the frivolous and the boring. Yet for very
       many people it is utterly impossible to avoid the one without falling into
       the other.

125   Happiness is the condition in which the higher psychic energies are not
       disturbed by the lower—comfort is the condition in which the lower are
       not disturbed by the higher.

126   In tolerance there always lurks a certain arrogance. When you say no,
       however impudently, you place yourself still on *one and the same* level
       with the person who has said yes. But if you tolerate him, you are his
       patron.

127   Innumerable love and marriage relationships run aground or at least
       lead to the deepest disillusionments because we tend to forget that an
       experience can never be repeated as the same thing—even the fact that
       it was already there once before creates different psychic conditions for
       the repetition than the original possessed. If today we had an hour of
       happiness, we believe it could be repeated tomorrow and the next day
       and forever because the outward conditions—and in broad measure the
       inner ones as well—have remained the same. Yet happiness is just as
       difficult to repeat as any other psychic condition. Only someone who can
       create a *new* happiness tomorrow can have the same happiness tomorrow
       as today.

128   The soberness of the drunk is remarkable—the drunkenness of the sober is appalling.[7]

129   I don't know: does a person's vulgarity show more when he becomes habituated to ugliness or when he becomes habituated to beauty?

130   Around all of the deepest and most beautiful things we enjoy is woven a double mystery: in the first place, the ultimate, unspeakable, unknowable region of the soul and of things that experience directly borders and from which its powers come without intervening stages; and then it is even a mystery confronting people, concealed to many, destroyed by each glimpse that comes only from outside.

131   By nothing is one so seduced (in every sense of the word) as by the ability to seduce.

132   Distinction: whether one plays *with* something or *on* something. One plays with a ball, but on a violin. Because it presupposes a greater meaning and objective value of the thing itself, the player's individuality can express itself more deeply and characteristically upon the latter. So it is with people: those with whom we play give us thereby no real opportunity to show our truest and best selves—while those upon whom we play . . . although we only release their own tones from them.

133   That is the wonderful thing: everyone knows himself a thousand times better, and knows a thousand times more about himself than about anyone else, even his closest intimate—and yet the other person never appears to us so fragmentary, so full of gaps and so little a coherent whole as we appear to ourselves.

134   Most men are born as nine-month children, but they die as seven-month[8] children.

135   To the proud person, it is the absolute degree of his value that counts—to the vain person, it is the relative degree.

---

7. Not fully translatable: G.S. puns on "nüchtern"—meaning (1) "sober," (2) "commonsensical," and (3) "vapid or philistine."—Trans.

8. That is, "premature."—Trans.

136   According to the content of his self-consciousness, the vain person is not
       dependent on others. He has—potentially—a very high opinion of him-
       self but not the power to realize it, not the courage for it. He only needs
       others in order for them to confirm this opinion, simply as a chorus that
       says yes to his own opinion of himself, because otherwise they invariably
       drift away from him. From this it often happens that the vain person
       often despises the masses without which he cannot exist.

137   Being underestimated often helps the small person to feel nevertheless at
       a certain height.

138   Sensational persons are also always egoists.

139   In objectivity vis-à-vis people, a boundless solipsism is often concealed.

140   The demand for happiness bears the contradiction of making the ego-
       point into the center of life and basing the value of the world fully upon
       the subjective reaction—yet declaring itself dependent upon objects and
       desiring more than the ego by itself can deliver.

141   A person must shudder to think of how much he can lose whose loss
       would cause pain. A person must shudder all the more, though, at the
       thought of how little he possesses whose loss would be a truly greater,
       more inextinguishable, and most pure pain.

142   Desire has already stepped beyond its climax when one recognizes
       it—sorrow, however, only approaches its climax at that point.

143   With many people, the depth of their life (and indeed an actual, by no
       means contemptible one) consists in suffering over its superficiality.

144   When a drop causes a glass to overflow, more always spills out than just
       that drop.

145   To C. F. Meyer's phrase, "Enough is not enough,"[9] one must counter with
       the following: enough is already too much. That is the deep contradiction
       in the relation of everything eudaimonistic/epicurean to the totality of
       our life—every such thing is for us either too little or too much. The first

---

9. From Conrad Ferdinand Meyer's poem, "Fülle."—Trans.

leaps into the second without passing through the equilibrium-range of "enough."

146   The passionate craving for life can itself lead to self-destruction. For it wells up from the ultimate *foundation* of all existence and leads back to it, so that the negation of the individual form lies in fact very close to it. The orgiastic or ascetic pain that one inflicts on himself has this double function—on the one hand to let the ego be felt as deeply and violently as no other sensation, and on the other to tread the path toward its destruction, its dissolution into universal being.

147   The essence of the tragic may perhaps be described thus: that a fate is aimed destructively against the vital will, nature, sense, and value of a particular being—and that at the same time this fate is felt to proceed from the depth and necessity of this same being. The tragic element in the loss of a wife is, as a rule, that the relation of dependency that destroys her is nonetheless established in the fundament of her essence. The falling roof slate kills a young, hopeful, vital person—this in itself is really only sad, not tragic. For the latter proceeds from the feeling that the death was in fact the necessity and meaning of this very person, but one whose fulfillment is aimed against others of his necessities and meanings. The amount of the tension by which what destroys a life was necessitated by an innermost element of this very same life—this is the measure of the tragic. This is quite evident in Shakespeare's tragedies. In ancient tragedy, rather than personal necessity forming the basis of the destroying process it is the necessity of fate—corresponding to the ancient way of thinking, which generally did not understand individual definiteness as the metaphysical basis for the life of the person. The relation of the comic to the tragic is described by the observation that what is directed against life's intention in comedy does not characterize the ultimate ground of life and its necessary destiny—but instead is simply arbitrarily opposed to it and has nothing whatever to do with it, so that it is ultimately overcome and is revealed as mere play. In tragedy, outward chance is inward necessity—in comedy, outward necessity is inward chance. In tragedy a deep harmony exists between the positive in the person and that which destroys the positive—in comedy, both contradict each other, and therein lies what is funny or ridiculous. Thus the betrayed wife is tragic because fate thereby consummates her weakness—the betrayed husband is comic because, as the stronger, it doesn't suit him to be betrayed.

148   In comedy a thoroughly individual fate is enacted by type characters—in
        tragedy, a universal fate is enacted by individual characters.

149   The essence of tragedy is that the person's deepest will is denied and that
        this denial is in the deepest sense willed. That the tragic hero so often
        ends with *suicide* is a very superficial realization of this constellation,
        but still a symbol of what comprises tragedy in general. The concept of
        guilt with which one tends to identify the essence of tragedy is only a
        stale, toned down expression for this state of affairs—it does not clarify
        or justify it, and into the puzzling tragic unity of what the person wants
        and does not want it places a link that is not a connection but more
        an indication that no such connection exists (just as Herbart regards
        "cause" as something introduced merely because change is an intolerable
        contradiction for the person). Guilt appears as the bridge upon which
        the will meets the fact that this will destroys its own basis—where the
        will encounters itself as opposed will. With guilt the paradox of the
        tragic is transposed into the conscience for the person, but its paradoxical
        character is thus recognized.

150   The poet—at least the dramatic poet—possesses the great love that gives
        rights even to one who is wrong. At least the right of existence. In actual-
        ity, evil does not exist on a basis of right, but only because it is there. In
        the work of art, though, it has an existence only because it is entitled to
        it.

151   Romanticism (in the superhistorical sense): longing for the cosmos, the
        infinite—and, as means to its fulfillment, only the pure subjective life.

152   The truly tragic element of *Don Quixote* seems to me to be this: we
        surely believe that the qualities of the soul—courage, nobility, idealism,
        magnanimity—have value through their existence in the soul, as facts of
        the personality, regardless of how they present themselves in the outward
        material of life. In Don Quixote, who possesses all of these, it is shown
        that such a belief is wrong, that it is truly irrelevant: that it is a flock of
        sheep rather than a cavalcade of knights—that the simple delusion of the
        intellect (though altering nothing at all in those qualities themselves) is
        capable of transforming the highest and most valuable things into a silly
        game, a meaningless and valueless foolishness. This power of the external
        and objective realm over what we had independently believed of its value,

over what had seemed to have meaning only as inner actuality proceeding from the center—that is the horrifying element of *Don Quixote*.

153   Leonardo da Vinci was perhaps the first person who grasped the world purely naturally, from the concept of modern natural law. Perhaps for that reason his age appears to have perceived him as something supernatural, as an uncanny sorcerer. To the still-medieval mind, absolute naturalness was magic. For us it is the other way around: nature has become perhaps too "natural." It is thus more difficult in our age than in any earlier one to find religion—but religion is thus even more needed in our age.

154   In primitive epochs, mystery had "use-value" and man lived with it, could not avoid it for his life—it was his form for possessing things, even to know—for everything demonic and superstitious is only the label on a sealed bottle. Now, though, when we know so much, mystery has "scarcity-value." The more it is repressed, and the more what was once mystery is now in essence knowable or actually becomes known, the more purely is revealed the range and essence of what is inherently mystery.

155   An animal unquestionably reveals its psychic processes in its bodily movements—it has no purely internal processes without a motoric correlate, processes that could satisfy their longing for expression through the nonsensory medium of speech (for the sensory sound of speech is only symbolic, and its physical aspect is only accidental and administrative.) Primitive man is close to this condition because he has not yet cultivated pure, psychologically self-sufficient innerness. Rather, his psychological process is expressed directly in the moment in a bodily event. The entirely unique cultural situation of the Greeks was that they already possessed fully that purely psychological element expressible in simple speech—but they had not yet lost the character of earlier epochs in which the psychological reveals itself directly in the physical.

156   The great act of Europe in contrast to the Orient (excluding India) in the history of ideas is the discovery of objectivity. The Oriental knows no objective price, only the measure of both negotiating subjects. No objective law, but only the dictum of the judge. No objectively decisive morality, but, rather, "Let him who is without sin cast the first stone." Plato discovered the objectivity of the spirit, Roman law the objectivity

of the law, and Catholicism the objectivity of religion—of which Jesus knew nothing.

157   All great forms of organization that mankind has either realized or dreamed of contain a mixture of rationalism and mysticism—State, Church, socialism. The rational element is obvious with all three. The irrational, arising from dark and opaque depths, is for the State the identity of the ruler—for without his giftedness (which divine right dogmatically anticipates or establishes), the State can neither arise nor persist (if it is not there in his person, it must reside with the officials.) For the Church, the irrational element is the mystique of the contents of belief. With socialism, it is the dark, communistic instincts of a probably atavistic nature, or the belief in a heaven on earth.

158   Whenever a great nation arrives at a concentration upon itself, at a passion for growth from its own roots and its own powers, there is bound to it a striving for domination, ideally over the entire world. The general correlation between freedom and will to power manifests itself at this point. The Italian Renaissance was a national movement, but it strove more or less willfully for its spirit's domination over Europe—and it almost seems to me as though reaching back to the ancients was only a means or a form for this because the ancients could be accepted most easily as a common mother, the common ideal. The correlation is perhaps repeated in the classicism of the Revolution and of Napoleon—a passionate accentuation of the French national spirit, which felt its urges to be the ideal with which it would, prevailing, bless the world. (Panslavism!) Likewise, English world dominion is the correlate of the strongest national consciousness; and likewise we experience it today with all parties—perhaps for us most strongly in the All-German Party. In national concentration, powers are created that extend beyond the national periphery.

159   Money is the only cultural formation that is *pure* power, that has fully eliminated material supports from itself, in that it is absolutely pure symbol. To this degree it is the most characteristic among all of the phenomena of our time, when dynamism has gained command of all theory and practice. The fact that it is *pure relationship* (and thus likewise characteristic of our time) without including any of the content of the relationship does not contradict this. For in reality, power is nothing but relationship.

160   There is scarcely any experience that could more surely cure us of exaggerating life's technical means into absolute values than war. For war shows that all of these wonders that have made life so comfortable, pleasurable, and secure for us now can serve equally well towards its frightful destruction, endangerment, and torture—that they are thus actually only value-indifferent *means* and nothing more.

161   What then is the greatest part of our culture? Really only this: that we create means gradually to assuage again the afflictions we have created for ourselves, the needs we ourselves have produced and the contradictions we ourselves have brought about—to relieve them a little, and to solve them in a very imperfect way. If it were perfect, it would not have to be changed continuously.

162   Only a person who has strength for the future will have a true appreciation for the past. A person may indeed immerse himself in a particular past epoch, believe it to be uniquely valuable, and renounce all else of the present and future. But this is not then the past at all that he understands and values but a particularity whose *content* is precisely suitable for him. The mere *laudator temporis beati* is a subjectively defined being who lacks an objectively defined relation to the past. The strength to move beyond the present belongs to such an objectively defined relation—and such a strength reaches unavoidably into the future.

163   Just as time is of varying length for different individuals (and even, perhaps, of variable length for the same individual), the same is true for whole peoples. This has many consequences.

164   How many values and motives are lost to us through the fact that the simple truth, the general validity, the fundamental has become banal to us and is thoroughly despised! Perhaps as a consequence of the war these will recover their honored status, and we will again place life on its broadest foundations, despite their triviality for *thought*. The war, too, was a consequence of intellectualism and the literary character of our intellectuality.

165   It has never turned out in the world as the prophets and the leaders intended and wanted—but without prophets and leaders it would never have "turned out" at all.

166   "Whoever is not for me is against me"—to my way of thinking this is
      only a half-truth. Only the indifferent person is against me—the person
      who is moved neither to a yes nor to a no by the ultimate questions I live
      for. But the person who is against me in the positive sense, who ventures
      onto the plains where I live and opposes me upon them—he is, in the
      highest sense, for me.

NOTES FROM SIMMEL'S "METAPHYSICS" FILE

Before his death, Georg Simmel said it expressly and on repeated occasions: that he was dying at the right time, that he had delivered his essential work; that he would only have been able to apply his manner of observing things again and again to more and more objects, but nothing truly new would have come.

Nonetheless, we sensed a certain reservation in these comments, something he alluded to when he might add: "Unless I had twenty more years of full strength ahead of me, such as could not be granted me given my age."

His reservation was directed particularly toward labors that would have continued in pursuit of the line of thinking laid down in his last book, *The View of Life*. In pursuit of this line of thinking, yet perhaps even in a broader application. He even started a work, "On the Essence of Truth," which was not fully worked out nor destined for publication, only for safekeeping by the family. Additionally, there is a folder of notes with the title "Metaphysics." The following text comes from that folder.

Gertrud Simmel

Gertrud Simmel, "Aus der nachgelaßnen Mappe 'Metaphysik,'" in *Georg Simmel Gesamtausgabe*, vol. 20, ed. Torge Karlsruhen and Otthein Rammstedt, 297–301 (Frankfurt: Suhrkamp, 2004). Originally published in *Aus unbekannten Schriften: Festgabe für Martin Buber zum 50. Geburtstag* (Berlin: Lambert Schneider, 1928), 221–26.

Cognition, work, and culture represent mediations between subject and object. Even the mere designation as subject and object contains the presupposition that the strict coexistence of life and world has been set aside. The peculiar difficulties with the concept of experience [*Erleben*][1] symbolize this.

Experience could be an absence of differentiation between subject and object, which nonetheless also in itself potentially contains cognition (that which arises after the separation of the two). Experience is immediate unity of subject and object; their separation then requires secondary unification in cognition—or rather, the separation and this subsequent synthesis take place pari passu.

Life is an absence of differentiation between process and content. Both of these are abstractions out of its unity. Experience regards this unity in consequence of the fact that a particular synthesis of subject and object occurs; yet as soon as content has become an object it transpires that the subject confronts it as something demanding recognition. Process and content are the primary pair of opposites, the first unfolding of the life-unity.

1. The reader should note the resonance throughout the German original between *Erleben* (rendered here as "experience") and *Leben* (life).—Trans.

If one poses quite generally the problem of the forms in which the givens of existence develop (in principle) into all-embracing syntheses, it is understandable that epistemology at once stands out. For cognition is still the most relatively closed, unambiguous, and comprehensible of the great categorical domains. Yet the same contents that we know also produce life in other syntheses. That is, contents have other *mutual relations*. It all has to do with the formulas of these relations. In what relations do the elements of a "given" stand to each other as they form a life-course, in distinction to those with which they form a cognition or a world of values?

In everything we think of as complete actuality there is something that is impermeable to our consciousness and with which we can do nothing more than bring these elements into syntheses. This occurs through the primary activities of our consciousness that form all of this into worlds. Now philosophy, as the reflective secondary activity, makes these forms alone its objects, as soon as it is at all clear about that premise.

When I see a sunset, epistemology asks: what is space? How do forms arise? How do I order this particular observation into a universal observational or cognitive context? Yet it is otherwise when I am aware of this as an *experienced* sunset. Then it is a factor of my continuing life, and indeed not only in that it is subjectively perceived—rather, this perception is an objective element in the objective fact of my life. The forms of this ordering—the laws of synthesis of elements through which they form a life and not only a cognition—this is the task of the philosophy of life.

By "life" I mean here naturally not the physiological process but the fact that the soul [Geist] subsists in the form of life. Not only does the soul form for itself a cognitive image of the given world—an existent representational world—but it also forms a life for itself from it. Functioning as a priori, these forms by which the material of life first becomes life must be determined. The fact that this can only occur in an abstract intellectual form is no more a hindrance and flaw than is the fact that with Kant we cannot accomplish the construction of the spatial world through the consciousness of geometric principles. Admittedly, it is immeasurably more difficult to determine the a priori of life than that of cognition, for the latter lies spread before us as a firm result in such a way that even an idea of the systematics of a priori forms can be grasped, while life is a continual gliding and oscillation that can be projected only with a certain artificiality and apparent forcing onto the conceptual plane on which cognition is present from the beginning.

The categories of theory and of viewability [*Anschaulichkeit*] describe in many ways also those of life, but they have a different meaning. With respect to life, for example, form means something completely different than it does elsewhere.

This is not at all a matter of psychology. Admittedly, all experience proceeds in the psyche, but here the focus is on the fact, not that it is the psychic at all, but rather that it is the *life process* of the psyche; on the form that must give specific existence to its contents so that it becomes a life; and on the fact that something objective is brought about. Just so, everything social and everything artistic are psychological and yet not psychology, because the selection, the synthesis, the vast particular cognitive construction of the world and consciousness now proceeds from a specific index concept [*Sachbegriff*], not from the neutral a priori that they generally proceed only psychically.

The principle of the excluded middle exists only between contents or results of thought. It finds no application to the life process itself—these forms of streaming, of continuity, of birthing follow completely different formative laws.

We create an artwork or enjoy it, we speak or we hear, we feel pleasure or pain or cause it for another—all of these are contents that we arrange into logically independent sequences: aesthetic, intellectual, ethical. When we say that we experience all of these, or that these are our life, an entirely different sequence is formed, and an entirely different object is constructed—just as the words of our language are something different when they stand in a dictionary, when they serve a scientific formulation, or when they are woven into each other in a poem. With respect to all of the contents of world and consciousness, it is an entirely distinctive matter of consideration that they form a life or life itself, and this naturally implies that life results from no mechanical assembly.

A philosophical science of life must proceed analytically. But this is an analysis of a peculiar sort. Life has the unique form that it is concealed as unitary and entire in each of the elements and aspects into which analysis can dissect it. Therefore one cannot put it together as Life out of these elements anymore than one can put together Being as a conceptual-metaphysical unity from the contents in whose summation it is presented as describable.

There must be forms of life that define it as life in the same way that mathematical-physical constructions are defined by forms like largeness and smallness, unity and multiplicity, raising and lowering—in short, the potentialities of measures and of the construction of series. To these mechanical—and ultimately always numerical—basic forms and ordering principles there must correspond similar ones for life, through which it develops into construct, order, and series.

A very deep theme: that the forms of our perception [*Vorstellen*] (i.e., our world) are defined by the fact that our perception indeed *is a life*, and therefore life itself has those forms from the outset and carries them over into the formation of the contents of perception.